AUBREY BURL was principal lecturer in archaeology, Hull College of Higher Education, East Riding of Yorkshire, and has carried out extensive fieldwork in Britain, Ireland and Brittany. His many books on stone circles include *Prehistoric Avebury* and *A Guide to the Stone Circles of Britain, Ireland and Brittany*.

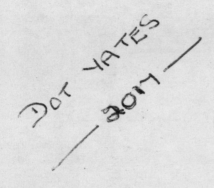

A peep into the Sanctum Sanctorum. 6 June. 1724.

William Stukeley's '*A peep into the Sanctum Sanctorum*' of 1724.

A BRIEF HISTORY OF

STONEHENGE

A Complete History and Archaeology of the World's Most Enigmatic Stone Circle

AUBREY BURL

From an utter darkness to a thin mist (John Aubrey)

ROBINSON
London

Dedicated to the memory of
Richard John Copeland Atkinson, 1920–1994, archaeologist,
scholar, authority on Stonehenge, my external examiner,
then mentor, and for many years a friend.

ROBINSON

First published in hardback by Constable,
an imprint of Constable & Robinson Ltd, 2006

This paperback edition published by Robinson in 2007

5 7 9 10 8 6

Copyright © Aubrey Burl 2006, 2007

The moral right of the author has been asserted.

A CIP catalogue record for this book
is available from the British Library.

ISBN 978-1-84529-591-2

Printed and bound in Great Britain by Clays Ltd, St Ives plc

Papers used by Robinson are from well-managed forests
and other responsible sources

MIX
Paper from
responsible sources
FSC
www.fsc.org   FSC® C104740

Robinson
An imprint of
Little, Brown Book Group
Carmelite House
50 Victoria Embankment
London EC4Y 0DZ

An Hachette UK Company
www.hachette.co.uk

www.littlebrown.co.uk

At the same time I have not scrupled to indulge in certain speculations of a kind which my more austere colleagues may well reprehend, upon the possible significance and interpretation of many aspects of Stonehenge where the evidence will not bear the full weight of certainty. Silence upon such questions is too frequently justified by an appeal to the strict canons of archaeological evidence, when in fact it merely serves to conceal a lack of imagination.

Richard Atkinson, *Stonehenge* (1956),
p. xiv; (1979), p. 23.

CONTENTS

NOTE ON MEASUREMENTS

Throughout the chapters metric dimensions are given for the convenience of those more accustomed to them. Decimalization was first suggested in 1585 by Simon Stevin, a Flemish mathematician and engineer, but metric measurements were not adopted in France until 1799. Even there, it was not widely accepted until the 1830s. It was not until 1989 that it was accepted in Britain – conditionally. Distances such as the mile, yard and foot were retained. So was the pint!

Imperial units, based on body measurements, are also provided in this book because it is probable that it was these lengths local and regional, of human arms, fingers, hands, heights and strides, that were used by the designers of the varying phases of Stonehenge. Examples include the foot of about 12in (30.4cm), similar to the Roman *pes'* of 11.65in (29.6cm), and the yard or pace (the Roman *passus*) of around 36in or 3ft (0.9m). There could also have been shorter or greater lengths, but it is doubtful in early prehistoric Britain that a distance as long as the mile, the Roman *mille passus* (thousand paces), was either thought of, needed or calculable.

Such natural lengths, especially the foot, were widely accepted in early times. Even on the far side of Europe the Sumerians had a 'foot' of 13.2in (33.5cm) and the Assyrians one of 12.96in (32.9cm). It is likely that the planners of any stage at Stonehenge used similar body measurements.

ILLUSTRATIONS

Unless otherwise stated, photographs are by the author. The maps and diagrams are © JB Illustration.

Tables

ACKNOWLEDGEMENTS

I am indebted to many friends, colleagues and learned bodies for the assistance they freely offered during the writing of this book. Those to whom I am most indebted are mentioned in alphabetical order to avoid being thought a batting order of importance.

Richard Atkinson for many discussions, in the field, at Stonehenge, at conferences and sundry inns; Rodney Castleden for his stimulating books whose subjects roved from Atlantis, the Cerne Giant and King Arthur to Stonehenge; Kate Fielden for encouraging several megalithic papers in *WAM*, for an idea about rivers and the Cursus, and for her staunch resistance to bureaucratic Stonehenge committees; Andrew Lawson for the photograph of Stone 57 and for information about other carvings at Stonehenge; Andy Manning of the Wessex Trust for Archaeology for his letter and plans of the Grooved Ware pit-circle on Boscombe Down;

Andrew Martin of the National Museums of Scotland and Alison Sheridan of the Department of Archaeology there for searching for a reference to a carved cist-slab; Neil Mortimer for transcribing the whole of a Stukeley manuscript about Stonehenge and for his splendidly useful *Stukeley Illustrated*; and Alexander and Archie Thom for their arithmetical, geometrical and astronomical researches in stone circles and megaliths in Britain and Brittany.

Invaluable help came from the Bodleian Library, Oxford; the Society of Antiquaries of London; the Society of Antiquaries of Scotland; the library of the University of Birmingham; and English Heritage.

Two colleagues at Constable & Robinson deserve gratitude: Carol O'Brien of Constable for encouraging the book from its beginning. I am especially indebted to my very conscientious editor, Miranda Harrison, whose vigilant patrolling through the text rejected a clutter of infelicities and condemned them to literary purgatory.

This book would never have reached a publisher without the encouragement and unyielding insistence of Judith, my wife. Except for the Taj Mahal, she has visited every place in this book and, other than Jerusalem and the Sphinx, always with me. As John Aubrey observed of another, she is 'very good company, and of a ready and pleasant smooth wit'. Even the most distant and unimpressive rain-dripping ancient stone became a pleasure when we were together.

PREFACE:

THE CHALLENGE

So many gods, so many creeds,
So many paths that wind and wind.

Ella Wheeler Wilcox, 'The World's
Need', from *Poems of Power* (1901).

Every day people come to Stonehenge, sometimes in hundreds, frequently in thousands. Outside the rope barrier they look at the stones, wonder, listen attentively to their audio-guides, and still leave asking the same question as Byron did 200 years earlier: 'What the devil is it?' Stonehenge survives, but the ghosts of the ring's builders are as silent as the circle itself. The questions remain, and for most visitors the only important one is exactly that of the poet. Similarly, the present writer has seldom been asked where the stones came from, how old they were or how they were put up. Almost always it is, 'Why were they raised?'

Occasionally an enquiry can be unusual, sometimes almost impossible to answer. Some years ago in Washington's Smithsonian Institute, an indignant member of the audience wanted to know why prehistoric people erected Stonehenge so close to the road. Resisting the impulse to make a joke that the highway made it easier to transport the heavy sarsen stones across Salisbury Plain, the polite response was that the metalled A344 was the modern successor to one of many ancient trackways across the chalk upland.

Less provocatively, there have been questions about Stonehenge as an observatory, but the most common enquiry remains 'What was it for?' The late Professor Richard Atkinson, leading authority on Stonehenge, wrote in reply: 'There is one short, simple and perfectly correct answer. We do not know and we shall probably never know'.[1]

That is likely to be true, but it is possibly pessimistic. Decade

Fig. 1: After centuries of decay and vandalism, today the stone circle of Stonehenge is viewed from the other side of a rope barrier.

by decade discoveries and insights are adding to our understanding of the monument. The advance is slow but persistent, despite the pessimist's negative whimper, 'If only we could speak to those distant societies'. We cannot. And even if we could it would not help. The Neolithic people who dug out the first Stonehenge around 3000 BC could not have anticipated what was to follow. More than 70 generations later, the Middle Bronze Age inheritors of a decaying monument of sarsens (boulders of ice-borne sandstone) would have had little understanding of what had been created so long ago, of what their forerunners – who were not necessarily their ancestors – had intended. It does not matter. What answers there are rest informatively in the remains that exist today.

Stonehenge was never still. Change was continuous. There were transitions from earth to timber to stone to a different type of stone. Posts were set up and withdrawn; pits were dug, then backfilled. Bodies were cremated and buried in selected places with selected objects. Entrances were dug, one was widened. Its predecessor had contained a bewilderment of postholes. A two-man high, heavy palisade, two-thirds of a mile or more long, was constructed to block the view. Later it was dismantled. There was always change, and always a reason.

Everything had meaning and contained an elusive answer. The outlying Heel Stone, the Slaughter Stone lying at the entrance, the two tumbled remnants of the Four Stations stones around the stone circle, the ring of insignificant Aubrey Holes that have been interpreted as an astronomical calculator and the prostrate Altar Stone can all be seen, and every one of them had and has a meaning.

There were lines of stone, isolated stones, stones treated like wood, stones removed. Stones were arranged in settings alien to those surrounding them. The history of Stonehenge was as unstable as windblown leaves. Creeds and fashions mutated unendingly in men's search for means of ensuring the safety of society. Certain instincts run through all of human history:

> Still climbing after knowledge infinite,
> And always moving as the restless spheres . . .[2]

If some of those changes and adaptations can be explained, some of the 'Why?' about the circle will be answered.

Contemplating prehistoric monuments, the antiquarian John Aubrey wrote in the late seventeenth century:

> This Inquiry I must confesse is a gropeing in the Dark: but although I have not brought it into a cleer light; yet I can affirm, that I have brought it from an utter darkness to a thin Mist; and have gone farther in this Essay than anyone before me . . . These Antiquities are so exceeding old, that no Bookes doe reach them, so that there is no way to retrive them but by comparative antiquitie, which I have writt upon the spott from the monuments themselves.[3]

More than three centuries later, today's researchers into the problems of Stonehenge share the same rueful sentiments.

Unlike John Aubrey in the 1690s, today's students do have the considerable advantage of having records of work undertaken since that time. First among them were the meticulous fieldworking notes of William Stukeley at Stonehenge, taken between 1721 and 1724. He observed many architectural details in the circle and detected inconspicuous features in the landscape that no one before him had noticed. He is sometimes disparagingly 'laughed at by fools' because he believed that proto-Christian priests had officiated at Stonehenge, but those notions were only published in 1740, after his ordination into the Church of England. Twenty years earlier in his site notebooks there are no such illusions. Those clear-headed archaeological records about Stonehenge, previously accessible only as a manuscript in the Bodleian Library, Oxford, have now been published.[4]

From 1720 there was a leap of 200 years to the excavations of William Hawley and R.S. Newall, between 1919 and 1926, during which time they explored almost the entire south-eastern half of the ring. The published reports, enlarged by later investigations by Stuart Piggott, Richard Atkinson and J.F.S. Stone (known as Marcus Stone), formed the basis of the seminal *Stonehenge* by Atkinson in 1956. This was revised, not entirely with the author's consent, in 1979.

It provided a clear and readable account of what was known about the circle, written in a lucid style, although (despite the author's expressed wish for objectivity) passages occasionally became poetic with a traveller 'humping his pack along the ridgeways of south Pembrokeshire' and visualizing the 'cloud-capped summit' of the Preselis as 'no less the house of the gods than . . . Mount Ida [was] to a voyager in the Cretan plain'.[5]

Without the imagination, and completely indispensable to any person seriously interested in the archaeology of Stone-henge, is the magisterial *Stonehenge In Its Landscape* (1995), assembled and edited by Rosamund Cleal, K.E. Walker and Rebecca Montague with the assistance of over a score of colleagues. Here every detail of the known excavations, situa-tion of stones, architectural phases, calibrated radiocarbon assays and previous interpretations is considered and ana-lysed. Its weighty and expensive 618 pages (with 4 detailed Parts and 9 Appendices) do not offer bedtime reading, but the result is the modern equivalent of John Aubrey's 'thin Mist', removing misconceptions and containing data never before put into print. Even with such an abundance of material one still gropes, but at last a guide exists with an archaeological lantern.

There is a necessary qualification. The volume is an indispensable record and analysis of excavations at Stonehenge. It does not attempt to explain why the ring had been built, nor, despite the *Landscape* in the title, why it stood where it did, nor whether it contained astronomical sightlines. Such questions were not part of its remit, which was to provide a well-considered digest of information for others to consider.

Peripheral assistance for today's student exists in other sources. Details of Salisbury Plain's long and round barrows can be found in Leslie Grinsell's exhaustive Wiltshire gazetteer of 1957, augmented in Paul Ashbee (1984) and Ann Woodward (2000). Material about stone circles and timber rings can be found in the present writer's book of 2000 and in Alex Gibson's overview of 1998. Astronomical considerations have been provided by Gerald Hawkins (1966), Alexander Thom (1967), Thom and his son, Archie (1978), and by Clive Ruggles in 1997. A delightful social history of Stonehenge – from earliest times to the present, complete with its whimsies, idiocies and common sense – was compiled by Christopher Chippindale in 1983. It was revised in 1994, and further expanded in 2004.

On an expensive day trip to Stonehenge in 1668, when horses had to be hired and guarded, Samuel Pepys wrote in his diary: 'The stones are as prodigious as any tales I ever heard of, and worth going this journey to see. God knows what their use was'.[6]

It was a different god or gods who knew the answers, the outcome of a medley of societies who created the enigma known as Stonehenge. If some solutions will always remain beyond us, we can at least ask many of the right questions. They help to clear the mist.

INTRODUCTION:

SOME QUESTIONS

The next day took another short tour to the hills, to see that celebrated peice of antiquity, the wonderful Stone-Henge.

Daniel Defoe, *A Tour Through the Whole Island of Great Britain*, Letter 3 (1724).

The best way to approach Stonehenge is not the direct but dispiriting one of the car park, the ticket office and the drab underpass. Instead, stroll across the downs to the circle.

Stonehenge was built at the eastern edge of Salisbury Plain, not far from the Christchurch Avon river and at the heart of a sprawling six-mile wide graveyard of prehistoric burial mounds (fig. 2). Long barrows rest like indolent whales in an ocean of grass, with crowds of round barrows resembling oversized, green beach balls floating around them.

The situation is puzzling. This is not because Stonehenge has several hundred Bronze Age round barrows around it. Many of them were raised centuries after the stone circle that the world knows as Stonehenge. The perplexity is the earlier spread of 17 Neolithic long barrows, more than a mile across. The earliest was laid out a thousand years before Stonehenge. As if the entire centre was a forbidden area, they surrounded an archaeological vacuum, something that both nature and archaeologists abhor.[1]

Round barrows, isolated or in lines, and occasionally clustered, are seen after the visitor has passed the weathered banks of the enormous earthwork enclosure of Durrington Walls and the enigmatic rings of Woodhenge, and has gone through Larkhill army camp and on to a bend of the Fargo Road with its pillar-box and alarming sign, 'Danger. Beware Of Children' (grid reference SU 137 434). To the left, south-wards, there is a footpath. The mile-long walk to Stonehenge starts here.[2]

It becomes open country, with the enticement of a gallery of prehistoric survivals. A few yards to the south and past a row of trees, through a gap on the right, one can make out the weathered banks of the long earthen rectangle of the Stone-henge Cursus stretching downslope then rising to the trees of Fargo Plantation almost two miles to the west. There is an information panel. There is also an illusion that nobody recognizes. For a score of paces the footpath rises very slightly, almost unnoticeably, because it lies over the 'huge body of earth, a bank or long barrow' discovered by William Stukeley, Stonehenge's first great chronicler, in August 1723. Ever since, archaeology has accepted that the Neolithic builders of the Cursus had chosen a venerable burial-place to be the fitting terminal to their enclosure. The opposite was true. It was a deliberate deception by its builders, adding an apparent anti-quity to the new earthwork. The prehistoric folly fooled Stukeley, Sir Richard Colt Hoare and even that doyen of barrow studies, Leslie Grinsell, until an excavation of 1983 exposed the fallacy.[3] It was the first of many illusions at Stonehenge.

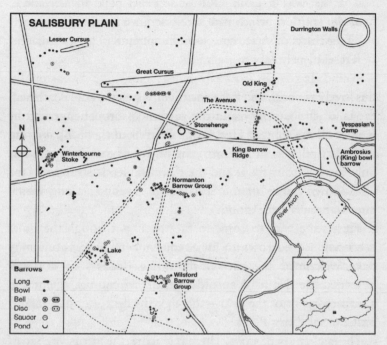

Fig. 2: Map of Salisbury Plain, showing Stonehenge, the Cursus, Durrington Walls and key barrow groups.

Beyond this ersatz mound of 5,000 years ago the path goes by two round barrows of the Old King group, past a copse with two more, before coming to a stile. Just ahead is a second copse on the other side of the path. It once contained a line of New King barrows before gales toppled the great trees covering them.

Over the stile, Amesbury Down descends to a second stile at the bottom of the companionable grassland. Stukeley loved it:

this delightful plain . . . naught could be sweeter than the air
that moves o're this hard and dry, chalky soil. Every step you
take upon the smooth carpet (literally) your nose is saluted
with the most fragrant smell of *serpillon* [wild thyme] and
apium [parsley], which with the short grass continually cropt
by the flocks of sheep, composes the softest and most verdant
turf, extremely easy to walk on.[4]

It is lovely ground, and it is evocative. When the stile is crossed,
the land climbs gently and the sarsens of Stonehenge can be
seen, with the solitary Heel Stone in front of them. By moving
until that pillar is in line with the centre of the circle one has
only to walk towards it and the direction leads straight to the
worn-down banks of the Stonehenge 'avenue', along which
lines of stones once stood.

This is the way to come to Stonehenge, through the quiet
necropolis of barrows to an avenue where processions may
have welcomed the arrival of a new leader, or cortèges
mourned the death of an old one, or ceremonies celebrated
a turning-point of the year – through the centuries of a far-off
past on Salisbury Plain.

The enchantment stops. There is fencing, the intrusive road of
the A344 and an exit that leads to a World Heritage Site beginning
with the disgrace of a car park and its Portakabins, then the steps
down to a concrete enclosure reminiscent of a compound on the
Gulag peninsula, a 'caff' unworthy of a lorry drivers' pull-in, a
cramped gift-and-few-books shop, a turnstile, an equally depres-
sing tunnel, and then one enters into the daylight of the roped-off
Stonehenge (another of the 'temporary' solutions to the feet of
thousands of visitors, successor to gravel and duckboards and 40
years of indecision and miserly bureaucracy).

The neglect and indifference began centuries ago but the
irresolution of committees has worsened it. Things were no

better in the past, but for different reasons. Rabbits were encouraged in the eighteenth century, burrowing destructively through postholes, loosening stones. Seventeenth-century plunderers dragged smaller stones away for walls, houses and bridges. Sightseers chipped souvenirs from the softest bluestones, but not from the sarsens, as diarist John Evelyn found in 1654: 'The stone is so exceeding hard, that all my strength with a hammer could not break a fragment'.[5]

On 7 July 1848 the American poet and essayist, Ralph Waldo Emerson, came to Stonehenge in the company of Thomas Carlyle ('Mr C') by train, carriage and foot. The Bostonian noticed the characteristic British reaction to the dilapidation. 'It is ironical', he wrote, that Britain 'leaves its own Stonehenge or *Choir Gaur* to the rabbits, whilst it opens pyramids and uncovers Nineveh'. Next day, by dog-cart from Amesbury, they took the ageing 'local antiquary' Henry Browne with them as an expert to explain the solar astronomy of the Heel Stone and the 'sacrificial stones'.[6]

There was a time, not many years ago, when having bought a ticket a person could enter the ring and, if sensibly informed, could go to the henge's north-eastern entrance and begin an exploration of the monument inside the earthwork. It is different today. Visitors must wander at a distance from the stones, trying to see the interior of the ring. They leave frustrated because there is so much to be seen – the earthwork and its entrances, the Slaughter Stone, the Aubrey Holes, the Four Stations stones, the sarsen and bluestone circles and horseshoes, the Altar Stone, the Heel Stone.[7] They are all unreachable without official permission, but they can be described and some of the uncertainties about them explained.

Measurements and counting systems

The sarsen ring of Stonehenge is surrounded by a three times more spacious circular earthwork, the henge, which is enclosed by a small outer and wide inner bank of earth, and is broken by two entrances (fig. 3). The inner diameter of the ditch is about 104m (341ft) and the central space of Stonehenge from the innermost edges of the bank is about 91.7m (301ft).[8]

For a note on why both metric and imperial measurements are given in this book, see page ix. That the planners of any stage at Stonehenge used measurements is clear from the precise layout of many structures of the Neolithic or the Bronze Age, whether extant or recovered by excavation. It is also likely that they had elementary counting systems.

The skill of those prehistoric planners is manifest at Stonehenge itself in the design of the large rectangle known as the Four Stations. If the four sarsens were intended to stand at the corners of an oblong measuring 260ft x 111ft (79.3m x 33.8m), then the greatest discrepancy, of only 11in (28cm), occurred in the short sides and was an error of less than 1 per cent. The long sides were almost perfect. The intended right-angled corners were also close to accuracy, little more than 0.7° below 90° or 0.2° above it. When coping with tons of rugged sarsens more than 3ft thick (over 1m), manhandled and erected in roughly dug big pits, the geometrical achievement was considerable. Almost 3,000 years later, referring to Iron Age tribes in Britain, Roman historian Tacitus wrote patronizingly: 'One must remember that we are dealing with barbarians'.[9] Had he lived three millennia earlier and known how symmetrical the Four Stations rectangle was, he might have been less dismissive.

The layout of the Four Stations was a remarkable instance of how well-developed the measurements and counting systems of Late Neolithic societies were. What has been forgotten, perhaps irrecoverably, is exactly what units of length those people used.

Attempts to recover some of these long-lost dimensions and computations were made as early as the 1720s by Stukeley with his deluded 'Druid's Cubit' of 20.8in (52.8cm); the original cubit was a body measurement from the elbow to the tip of the extended middle finger, measuring 18in to 22in (46–56cm). Two hundred years later, in 1930, Ludovic Mann offered the alternatives of tiny 'Craftsmen's Measures', an a Unit of 0.6in (1.572cm) and a ß Unit of 0.55in (1.406cm). Alexander Thom in the late 1950s provided statistical evidence

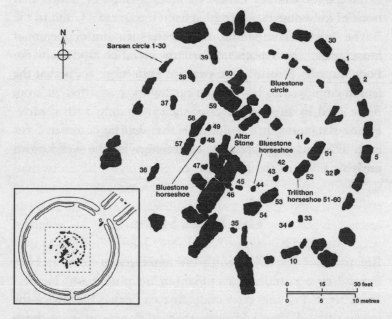

Fig. 3: Diagram showing the stones, stoneholes and pits of the henge.

for his national Megalithic Yard of 2.72ft (0.829m) and Megalithic Rod of 6.8ft (2.07m). The present writer analysed possible counting systems, the limited evidence suggesting that bases of 3 and 4 were common but, despite human fingers and toes, 5 was less so.

He has also proposed that slightly different units of measurement existed in regions as far apart as central Scotland, south-west Ireland and the Lake District. There were local yardsticks in Cork and Perth, 3ft 1½ in (0.95m); Cumbria, 2ft 7½ in (0.8m); and by the Beaker people, 2ft 4½ ins (0.732m). From Powell's analysis of the plans of some Irish passage-tombs there could also have been a Boyne Yard of 2ft 8½ in (0.82m) that was used in the construction of the gigantic passage-tombs of Newgrange and Knowth.[10]

Except for Mann's minuscule units it must be added that none of these suggested lengths, from the Druid's Cubit to the Boyne Yard, is compatible with all the differing diameters at Stonehenge. The hypothetical lengths could be modern inventions. Equally possible, and perhaps even more so, is that the length employed to lay out the earthwork was different from those used by the architects of the sarsen ring and of intervening structures. It is a question that will be considered for each of Stonehenge's phases, beginning with the well-known outlying pillar of the Heel Stone.

The Heel Stone

Isolated some 79ft (24m) north-east of the sarsen circle, the Heel Stone itself is a crude sarsen pillar (an 'uncouth mass', Herbert Stone termed it) that rises clumsily to a peak. Over twice the height of a tall man and more than 30 dangerous tons dead-weight, it would have taken an apprehensive, large gang of labourers, workers in wood who were unused to dealing with ponderous boulders, to manoeuvre it into its deep hole and edge it erect. Gradually, over centuries of insidious rain, snow and gale, it tilted towards the ring, as though piously inclined. Stukeley thought so, perceiving it as a *crwm leche* (bent stone) that his druidical priests had intentionally set leaning piously towards the circle in a 'silent bowing'.[11] At some time a ditch was dug some distance away to surround it. Then, for an unknown reason, that little trench was filled in and hidden.

The name 'Heel' dates back no earlier than the mid-seventeenth century, but since then the outlier has also been known as the sun-stone and the Hele Stone. Predictably in the superstitions of folklore it has also been associated with Merlin the magician, King Arthur and the Devil.

More recently it has been speculated that the high pillar was a foresight (or sighting device) beyond which an observer, standing near the Altar Stone at the centre of the sarsen circle, would have seen the midsummer sun rising. Just as predictably, that was incorrect. What its function was, at what period the stone was set up and whether it was a component of a more elaborate complex of stones are matters to be debated later. First the henge and the stone settings it contains must be considered.

The Slaughter Stone

From the north-eastern entrance of the earthwork and lying to the right (east) against the bank is the tumbled Slaughter Stone, a partly smoothed sarsen pillar as big as many in the circle, 21ft 6in long and 6ft 9in wide (6.6m x 2.1m) and weighing some 30 tons. Like other isolated stones at Stonehenge, the name is as fanciful as the Heel, Four Stations and Altar. None is earlier than 1655. Early chroniclers simply recorded the stone's existence, and it was not until 1799 that Edward King called it 'the slaughtering-stone . . . manifestly to have been designed for the slaying or preparing of victims'.

He had first seen Stonehenge by moonlight and was 'filled with a degree of horror, on reflecting upon the abominations of which this spot must have been the scene . . . in the most corrupted age of druidism'. The source of this fantastical imagery was an anonymous writer of 1776, who had referred to the innocent stone as a 'table, upon which the victims were dissected and prepared'. 'Prepared' was a word that thrilled imaginative readers in the late eighteenth century, the age of Gothic horror stories where lasciviously demented monks prepared to ensnare innocent maidens.[12]

The Aubrey Holes

Passing the Slaughter Stone and entering the earthwork there is a ring of 56 earth-filled pits, lying in a fairly regular circle about 87m (285ft) in diameter. They are known as the Aubrey Holes after the first careful explorer of Stonehenge, John Aubrey, who noticed some in the hot summer of 1666. Their circle was tidy but the holes were not; some were deep, others less so, some neat, others badly dug. Their positions are marked today by weather-stained and grass-encroached concrete discs.

What their function was and to which age of Stonehenge they belonged are contentious questions. Atkinson, who excavated some, was adamant that they had never held posts. Others are certain that they had. It is known that cremated bone was recovered from them, but when those deposits were buried is debatable. Gerald Hawkins, and Fred Hoyle after him, calculated that the number 56 could have been chosen to permit predictions of eclipses of the sun. Statisticians have been sceptical.

It was once suggested to the writer that the Aubrey Holes, surrounding the gaunt sarsen circle, could have had flowers planted in them, the memorial offerings of funerary ceremonies. It is an attractive horticultural image and not as implausible or archaeologically ridiculous as it might seem. Broken pottery fallen from a ledge outside the façade of the splendidly linked and transepted passage-tombs of Les Mousseaux in southern Brittany offered the possibility that the vessels had contained bouquets left by mourners. Like every aspect of Stonehenge, early or late, the Aubrey Holes provide easy questions and elusive solutions.[13]

The Stations

Connected with the Holes because they stood between four pairs of them, the so-called Four Stations – four stones, of which only one and a half survive, once standing at the corners of a rectangle – are no less perplexing and contradictory. Of no known date, they were set between the Aubrey Holes at SE, SSE, NW and NNW. The north-eastern 'station' is now toppled and shifted, its partner opposite at the south-west is a reduced relic and the others have disappeared, their places shown by low and irregularly circular mounds.

Such oblong shapes are almost unknown in prehistoric Britain and Ireland. That the Four Stations should stand inside Stonehenge is almost as incomprehensible as finding the Taj Mahal at the centre of Jerusalem.

Their name was not given until very late (1923), but its origin came almost a century earlier when the Rev. Edward

Duke, of the nearby Lake House, remarked that the short sides stood like observation stations pointing towards the midsummer sunrise and midwinter sunset. A hundred years later Gerald Hawkins analysed the longer sides and noticed that there was an alignment on the northernmost setting of the moon. By the 1990s fashionable revisionism claimed an even more accurate sightline in the opposite direction, towards the midsummer southern moonrise.[14] How such a well-planned oblong was achieved and whether such astronomical orientations were ever intended is one more problem confronting Stonehenge investigators.

The sarsen circle

Set well inside those stones is the dark circle that the world knows as Stonehenge. From the outside it appears disappointingly small. Inside it becomes domineering and claustrophobic. Parts of it are easy to make out. Other settings are best described as confusion.

The most recognizable is the great outer ring, a perfect circle some 97ft 6in (29.7m) across.[15] Of the original 30 tall sarsens, each weighing some 26 tons, only 17 stand and most of them are now set in concrete. They came from the Marlborough Downs about 20 miles to the north. To bring them so far was an arduous undertaking, with the marshes of the Vale of Pewsey to be met before the steep slopes that rose to Salisbury Plain. But what made this monument so remarkable was that it was unique among the stone circles of Britain and Ireland (and the comparable cromlechs of Brittany), because of its lintels that crowned the uprights like a simple but imposing coronet.

From the same Downs came ten even higher pillars, whose five lintelled archways formed a horseshoe open to the north-east and increasing in height from 20ft to 24ft (6m to 7.3m) to the south-west. Stukeley called them 'trilithons' from the Greek *tri-lithos* (three stones).[16] Nowadays the title is invariably applied to Stonehenge, but in classical times it had been used to describe three startlingly long slabs in the walls of the Temple of Jupiter at Baalbek (later Heliopolis, 'City of the Sun'), near Damascus.

It is the ring and the trilithons that awe spectators. In contrast, the never symmetrical and now ravaged higgledy-piggledy 75ft to 78ft (22.9m to 23.8m) inner circle of 60 rough bluestones, and an equally devastated neat horseshoe of 19 smoothed stones, are seldom considered or even noticed as having significance.[17] In several ways they are very informative about some of Stonehenge's secrets. In contrast to the towering sarsens, they are like unkempt urchins slouching and flopping beneath the disapproving glares of their elders.

Of their 70 or so stones – a mongrel collection of dolerites, rhyolites and tuffs, from various parts of south-west Wales – three-quarters have disappeared, despoiled by centuries of plundering in medieval, Tudor, Stuart and Hanoverian times. They were carted away to be shattered for trackways, used as footbridges, lintels and doorsteps, or embedded in walls. Weighing on average 4 tons, about a seventh of the weight of the sarsens, they were no challenge to the wagons and horses that dragged them. It is some consolation that many holes of these looted stones have been discovered during twentieth-century excavations. The remaining stones exist in untidiness. A few stand, some tilt, more are fallen and a few are eroded almost out of sight.

The Altar Stone

The last of the internal Stonehenge features is the Altar Stone, which lies pressed into the earth near the middle of the ring, half-buried under the crushing heaviness of a pillar of a collapsed trilithon at the south-west. The Altar Stone is neither a sarsen nor a bluestone. It is a fine-grained, glittering, greenish sandstone, 16ft long and 3ft wide (5m x 1m). Its name was a speculation of Inigo Jones, the royal architect, who first saw it in 1620: 'Whether it might be an *Altar* or no, I leave to the judgement of others, because so overwhelmed with the ruine of the Work, that I could make no search after it'. It could have been for sacrifices, 'Wherein the *Victims* for oblations were slain'.[18]

Whether that had been the function of the Altar Stone is debatable, even unlikely, but exactly where it came from is important when considering the question of how the bluestones came to Salisbury Plain. Even more important – although the matter seems trivial – is whether it had ever stood erect rather than intentionally laid flat.

Numbering systems

The numbering system used to identify the stones and other features at Stonehenge needs some explanation (fig. 4). There had been maladroit attempts by early workers – John Wood in 1747 with each setting numbered individually; John Smith in 1771, numbering circles and the bluestone horseshoe individually, but giving trilithons planetary symbols (Mercury to Saturn plus the Earth and its moon); Sir Richard Colt Hoare in 1812 with letters A, B, C, D, E, F for the settings inwards and each stone numbered, from A1 to F2.

Rejecting these it was Flinders Petrie, later to win fame as an Egyptologist, who in 1877 proposed the system that has been used ever since. With his father he had made a plan of the circle in 1874. Being an excellent surveyor, and dissatisfied with the outcome, he returned in 1877 with an improved 1,000in (25.4m) steel measuring chain. The result was the first really accurate and thorough survey of Stonehenge.

Petrie was logical. Although in his book he listed the conspicuous sarsens first and the less noticeable bluestones later, his numbered sequence worked inwards, setting by setting, from the outer ring to the central Altar Stone.[19]

The stones of the great circle were numbered 1–30, clockwise from the north-east; then 31–49 for the 19 remnants of the ruined circle of once 60 bluestones inside the sarsens. The uprights of the trilithons followed as 51–60, succeeded by 41–49 for the survivors of the elegant inner horseshoe of 19 bluestones. The Altar Stone became number 80.

Lintels were numbered by adding 100 to the higher numbered of its two supporters. The three lintels in position at the north-east of the sarsen circle, resting on the tops of stones 29, 30, 1 and 2, became numbers 130, 101 and 102. The lintel of the eastern trilithon, 51–52, became 152. Prostrate fragments were lettered according to their former stone, so that the two pieces of the gigantic fallen trilithon pillar 55 became 55a and 55b, the latter lying on top of the fallen Altar Stone.

It was an ingenious scheme and it has remained workable – although, perversely, it is not always followed. Outside the circle and its internal settings, the rectangle of the Four Stations, again starting at the north-east, became 91–94 even though two were missing. The Slaughter Stone lying by the entrance to the earthwork was number 95. Because its one-time partner had disappeared, the missing pillar was allotted not a number but the letter E. Stone 96 was the outlying Heel

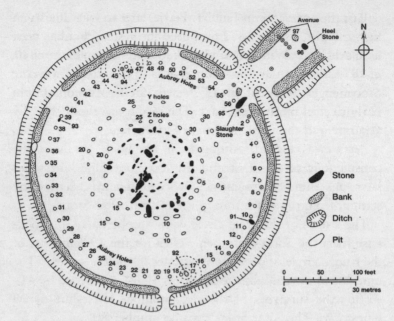

Fig. 4: Diagram showing Flinders Petrie's numbering system, established in 1877.

Stone. Alongside it, the stonehole discovered in 1979 illogically became number 97. Because it no longer existed, it should have been F in accord with the lost E that had partnered the Slaughter Stone. Teutonic inflexibility is not a characteristic of British archaeology.

The 56 Aubrey Holes were first numbered by Hawley, their excavator, in 1921.[20] They also run clockwise from the northeast entrance of the henge – first the excavated pits, 1–32, followed by 33–54 which have been located but not excavated and finally, numbers 55 and 56 which are the last, lying across the entrance just to the north-west of Aubrey Hole 1.

There are also features that are invisible to visitors – two separate semi-circles of holes that are unmarked and the Q and R Holes inside the ring where bluestones once stood. In the

1950s they were numbered Q1 to Q30 and R1 to R30. The Y and Z Holes, now grassed over around the sarsen circle, were similarly numbered by Hawley, Y1 to Y30 and Z1 to Z30, clockwise from the north-east. Little of this was known to Stonehenge's first chronicler, Henry of Huntington, in the early twelfth century AD.

CHAPTER 1:

ANTIQUARIANS; RECOVERING STONEHENGE; TO AD 1900

The island was Britain 'and [as Oldcastle wrote] "the sacred precinct" of Apollo would be the famous Stone Age remains of Stonehenge'.

Oldfather (1929), p. 37n.

Monastic writings and medieval myth-making

Stonehenge entered written history in AD 1129 when it was mentioned in the first edition of Henry of Huntingdon's *Historia Anglorum (*The History of England) as the Second Wonder of Britain – *Secundum est apud Stanhenges*.[1] Spelled variously as Stanhenges, Stanenge and Stanhenge', the name is a conjunction of two Old English words, *stan* (stone) and *hengen* (hanging), due to the resemblence of the framework of the sarsens, especially the trilithons, to gallows.[2] Stukeley understood that the word was 'plainly Saxon & signifys only the hanging stones', a 'stone gallows'.[3]

Henry, an early twelfth-century archdeacon of Huntingdon, may never have seen the monument but he had heard of its astonishment. 'The Second Wonder is Stonehenge, where stones of extraordinary dimensions are raised as columns, and others are fixed above, like lintels of immense portals; and no one has been able to discover by what mechanism such vast masses of stone were elevated, nor for what purpose they were designed'.[4]

Ten years later, in 1139, when Henry was accompanying a newly appointed Archbishop of Canterbury to Rome, the entourage rested at the Abbey of Bec in Normandy. Here Henry met Robert de Torigny, monk and historian, who showed him Geoffrey of Monmouth's recently issued *Historia Regum Britanniae* (History of the Kings of Britain) with its fantasies about Stonehenge, Merlin and Irish giants.[5] But it had been Henry who was the first to mention the wonderful stone circle on Salisbury Plain.

It has been claimed, mistakenly, that Stonehenge had been described a thousand years earlier by the first-century BC historian, Diodorus Siculus. In Book II of his *Library of History* he referred to a distant island with a 'renowned temple of a round form', obtaining his information from the late fourth-century BC chronicler, Hecataeus of Abdera, who in turn had copied it from *On the Ocean* by the Greek explorer Pytheas of Marseilles.

This temple could not have been Stonehenge. Diodorus recorded that the moon as viewed from this island, appears to be but a little distance from the earth, a lunar phenomenon that could never have happened in southern England. The only

possible latitude for it was 58° north, a full 500 miles from
Salisbury Plain. Diodorus added that the temple was associated with the vernal equinox and the bright constellation of
the Pleiades. Links with the moon, the equinox and the stars all
exist at the marvellous stone circle of Callanish with its avenue
and rows on the island of Lewis, in the Outer Hebrides. It was
not Diodorus Siculus who introduced Stonehenge to history. It
was Henry of Huntingdon.[6] The man who brought chaos to
the story of Stonehenge was Geoffrey of Monmouth.

His *Historia Regum Britanniae* purportedly was a learned
chronicle of the years after the departure of the Romans. In
reality it was a scrapbook of genuine annals mixed with
legends, folk-stories and guesswork that introduced his recep-
tive audience to a land of giants, King Arthur and Merlin.

Few readers would have been excited by Geoffrey's report
that St Augustine had come to Britain 'to preach the word of
God to the Angles, who, blinded by their pagan superstition,
had done away with Christianity'. Every literate person knew
that it had been done better by the Venerable Bede 400 years
earlier. Much more enthralling was the story about the mas-
sacre of British nobles at Amesbury by treacherous Saxons.
Vortigern, King of Britain, vowed to build a cenotaph as a
memorial to his murdered subjects. Merlin the magician
advised him to 'send for the Giants' Ring' – called Chorea
Gigantum (the dance of the monsters) – which was an immense
stone circle on Mount Killaurus in Ireland. 'The stones are
enormous and there is no one alive strong enough to move
them'. They were doubly desirable. Not only were they huge,
but they had medicinal powers if water were poured over
them.

Arriving at the ring the Britons 'strove their hardest to take
the Ring down' but failed. Merlin succeeded. Later elabora-
tions had him put them on his back and fly over the sea to

Salisbury Plain, but Geoffrey was content to have the wizard dismantle the circle and have the stones carried down to the sea. It did not matter. The damage was done. Stonehenge was magically accounted for. The stones were curative and they came from Ireland.

Myths have a permanence that facts cannot always efface. Even a thousand years later, in the present day, Ireland remains a part of the Stonehenge archaeological canon. The credulity and ignorance is unsurprising. A recent history poll found that one person in ten believed that Adolf Hitler was a fiction, whereas half thought that Robin Hood and Lord Edmund Blackadder were real people. As King Arthur was another of these reincarnations, it demonstrates how history and fable can blur. Geoffrey of Monmouth's whimsies are not dead.[7]

Yet even in his lifetime not everyone accepted those fantasies. Just a few years after the *Historia Regum Britanniae* appeared, a fellow monk, William of Newburgh, accused Geoffrey of 'the most ridiculous fictions', of being a storyteller who 'promulgated the mendacious predictions of one Merlin' in a so-called history which he 'impertinently and impudently falsifies in every respect'.[8] Nobody cared. *Historia Regum Britanniae* was the most popular pot-boiler of medieval times, had many copyists and still lures the misguided today.

One might wonder that so little attention was given to Stonehenge between its gradual decline around 1500 BC and Henry of Huntingdon's words almost 2,500 years later.

Once people had abandoned the ruin of Stonehenge in the middle of the Bronze Age, the stones had been deserted. Similar superstition and indifference kept later people away from ancient monuments elsewhere in Britain and Ireland, where not one of more than a thousand stone circles contained Iron Age objects.

At Stonehenge no clear picture emerges of Iron Age activity.
A tinker's hoard of scrap metal was secreted by Stone 7 but
never recovered. The corpse of a young man was buried in the
ditch of the long-abandoned Palisade.[9] The only substantial
first-century BC structure in the area was the spacious triangular earthwork of Vespasian's Camp hillfort a long mile to
the east.

Even in Roman times there was nothing permanent. Coins
were dropped inside the ring by casual sightseers from the first
to the late fourth century AD. Little more. That the ring had
been partly dismantled because it had been a centre of druidical resistance is improbable. Writers about Britain like
Caesar and Tacitus never mentioned the ring nor any incident
about it. Nor is there archaeological evidence to connect any
other stone circle with the Iron Age druids. The Romans had
no need to despoil the monument. Weather and makeshift
workmanship had already done that.[10]

Yet according to the antiquarian and traveller, William
Camden (whose pioneering survey of Great Britain, *Britannia*,
was published in Latin in 1586 and in English in 1610), even in
ruin Stonehenge may have been used in those remote years:

> I have heard that in the time of King Henrie the Eighth, there
> was found neere this place a table of metall, as it had been tin
> and lead commixt, inscribed with many letters, but in so
> strange a Caracter, that neither Sir Thomas Eliot, nor master
> Lilye Schoole-master of Pauls, could read it, and therefore
> neglected it. Had it been preserved, somewhat happily might
> have beene discovered concerning *Stonehenge*, which now lieth
> obscured.

John Aubrey mused, 'The Inscription in Lead found at Stone-
heng, wch Mr Lilly the Schoolmaster, and Sir Tho. Eliot could

not read, might be made by the Druides'. Stukeley added his regrets:

> But eternally to be lamented is the loss of that tablet of tin, which was found at this place . . . inscrib'd with many letters . . . No doubt it was a memorial of the founders, wrote by the Druids, and had it been preserv'd till now, would have been an invaluable curiosity.

The enigmatic object has disappeared with no record. It may have been a 'curse', like those offered in Roman times to the goddess Sulis and other deities. Known as *defixiones* and written on imperishable lead, such tablets were intended to harm. At chariot-races in ancient Rome gamblers buried them near the starting-line, specifying which rival team was to be upset, even killed. It would have been fitting if in the dying ages of Stonehenge someone had come to the silent circle begging its almost forgotten spirits for revenge against an enemy.[11]

Saxon settlers provided a new name for the site (the original long forgotten), calling it 'stan-hengen', the stone gallows title that Henry of Huntingdon knew. The image of the gibbet was probably deterrent enough to keep superstitious settlers away. There were Saxon farmers nearby at Amesbury (Ambresbyrig, meaning 'Ambre's burgh' or 'land-holding') and Durrington (Derintone, 'Deora's farm', in the Domesday Book),[12] but the incomers left no souvenirs at the deserted and forbidding stones.

By the twelfth century a combination of Christianity, literacy, a network of trackways and visits to shrines had brought Stonehenge back into the world. Ever since the late eleventh century when Lanfranc, the Norman-appointed Archbishop of Canterbury, asserted his dominance over York and then demanded the same obedience from Christian houses

in Ireland, bishops from that country had been making journeys to Canterbury, while English and Welsh clerics visited
Ireland. It was monasticism, not Merlin, that created the
overseas connection with Stonehenge.[13]

Not many years after Geoffrey of Monmouth's Arthurian
stories, the monk Gerald of Wales went to Ireland five times,
once in 1085 in the retinue of Prince John. Like others he rode
from Dublin to the wondrous abbey of St Brigid at Kildare,
'the church of the oak grove'. 'Great is victorious Brigid', he
exulted, 'and lovely her thronged sanctuary' with its eternal
flame and beautifully illustrated manuscripts.[14] That ride from
Dublin to Kildare was the cause of one of the most enduring of
all myths about Stonehenge. The prelates and the priests
passed several towering standing stones, just like those on
Salisbury Plain, and clerical minds imagined that others had
been stolen to build Stonehenge. That is why Geoffrey of
Monmouth, another cleric, wrote of the Irish Giants' Ring.

Prelates travelled to Ireland from as far away as south-east
England, riding along the Harroway (the 'hard' or 'old' road),
a gradual linking of age-old, local tracks that followed higher
ground, avoiding swamps and forests, to cross England from
coast to coast. Part of it is now Chaucer's Pilgrims' Way to
Canterbury, but it was far more ancient than that medieval
road. Prehistoric pilgrims knew parts of it. The Harroway led
for miles westwards from Dover, Canterbury and Rochester,
past Farnham and Basingstoke to Amesbury, then, near to
Bulford, across a ford whose marshy banks were pink with
ragged robin flowers. Then the way rose to Salisbury Plain and
Stonehenge. Marvelling bishops and passers-by stared at the
impossibly high, weathered pillars, understanding nothing
about them.[15]

What they never remarked on were the dwarfed bluestones.
Even a fanciful fourteenth-century sketch shows only Merlin

handling a lintel into place, 'more easily than anyone would believe', in sight of two astonished onlookers. Not one bluestone is shown. Another contemporary drawing, 'the earliest known image of Stonehenge', depicted a strangely rectangular 'circle' of sarsens but no bluestones. Nobody noticed them.[16] The absence is stressed because the evidence becomes vital to an understanding of one of the early phases of Stonehenge.

Elizabethan and Stuart responses to Stonehenge

Towards the end of the sixteenth century a proper sketch of the circle was made. Around 1568–69, Joris Hoefnagel, a topographical artist who specialized in perspective drawings of monuments (a rare technique for his time), visited Stonehenge, perhaps with a Flemish friend, Lucas de Heere. Hoefnagel's drawings are lost, but four Elizabethan half-aerial copies of his Stonehenge from the north-west have survived – de Heere's; a tinted drawing by William Smith, a royal herald; an engraving dated 1575 by an unknown 'R.F.' (fig. 5); and a clumsy engraving for the 1600 edition of Camden's *Britannia*. Of these, de Heere's and Smith's show only the sarsen circle, but both 'R.F.' and the Camden version include extra features.

There are absurdities in the Camden, such as a walled castle in a mountainous background instead of Vespasian's Camp Iron Age fort on its low hill, presumably a misunderstanding of the Latin *castrum* (fort). The ring itself is a travesty. The trilithons are skewed, as curvaceous as a Modigliani nude, and linked together like a medieval mass gallows but with stones missing or misplaced. Despite these blunders, the engraving has merits. Station Stone 93 is in the foreground. The bank and ditch are shown, and also two adjacent stones standing outside the ring at the north-east. They must be the Slaughter Stone and the now-missing Stone E, showing that they were still erect in 1575.[17]

Fig. 5: The first-known sketch of Stonehenge, made in 1575 by 'R.F.'.

Realism about Stonehenge began in the late sixteenth century. Camden admitted complete ignorance of the circle's history because there were no books to guide him. The ring was a 'huge and monstrous piece of worke' inside whose ditch were 'certain mightie and unwrought stones' with lintels 'so that the whole frame seemeth to hang'. He added that some believed the stones to be artificial, stuck together 'by some glewie and unctuous matter knit and incorporate together'.

Camden did not speculate about origins. 'For mine owne part, about these points I . . . lament with much griefe that the Authors of so notable a monument are thus buried in oblivion'. He continues:

> I feare me greatly that no man is able to fetch out the truth, so
> deeply plunged within the winding revolutions of so many
> ages . . . they lie so hidden in the utmost nooke and secretest
> closet of Antiquitie, as it were in a most thicke wood, where no
> pathwaies ae to be seene . . . oblivion hath so long removed out
> of sight of our ancestours.[18]

The reluctant acceptance that the present was helplessly ignorant of the prehistoric past was to endure throughout the
seventeenth and eighteenth centuries.

In 1620 James I visited the Earl of Pembroke's great house at
Wilton, seven miles south of the circle. Some of the royal party
rode out to the ring and, not content with looking, dug into
various parts, finding skulls of bulls, oxen 'or other beasts'.
Prominent amongst these primitive archaeologists were Dr
William Harvey, discoverer of the circulation of the blood;
Inigo Jones, the royal architect; and George Villiers, Duke of
Buckingham and favourite of the king.

Inigo Jones – appointed five years earlier as the prestigious
Surveyor of the King's Works – was commanded by the king,
'out of mine own experience in *Architecture,* and experience in
Antiquities abroad, what possibly I could discover concerning
this *Stoneheng*'. The result was to be the first book entirely
devoted to the circle.[19]

Having pitched his tent near the ring, Jones cleared the
ground and began his investigations. Being a meticulous
architect Jones was not content merely to measure diameters
and record the heights of stones. By excavation he also discovered how deeply they were set in the chalk. He 'digged
throughout all the Foundations'. He checked that there had
been no stones between the circle and the surrounding earthwork, proving that 'there could never be found, by whatever
digging, though no Cost or Pains was spared, the Footsteps or

Fragments of any Courses of Stone between those of the Trench, and the outward Circle'.

The result was the first plan of the circle, 'The Groundplot of the work as it now stands'. Some stones had gone, a lintel-less trilithon 57–58 was leaning, to fall two centuries later, and many lintels were missing from the outer circle.[20]

From faulty reasoning Jones deduced there had been three gaps through the bank, placed geometrically at the corners of an equilateral triangle – a wide one at the north-east, a narrower at the south, and a mistaken one at the north-west, each with four portal stones that gave dignity to the entrances. Forty years later John Aubrey called this trio 'absolutely false', and on the plan he made for Charles II he drew in only the north-east entrance with two stones inside the bank and one more outside the ditch. Jones' nephew, John Webb, using his uncle's posthumous and 'indigested' notes, corroborated this. 'He hath described in his Draught two Stones . . . these were the two parallel stones that *stood* upon the inside of the Trench, at the Entrance from the North-East'.[21]

Presumably writing several forgetful years after 1620, Jones was also wrong about the condition of the portals, 'At each of which was raised, on the Outside of the Trench aforesaid, two huge Stones gatewise, parallel where unto on the Inside two others of less Proportion'. He had confused the inner with the outer pair. It was the external pillars that were smaller and smashed. He described them as 'four foot broad, and three foot thick; but they lie so broken, and ruined by time, that their proportion in height cannot be distinguisht, much less exactly measured'. The inner pair – the Slaughter Stone (number 95) and E – still stood, 'seven foot broad, three foot thick, and twenty foot high'.[22]

His great strength was his wide knowledge of classical architecture. From his plan he decided that Stonehenge was

1. *The Trench.*
2. *The Entrance thereat from the North-East.*
3. *The two Pyramids thereof, on the outside of the Trench.*
4. *The other two on the inside.*
5. *The Pylasters of the outward Circle, or Supporters of the o[   ]
   Gallery, as G. Cambrensis hath it.*
6. *The Architraves incumbent on them.*
7. *The Perpendicular Stones of the inner Circle.*
8. *The Pylasters of the greater Hexagon.*
9. *The Architraves that adorn them.*
10. *The Pylasters of the lesser Hexagon.*

Fig. 6: Engraving from John Webb's *Vindication of Stone-heng Restored* (2nd edition, 1725). This speculative plan is that of Webb's uncle-in-law, Inigo Jones, and was drawn in the 1620s.

Roman, of the Tuscan order, 'rude, plain, simple'. He wrote, 'The *Order* is not only *Roman*, but the *Scheam* also (consisting of four [intersecting] equilaterall triangles, inscribed within the circumference of a Circle) by which this work *Stoneheng* formed, was an *Architectonicall Scheam* used by the Romans', as described by the famous architect, Marcus Pollio Vitruvius, whose *De Architectura* was the standard work on the architecture of classical theatres. It followed that Stonehenge was a Roman work.

Jones realized that there would have been a sixth trilithon to complete 'the greater Hexagon', most of whose stones 'after so long a contest with the violence of time, and injury of weather, are for the most part standing at this day'. But integrity made him omit the speculative trilithon from his objective Plan 7. His conclusion was erudite, intelligent, logical and wrong.

The architect died in 1652. His book was not published until his nephew, John Webb, had it printed in 1655. It was an anticlimax. Few copies were made, sales were poor and slow, and the remaining stock was destroyed in 1666 in the Great Fire. There was a minor revival. Existing copies became 'extremely scarce, and at the same time much sought after by the Curious'. They remain collectors' items even today.[23]

As Horace Walpole acidulously observed much later, 'It is remarkable that whoever has treated of the monument has bestowed on it whatever class of antiquity he was particularly fond of'. It was true of Jones and it was true of Walter Charleton half a century later.[24] Eight years after the posthumous publication of Jones' book, Walter Charleton, a royal physician, contradicted it, deciding that Stonehenge was the handiwork of Danes, using learnedly literary references to ancient monuments in Denmark, but making no attempt to describe Stonehenge itself. Inigo Jones introduced the reading world to what could be seen at the site. Charleton added nothing.[25]

John Webb, who had married Jones' niece, resolved to counteract Charleton's Danish assertion by writing a tedious vindication of Jones' beliefs in 1665. Seventy years later an enterprising but probably over-optimistic publisher printed an omnibus trilogy of Jones' *Stone-Heng* (1655); Charleton's *Chorea Gigantum* (1663); and Webb's *Vindication of Stone-heng Restored* (1665; fig. 6). Together the books formed, as Stuart Piggott observed in a facsimile reprint of 1971, 'a forgotten controversy conducted on forgotten lines of argument . . . It is a microcosm of the battle of the ancients and Moderns, with Jones, Webb and Charleton on the far side of the intellectual gulf, Aubrey and Stukeley on the near side, which is ours today'.[26]

Royalty, in the form of James I's grandson, intervened again in the history of Stonehenge. As a refugee after the Battle of Worcester, Prince Charles had passed an anonymous 7 October 1651 at Stonehenge with Colonel Philips, 'reckoning and re-reckoning the stones'. After his restoration to the throne in 1660 Charles II was astonished to learn from his physician, Walter Charleton, that John Aubrey believed Avebury 'does as much exceed in bignes/greatness the renowned Stoneheng, as a Cathedral doeth a parish Church'. Intrigued that 'his' circle could be so belittled, the king commanded Aubrey to attend court.[27]

Today John Aubrey is best known for his popular and amusing *Brief Lives*, a compendium of facts, suppositions and gossip about contemporaries, often needing little more than a succinct line or two to sketch a character – the historian, Sir William Sanderson who 'dyed at Whitehall . . . went out like a spent candle'; Thomas Willis, physician and a founder of the Royal Society, who with his 'dark, brindled hair (like a red pig) stammered much'; Gwyn, the Earl of Oxford's secretary, was 'a squeamish, and disobligeing, slighting, insolent, proud fellow . . . [who] cutt some sower faces that would turne the milke in a faire ladie's breast'.[28]

But John Aubrey was more than a witty purveyor of tittle-tattle. He was Britain's first great archaeologist. For more than 30 years, through fieldwork and correspondence with fellow enthusiasts, he accumulated information about stone circles and other ancient monuments, a corpus that has remained an invaluable source-book, often providing details of sites that no longer exist.

He was tireless, 'never off horseback' in his search for antiquities. Having discovered Avebury by accident in 1649 while out hunting with friends he started to gather facts about prehistoric rings. Learning that many were in parts of Britain such as north-eastern Scotland, western Wales and Ireland where Romans, Saxons or Danes had never been, he realized that the rings were pre-Roman. 'I am perswaded that the monument was built long before the Romans ever knew Britaine . . . a work of a people settled in their country', and therefore 'tis odds, but that these ancient Monuments (sc. Aubury, Stoneheng, Kerrig y Druidd &c) were Temples of the Priests of the most eminent Order, viz, Druids, and it is strongly to be presumed that Aubury, Stoneheng to be as ancient as those times'. It was an insight that proved seminal to the study of megalithic rings. He was realistic. 'The retriving of these forgotten things from oblivion in some sort resembles the Art of a Conjurer'.[29]

When he attended Charles II in 1663 he took with him a plan of Avebury 'donne from memorie alone', interested the king, and in late August joined the royal party at the ring where Charles and his brother James rode up the nearby Silbury Hill. Aubrey, however, was embarrassed to see how inaccurate his early plan of Avebury was, and the following

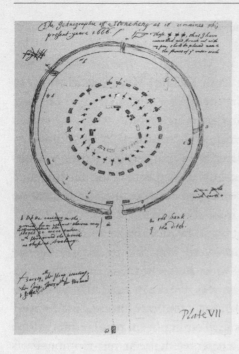

Fig. 7: John Aubrey's accurate plan of 1666.

month he 'surveyed the old Monument of Aubury with a plaine-table'. Three years later he took a 'Review of Stoneheng', a site he 'had knowne since eight yeares old'. He entitled it 'The Ichonographie of Stoneheng as it remaines this present yeare 1666'. His plan was good, measured accurately despite the litter of stones. 'From the circular Trench to the grand circle of stones is thirty-five yards [105ft; 32m]. The Diameter of the grand circle of stones is thirty two yards ½'. At 97ft 6in (29.7m), this distance accords exactly with Thom's precise survey of 1973.[30]

Aubrey disagreed with Jones' hypothesis, and 'this gave me an edge to make more researches'. At the north-eastern entrance of the circle, Aubrey's plan, drawn almost 50 years after Jones' investigations, showed only the eastern outer portal. The shattered fragments of the west had disappeared. The Slaughter Stone and its partner remained standing.[31] Beyond them was the yet-to-be misnamed Heel Stone 'of which there hath not been any notice taken'. It was, he decided, 'the remaines of the Avenue', like those he had seen at Avebury and Stanton Drew. Two dotted lines stretching northwards past the Heel 'signifie the imaginarie Walke of Stones which was there heretofore'.[32]

He ridiculed Geoffrey of Monmouth. The sarsens had not been brought by Merlin from Ireland. 'They are of the very kind of Stone with the Grey-weathers about 14 miles off: that tract of ground near Marleborough'. Nor were the stones artificial and carried by magic to Salisbury Plain. Common-sense told him that they had been dragged on 'Rowlers' from near Avebury. He did not, however, speculate on the origin of the bluestones, perhaps did not even notice their different appearance and texture from the sarsens.

He found no stone that could be recognized as an Altar, but his keen observation did make him the discoverer of the famous pits now named after him, the Aubrey Holes. Late in 1919 William Hawley was working near the Slaughter Stone and, knowing of Aubrey's findings, probed with a steel bar and found several of the filled-in pits 'at regular intervals of 16 feet [4.9m] . . . To these we have given the name of "Aubrey Holes" to distinguish them from others which may hereafter be found, and as a compliment to our respected pioneer who left such a useful record'.

They were, wrote Aubrey, 'little cavities in the ground, from whence one may well conjecture the stones c, c, were taken', referring to the two remaining Four Stations, 91 and 93, that he supposed had once been part of a ring around the inner edge of the ditch '(ornamentally) as at Aubury'. Had he guessed 'posts' rather than 'stones' he would have been more than 300 years ahead of later suppositions.

Sceptics doubted that he could have discerned such insignificant traces of holes that had been filled for more than 4,000 years, but the sceptics were sadly ignorant of English history. The year preceding Aubrey's discovery, 1665, had been the time of the Great Plague, while 1666 was the year of the Great

Fire of London. They were also two years with insufferably hot
summers when prayers were said daily for rain, and Aubrey's
'cavities' would have retained some moisture, vegetation and
colour unlike the aridly hard and bleached chalk around
them.[33]

He also mentioned a folk-story about a fallen stone that lay
at the west of the ring:

> One of the great Stones that lies downe on the west side, hath a
> cavity something resembling the print of a man's foot; con-
> cerning which the Shepherds and countrey people have a
> Tradition (w[ch] many of them doe steadfastly believe) that when
> Merlin conveyed these Stones from Ireland by Art Magick, the
> Devill hitt him in the heele with that stone, and so left the print
> there.

The particular 'great' supine pillar was possibly the tumbled
number 19 at the west of the outer circle, some 20ft by 6ft (6m
by 1.8m) according to John Wood. Aubrey never specifically
identified it, and it was not until 1771 that John Smith wilfully
ignored the legend and, for the sake of his astronomical
theories, transferred the name to the 'solar' Heel Stone which
had never lain down and had no sign of a footprint on it. The
Devil and sarsens were almost bedfellows in Wiltshire. Villagers claimed there was an imprint of his foot on one of the
Broome circle stones, and the fiend lurked everywhere in and
around Avebury.[34]

Aubrey did not limit his description to the circle. 'Round
about Stoneheng', he noted, 'one may number 43, or 45
Barrowes, some much bigger than others'. Camden had
known of them: 'Mens bones have beene digged up here',
and his engraving portrayed two treasure-hunters, unearthed
skull and bones beside them, trenching into a ditched round

barrow, perhaps a foreshortened view of a bell barrow in the Cursus group. The engraving was a copy of R.F.'s sketch of 1575, which 'sheweth wher great bones of men ar found'. Camden believed the bones had been buried by the comrades of warriors killed in battles. Aubrey doubted it. 'Soldiers have something else to do'.[35]

As early as 1620 there had been digging inside Stonehenge itself, not only by Jones but by the king's favourite, George Villiers, Duke of Buckingham, who had a huge pit dug near the centre. He also had several barrows opened, but by Aubrey's time any finds had been forgotten and lost. Dissatisfied by his profitless efforts the nobleman decided to purchase the ring and 'offered Mr. Newdick (then Owner of this place) any rate for it but he would not accept it.'[36]

John Aubrey was very much a man of his time, intelligent, educated but conditioned from childhood by popular beliefs, of fairies, witchcraft and giants, and that church bells could drive away thunder. His mind was a medley of scientific curiosity and medieval credulity. He recorded without scepticism the local tradition that pieces or grains of sarsen dropped into wells would drive away toads. Yet he dismissed the notion that 'no Mag-Pye, Toade, or Snake was ever seen here' as though the animals were terrified of the stones. To the contrary, he explained, weaker birds would not fly over the open plain 'for fear of Hawkes and Ravens', toads would not move far from their spawning-grounds, and snakes and adders preferred the protection of shade and shelter.

Although he rejected Jones' explanation for his 'greater Hexagon' he did wonder, 'Why might not be then, the seaven-sided figure in the foregoing scheme be made in relation to the seaven Planets, & seaven daies of the Weeke? I cannot determine. I only suggest'. It was speculation without foundation. In early prehistoric Britain there were no days of the week, only daytime and night, the waxing and waning of the moon and the slow changing of the seasons.

Nor, in the early seventeenth century, were there seven planets. Still to be discovered were Uranus (1781), Neptune (1846) and Pluto (1930). Aubrey's seven were Mercury, Venus, Mars, Jupiter and Saturn plus the Earth and its moon. As late as 1771 John Smith used an almost identical combination when labelling the trilithons on his plan. 'I call them the seven planets, which at present give names to the seven days of the week'.[37]

John Aubrey's Stonehenge can be left with his words about starlings. 'I thought of *Aves Druidum* when I saw the Stares breed in holes of the Stones of Stoneheng. The Welsh doe call Stars *Sturni Adar y Drudwy, i.e. Aves Druidum,* "birds of the druids" because they could talk'. Then came a comment that could have come straight from his *Brief Lives,* a characteristic Aubreyism. 'Pliny tells of a stare that could speake Greek. Why not?'[38]

Georgian and Victorian findings

There were three literary giants in the early history of Stonehenge. Inigo Jones had been a limping one; John Aubrey, an innovative one. Towering above them was the brilliant William Stukeley, who spent years not only inside Stonehenge, measuring, finding, recording, but also outside it, exploring the countryside, recognizing features that had been forgotten for millennia.

He is often derided for his improbable druid-as-a-proto-Christian theory first put forward in his book of 1740, *Stonehenge a Temple Restor'd to the British Druids.* Almost unknown are his much earlier, clear-headed notes of fieldwork at

Stonehenge from 1721 to 1724. Stukeley's manuscript about his work at Stonehenge, 'The History of the Temples and Religion of the Antient Celts. Par. II', remained almost forgotten in the Local Studies Department of Cardiff Central Library for years, and has only recently been published. Its revelations were a triumph for archaeology, and it is that manuscript's objective records rather than the later book's polemics that are cited here.[39]

There were inevitable mistakes. Stukeley miscalculated the date of the circle by over 2,000 years. His despairing use of classical references to illuminate the customs of prehistoric societies in western Europe resulted in confusion, rather than clarity. Yet this was a minor fault amongst the perceptive discoveries, and came from an eighteenth-century ignorance of the Neolithic and Early Bronze Age in southern England. It was Stukeley's archaeological insights that were the triumphs.

Having visited and explored Avebury six times between 1719 and 1724 he turned to Stonehenge, a monument that had

already attracted him. In 1716 he had recorded, 'Happening to fall into a Set of thoughts about Stonehenge in Wiltshire . . . I undertook to make an exact Model of that most noble and splendid piece of Antiquity'.

Fig. 8: Engraving of William Stukeley by Gerard Vandergucht, 1740. 'Chyndonax' was Stukeley's druidical nickname as President of the Society of Roman Knights.

Stukeley worked at Stonehenge between 1721 and 1724, admiring it, although reluctantly agreeing with John Aubrey that Avebury 'did as much excell Stoneheng, as a Cathedral does a Parish Church'. In his notes, after three years' field-work, Stukeley stated, 'Great as were the Conceptions of the Founders of Abury yet Stonehenge will not be dispensd with claiming the second Place to it'.[40]

Despite this reservation, in the company of colleagues such as his friends Roger Gale and Edmond Halley, and the noble-men, Lords Pembroke and Winchelsea, he measured, planned, examined the diverse mineralogy of the stones, excavated, devised the word 'trilithon' and discovered unsuspected fea-tures of the landscape such as the Avenue and the Cursus.

At Avebury he had stayed at the Catherine Wheel Inn inside the earthwork. For Stonehenge he sometimes lodged in Ames-bury. More often he was a guest at Wilton House, the palatial ancestral home of Henry Herbert, 9th Earl of Pembroke. By an archaeological coincidence Stukeley was there almost exactly 100 years after Inigo Jones.[41]

Stonehenge fascinated him. It was, he thought, 'more antient than the arrival of the Romans here', but unfortunately, by a

Fig. 9: Drawing of Stonehenge by William Stukeley, 1722.

wrong choice of calculations, he decided that the druids had built but only used the ring from about 480 to 100 BC. Had he accepted the judgement of Edmond Halley, astronomer and mathematician, who inspected the weathering of the sarsens and calculated an existence of 'not less than 3,000 years, perhaps longer', Stukeley would have been extremely close to the true date.[42]

Despite this chronological lapse Stukeley was correct in many observations. He rejected the opinions of Geoffrey of Monmouth, Inigo Jones and John Webb. The circle was the handiwork of skilful British druids who had used a cubit of precisely 20.8in (52.8cm) for their measurements. 'Stonehenge' was a Saxon word, 'the hanging stones or gallows'. He was also a geological pioneer, realizing that the outer circle, the low and inconspicuous horseshoe-shaped setting inside it and the Altar Stone were all from different sources – the sarsens of the circle from the Marlborough Downs, the bluestones of the horseshoe 'from the west', and the Altar a 'blue coarse marble' like boulders in the Peak District.

Evidence of the builders' dedication was obvious. However bulky and tough, every side of a sarsen above ground had been dressed, smoother on its inner face and tapering gently upwards, an architectural device known as entasis ('to create an optical illusion of straightness', added Richard Atkinson 300 years later).[43]

There was further refinement. In the great horseshoe the five pairs of lintelled sarsens, which he termed 'trilithons' (three stones), were graded in height, rising towards the Great Trilithon at the south-west. Inside the horseshoe lay the Altar Stone, not quite central to the circle, 'whereon no doubt the matter of their sacrifices was consumed by fire'. Stukeley dug under it but found nothing but 'solid chalk mixt with flints which had never been dug'.[44]

Outside the circle Stukeley recorded the two survivors of the Four Stations stones, the tumbled Slaughter Stone and the tilted Heel Stone, 'perhaps the place of bowing adoration upon approach'.[45] It stood inside a ditched and earth-banked avenue which 'was never observ'd by any who have wrote of it, tho' a very elegant part of it, and very apparent'. Several times over two years Gale and he measured and re-measured it with a theodolite. It had been lined with standing stones, although 'there is not one stone left therof, yet a curious eye without difficulty will discern a mark of the holes whence they were taken'. There had been 50 on each side.

Yet in his book of 1740 Stukeley made no mention of them, and a few days after its publication Gale chided him for the omission: 'For I well remember we observed the holes where they had been fixt'.[46]

On 6 August 1723, riding through the surrounding countryside, Stukeley's experienced eye detected the worn-down banks of the Cursus, that enormous and controversial rectangle just north of Stonehenge, almost two miles long and a fifth of a mile wide (2.8 x 0.3km). From its length and shape he thought it to be a racecourse for chariots, 'a noble ippodrom'. Some modern opinions concur with him.

During those years of long weeks in the open air Stukeley must have known the icing winds of Salisbury Plain, rain and storms as well as sunshine, but in his enthusiasm he never spoke of them. He was too busy noting the crowds of barrows around Stonehenge for 'families, friends, wives . . . and some lower in dignity'; the rare long barrows for distinguished Archdruids, whose 'paucity seems to confirm the notion'; 'fancy' ditched-and-banked bell barrows for kings; plain round barrows for the nobility; and disc barrows with their tiny central mound for ordinary druids. With the 30-year-old Lord Pembroke he excavated some, not for plunder but out of curiosity about the skeletons of the men, women and children buried there, interested to see that many were buried with their heads to the north.

Stukeley was tireless. He took magnetic bearing after bearing from barrows towards Stonehenge and from Stonehenge to the barrows. Sadly, his theodolite had been damaged, perhaps by the jogging on horseback, with the result that it had a consistent error of $\pm 4°$, $-4°$ to the east of Stonehenge, $+4°$ to the west.[47]

A different mistake was caused by chronological ignorance. Despite Inigo Jones, he saw that there was only one entrance at Stonehenge, at the north-east where the space between two sarsens in the circle was twice as wide as anywhere else, creating an imposing portal. Beyond it 'the entrance of Stonehenge is 4 degrees East from the true Northeast point. They set it to the Northeast because that is the suns utmost elongation in somer solstices'. In 1740 he added a rider, 'being the point where the sun rises, or nearly, at the summer solstice'.[48]

'Or nearly'. It was not just his theodolite that betrayed him. It was a mistaken 21 June from 1721 to 1724, a calendrical confusion that would take almost 30 years to resolve. In 1752, 11 days were deducted from the outdated Julian calendar.

Everything in Stukeley's manuscript was objective, whether lists of measurements, descriptions of stones or clear-minded thinking about the reasons for circles and ellipses. His druids were capable men who lived before the Romans came to Britain. But in 1740, in *Stonehenge a Temple Restor'd to the British Druids*, they were transmuted into descendants of Abraham, transformed into religious predecessors of a Christian priesthood. These proto-Christian druids were clerical idiocies that Stukeley zealously developed after being ordained into the Church of England in 1729. He wrote:

The patriarchal history, particularly of *Abraham*, is largely pursu'd; and the deduction [immigration] of the *Phoenician* colony into the island of *Britain*, about or soon after his time; whence the origin of the *Druids*, of their Religion and writing; they brought the patriarchal Religion [Old Testament] along with them . . . they had the notion and expectation of the Messiah, and of the time of year when he was to be born, of his office and death.[49]

He became obsessed with the origins of Christianity in England, and slid quickly downhill as an archaeologist. Before that, his meticulous fieldwork had resulted in a masterpiece of discovery.

Since his time, excavations and radiocarbon dating have added much to our understanding of the challenges that Stonehenge provides, but little more has been noticed physically about the circle except for some carvings on the stones. Stukeley was an archaeological giant among the giants that lived before and after him.

There were worthy successors. John Wood, John Smith, Sir Richard Colt Hoare and Flinders Petrie all added something to Stukeley's foundations. In contrast, when Daniel Defoe visited Stonehenge in 1724, he offered only pessimism about the stones and their age. 'How they came thither, or from whence, no stone of the kind now to be found in any part of England near it, is still the mistery'. 'No history has handed down to us the original, as we find it then uncertain, we must leave it so'.[50]

In 1740 the architect John Wood visited Stonehenge twice to make a detailed survey. He was not a critical archaeologist. Accepting the illusions of Inigo Jones and criticizing Stukeley for his equally illusory druids' cubit and other supposed blunders, Wood, following Jones' belief in three entrances, whimsically designed the elegant Circus in Bath with Gay

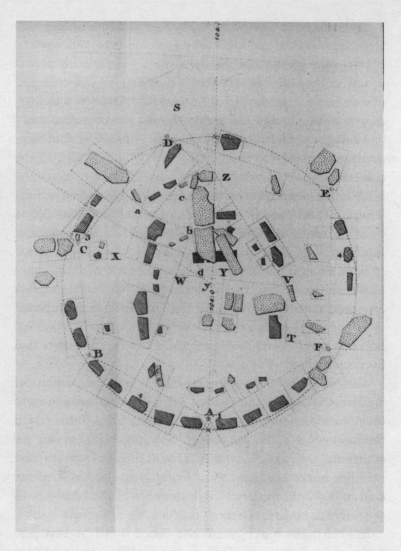

Fig. 10: John Wood's plan of 1747.

Street leading to it like an avenue at Stonehenge, adding Brock
Street and a short third approach from the Assembly Rooms.

His book of 1747 mostly consisted of imaginary colleges for
druids at Stanton Drew, Avebury and elsewhere, but he did
make the first accurate set of measurements for Stonehenge,
despite such a violent storm that several spectators 'thought I
had raised the Devil, or some guardian spirit over our Antiquity'. Being an architect he was fastidious in recording the
size and position of every stone in such detail that by hatching,
cross-hatching and dotting he distinguished between 'the erect
Stones in the Body of the Work, together with those in a
Leaning Position, and such as are buried in the Ground from
those that lye flat on the Surface of the Earth, or on the Surface
of other Stones' (fig. 10).

In 1880 Flinders Petrie commended Wood. Following his
own punctilious survey of Stonehenge in which 'no distinction is
made . . . between perfect stones and mere stumps of which the
upper part is removed', he was able to assert that 'No stones are
missing since Wood's plan in 1747'.[51] Marauders and treasure-
hunters may have been deterred by the activities of successful
and dangerous eighteenth-century highwaymen on Salisbury
Plain, such as James Boulter, who had been publicly flogged in
Devizes market-place, and William Davis, 'the Golden Farmer'
who had a public house named after him. Stagecoaches, private
carriages and individuals on foot or horse were all at risk, losing
gold guineas, silver shillings, rings and watches. Eventually both
men were caught and hanged.[52]

Stukeley was venomous about Wood's book and its pre-
tensions to exactness. 'Tis such a heap, a ruin of trifling,
nonsensical, impertinent and needless measuring of the stones,
designed to be rude, as if they were the most nice and curious
Grecian pillars . . . a tedious parade of twenty pages of feet,
inches and halfs and quarters'.[53]

Thirty years after Wood came John Smith, a 'kill-or-cure' inoculator of the smallpox, a quarter of a century before Jenner and vaccination. For his practice Smith rented Boscombe House, a hospital being used for smallpox patients near Stonehenge. Villagers drove him out 'by every act of violence in the pursuit of my business, by these malevolent villains, NOYSEY WRETCHES!', probably resentful of being treated as suicidal guinea-pigs. Smith escaped to the comparative peace of Stonehenge. He was the first of a queue of astronomers endeavouring to make Stonehenge an observatory.

Plotting the circle at Stonehenge he decided its diameter was 110ft (33.5m), the same length as Inigo Jones had proposed. Stukeley thought the length was 60 druid cubits or 104ft (31.7m), and John Wood 97ft (29.6m). Petrie was more precise with 97ft 4in (29.7m). Even more exactly Alexander Thom found the distance to be 35.8 of his Megalithic Yards or 97ft 6in (29.7m). Amongst this cavalcade of architects and surveyors it was an amateur, John Aubrey, with his 'thirty two yards ½' or 97ft 6in, who agreed with Thom.

John Smith had one considerable benefit that Jones, Aubrey, Stukeley and Wood had lacked. He knew when 21 June occurred. The others had lived when the old Julian calendar of 46 BC was still used in Britain, even though it had been losing time for centuries. In 1582 Roman Catholic countries adopted the more accurate Gregorian calendar. Suspicious of anything Catholic, the Protestant nations hesitated, and it was not until 1752 that Britain accepted it. The discrepancy had become so bad that over a week had to be cancelled, and the day after 2 September became 14 September to an hysterical background of 'Give us back our 11 days!'

Stukeley's 21 June was really 3 July, when the rising sun had moved several degrees southwards from its solstitial position at 50°. Hence Stukeley's rider, 'or nearly'. Smith was luckier.

The Heel Stone, a name that ironically he gave to the wrong stone, was 'the Key, or Gnomon':

At the summer solstice, when the days are longest [the sun] seems to rise in the same point of the horizon three days together. The Arch-Druid standing against his stall and looking down the right line of the temple, over the stones II and I [Slaughter and Heel] . . . he there sees the sun rise from behind the hill [Silbury].

By a calendrical fluke Smith became an innovatory member of Stonehenge scholarship. The vacuous remainder of his book was a melange of solar, lunar and planetary guesswork. Smith himself vanished from history. In spite of his radical discovery, he had no entry in the *Dictionary of National Biography*.[54]

At the beginning of the nineteenth century Sir Richard Colt Hoare, the rich landowner of Stourhead House and parkland, subsidized the excavations of his colleague William Cunnington, a wool merchant of Heytesbury whose health was such that doctors told him, 'I must ride out or die – I preferred the former'. Ride out he did with his pick-axed digger, John Parker, plunging into barrows and parts of Stonehenge. In 1812 Hoare conscientiously published some of the Stonehenge results in a sumptuous volume. For this book his surveyor, Philip Crocker, produced a very useful plan of the ring in 1810.[55] Seventy years later Flinders Petrie published his own meticulous survey, providing the stones with his definitive numbering scheme.

There are several books that are informative about the assiduous field-workers whose studies have provided so many insights about Stonehenge.

In 1876 William Long, in his *Stonehenge and its Barrows*, summarized the literary history of the ring from Geoffrey of

Monmouth up to the publication of Algernon Herbert's *Cyclops Christianus* of 1849. At the beginning of the twentieth century Jerome Harrison produced a comprehensive summary of books and articles written about Stonehenge and Avebury from Geoffrey of Monmouth to the last years of the nineteenth century. The best of these compendia is Christopher Chippindale's *Stonehenge Complete*, now in its third edition of 2004, well-written, scholarly, finely illustrated and entertaining. As the present writer thought in 1992, it 'will for years to come be a standard reference work'.

Yet, in the mid-twentieth century, despite all this research, an authority on Stonehenge was able to reply to questions such as *What* is it? *When* was it built? *How* was it done? *Who* did it? with the words 'We do not know, and we shall probably never know'.[56] But as suggested in the introduction to this book, this was probably too pessimistic. By 1900 so much had already been learned – the varied architecture, the differences between the types of stone, the intentional grading of the trilithons, the idea of numeracy, the solar alignment.

By 1956 excavations were providing even more answers to the questions that were being asked.

CHAPTER 2:

EXCAVATIONS AND REPAIRS FROM TUDOR TIMES TO AD 1949

Colonel Hawley replied that his object had been to report all that he came across during the excavations, and to collect facts without indulging in any theory concerning them.

Hawley (1923), p. 20

Early excavations

If every hole, trench and pit gouged into Stonehenge were abruptly exposed, the ring would look as though it had been bombarded by meteorites. Everywhere there would be cavities, some dug by looters, some by sentimentalists seeking souvenirs, a minority by scholars hoping for information about a lost past. There were gaping sprawls of earth and chalk around sockets where stones had stood. Most of the culprits had been local villagers. Some were of a higher social status.

Some 50 years after 1620, when James I had visited Wiltshire to sell lucrative £30 knighthoods, John Aubrey saw that near the centre of Stonehenge 'is a Pitt, which the Duke of Buckingham ordered to be digged . . . at which time, and by wch meanes, the Stone [55] twenty one foote long [now out of the ground] reclined by being under-digged . . . it is about the bignesse of two sawe-pitts'. It was big enough for two men to stand sawing through a log lying above them across the top of the hole.[1]

Aubrey was misled about Buckingham causing the toppling of Stone 55. The Stonehenge sketch of 1574 showed that the sarsen had already fallen and that its partner, 56, tilted forward. By Aubrey's time of around 1660, Stone 56 was leaning at an angle of 75° and the inclination would increase steadily over the centuries. Aubrey had been given the information about Buckingham by Mrs Mary Trotman of West Amesbury Farm, wife of Anthony, a tenant of the then owner of Stonehenge, Lawrence Washington. Aubrey was able to recognize where Buckingham's outrage had been, and marked the spot at the centre of the circle about two paces north of the broken 55's tip.

In 1994 his location may have been confirmed by augering, using a metal tool to probe the ground. It is a technique used sparingly by archaeologists after a similar exploration at Lullingstone Roman villa in 1949 resulted in cries of 'Coming up red' as the workers enthusiastically prodded with their steel rods, neatly piercing the coloured cement at the edge of a buried mosaic. At Stonehenge more delicate augering through a parchmark suggested a backfilled pit 'at the centre of the monument'.[2] Just as possibly it was the result of a further disruption in 1829.

People had been ransacking the circle for years before Buckingham. In a print of 1575, two robbers spaded into a round barrow near Stonehenge, a piratical haul of a skull and crossbones alongside them but nothing of mercenary value. The sketch 'sheweth wher great bones of men are found'.[3] In *Britannia* William Camden repeated 'that mens bones have many times beene digged up here' by the treasure-hunters, adding 'ashes and pieces of burnt bone here frequently found'. Tudor fortune-seekers had even dug across the north-east entrance, wrecking two postholes and leaving broken pots and bottles behind them but finding nothing of mercenary value.[4]

More significantly for archaeological research, many skulls of bulls, oxen 'or other beasts' interred in pits were dug up in 1620 by Inigo Jones, Buckingham and William Harvey. All of them noticed the 'great Quantities of burnt Coals or Charcoals digged up likewise; here lying promiscuously together with the Heads, there, in Pits by themselves apart, here more, there less', both inside the circle and outside it in the henge, 'in several Parts of the Court surrounding Stonehenge it self'.

They could have been funerary offerings. The presence of skulls of oxen supports what archaeologists have suspected, that in the Late Neolithic of the final quarter of the fourth millennium it was only certain members of society – men – who were privileged to be buried in the later long barrows. Alongside such dead the ox skull was dominant, perhaps as a totem, perhaps as the epitome of strength, perhaps even as the emblem of a richer, more powerful member of the group, the badge of an emergent aristocracy in what had previously been an egalitarian society.

Inigo Jones believed the skulls were the remains of sacrifices: 'Now that there hath oftentimes been digged out of the Ground at Stone-Heng the heads of such Beasts, in all probability in that Place sacrificed, I need not again remember, it being so well known'.[5] Other finds went almost unnoticed, yet the stone and flint tools, the antler picks and the sherds of pottery were to give information about the successive stages of Stonehenge from the Late Neolithic to the Early Bronze Age and, also, the tantalizing rituals performed by the makers of vessels such as Grooved Ware and beakers.

A hundred years after Inigo Jones, 'Mr Hayward, late owner of Stonehenge, dug about it . . . He found heads of oxen and other beasts' bones, and nothing else'. The owner had also encouraged rabbits to breed near the ring. The results may have been good for his table, but they were certainly bad for the stability of Stonehenge. Since 1574, Stone 56 had tilted a further 6° from the vertical.

Stukeley grieved. 'But what is most to be lamented is the colony of rabbits adjacent [to the north-east entrance] which in my own observation have done prodigious damage & will in a little time infallibly ruin the whole if not destroyd. For they have undermind several of the stones [29, 30, 1, 2] very lately'. He was appalled to see how quickly and far they bred, with warrens at the Winterbourne Stoke barrow cemetery well over a mile to the west. 'They are the nearest barrows planted with rabbets, which do much damage too at Stonehenge, and threaten no less than the ruin of the whole'.[6] By 1771 rabbit warrens were apparent under the Slaughter Stone.

It was only in the early eighteenth century that any prolonged and serious attempt was made to understand what Stonehenge was. The first systematic and serious examination of its stones and plan began in 1719 with the visits of William Stukeley. He was the first of a noteworthy quartet of Williams archaeologically associated with the circle. After him came William Cunnington, who dug enquiringly into parts of the ring. Ninety years later Professor William Gowland supervised the re-erection of the stupendous Stone 56. There followed Lt.-Col. William Hawley, who is respected for his methodical excavations there from 1919 to 1926.

A fifth William might deservedly be included, William Long, who in 1876 compiled an account of writers about Stonehenge, from the early twelfth-century Henry of Huntingdon down to the publication in 1812 of Sir Richard Colt Hoare's account of the work of Cunnington between 1798 and 1810 at the Altar and Slaughter Stones and elsewhere. Stukeley was the forerunner of the distinguished quintet.

Depredations by robbers, romantics and rabbits continued. But commendable excavations began. From scholarly curiosity Lord Pembroke told Stukeley to have the ground near the Altar Stone dug. The work was probably done by Abraham Sturges of Amesbury. (Stukeley termed the man an architect, but John Wood derided him as 'a jobbing Bricklayer'). Stukeley wrote:

5. July 1723. By Lord Pembrokes direction I causd a pit to be sunk on the inside of the altar at the middle of the stone. It was 4 f. long [1.2m] upon the edg of the stone & 6 f. fowards [1.8m] or towards the grand entrance. at a foot we came to the solid chalk mixt with f[l]ints which had never been dug we went 2 f. & ½ perpendicular [0.8m] under the Stone and found it perfectly solid chalk that had never been stird. I found the altar 20 inches [50.8cm] thick, but broke in two or 3 pieces by the upright [Stone 55] & architrave [lintel 156] falling upon it.[7]

It was good observation and good archaeology. Stukeley and Pembroke also dug into several barrows around the circle.

Stukeley railed against the vandalism of superstitious visitors chipping pieces off the obstinate stones as lucky charms. Rabbits and souvenir-hunters were not the only threat.

Weather on the bleakly exposed wastes of Salisbury Plain was as dangerous. Late in the autumn of 1796 gypsies waiting for local fairs sheltered at Stonehenge, digging a deep hollow against trilithon 57–58 to protect them from the south-west wind and rain. The hole was never filled. On 3 January 1797, ploughmen half a mile from the circle 'felt a considerable concussion, or jarring, of the ground' as 90 tons of trilithon crashed outwards. The lintel, itself 16 brutal tons, smashed 'an impression in the ground to the depth of seven inches or more' (18cm).

At the end of 1796 the trilithon had already been 'observed for two or three days to be out of its perpendicular position'. The collapse was inevitable. There was 'a sudden and rapid thaw that began the day before the stones fell, succeeding a very deep snow'. The disaster was exacerbated because the builders, in their determination to make the trilithon high enough, had allowed stoneholes only a few feet deep to support lintelled pillars over 20ft (6m) high.[8]

Hoare and Cunnington

At the beginning of the nineteenth century Sir Richard Colt Hoare became engrossed in the excavations of William Cunnington, a wealthy, retired wool merchant whose doctors advised him to take prolonged exercise in the open air. Interested in antiquity, he began excavating barrows in south Wiltshire. Between about 1800 and 1818 Cunnington and Hoare opened some 500 mounds, usually having their workmen plunging down from the centre, using picks and shovels but seldom trowels. In some compensation for such crude methods Hoare did publish the results, many with informative diagrams by his surveyor, Philip Crocker. Such conscientiousness was quite unlike the unrecorded pillaging of many rapacious and irresponsible contemporaries (fig. 11).

Barrow digging became a preoccupation of Cunnington, and the results of many excavations such as that of the famous Bush Barrow near Stonehenge are described later. One of his earliest explorations was at Boles Barrow, not three miles north of Heytesbury but well over eleven west of Stonehenge. The barrow is categorized as Heytesbury 1.[9] Cunnington trenched into the side of the long mound in July 1801, and near ground-level his men uncovered a large block of bluestone, over half a ton of fine-grained dolerite, 'y^e same to those of the upright stones in y^e inner circle at Stonehenge'.[10] This discovery is still disconcerting geologists.

Group of Barrows, South of Stonehenge.

Fig. 11: Watercolour depicting Hoare and Cunnington (on the left) watching the Parker brothers digging at Lake cemetery, c.1805.

Cunnington had already dabbled at Stonehenge in 1798, prodding 'with a large stick' into the disturbance caused by the tumbling of trilithon 57–58, and raking up sherds of fine black

Roman pottery not under but alongside the sarsens. He returned more earnestly to the circle in 1802. In September of that year he dug at the Altar Stone. He sank a pit almost 6ft (approximately 2m) deep, close to Stukeley's central hole, finding Roman sherds halfway down and well below them charred wood, animal bones and three fragments of coarse, half-baked pottery, 'similar to the rude urns found in the barrows'. There were also antlers that had been used to prise out the chalk of the stonehole.[11]

Knowledgeable in geology, Cunnington deduced that the different kinds of stone in the circle indicated two quite distinct architectural periods, but although he knew the source of the sarsens the origin of the bluestones baffled him. He first thought of Frome in Somerset, and later speculated on an origin in Devon or Cornwall. He knew, however, that Geoffrey of Monmouth had been wrong about Merlin. Jokingly in a letter of 12 April 1803 to the antiquarian John Britton, he laughed, 'Please don't send your readers to Ireland for them!'

He returned to Stonehenge the following year, 1803, becoming certain that the prostrate Slaughter Stone had once stood upright. He was frustrated from digging in 1804, having forgotten to obtain permission from the landowners. By that time Hoare had become his patron and gently rebuked him for the omission, 'in future [do] not begin before you are sure of no impediment'. Despite the admonition Cunnington was prevented from digging near Sidbury two years later.

Their places marked by surrounding ditches, the two missing Station stones, 92 and 94, intrigued the two men. They had the centre of 94 trenched, discovering 'a simple internment of burned bones', probably a cremation from Aubrey Hole 46 rather than a cremation at the foot of the Station stone. A similar search at 92 had 'nothing in it'.[12]

More and more was being learned about the comparative

age of Stonehenge. In September 1807 Cunnington turned to a rather battered round barrow near Stonehenge (Amesbury 4). It had already been attacked by Stukeley in 1723, 'a great and very old flat barrow'. In it were 'several bits of a blue hard kind of marble . . . [and] more bits of a red marble'. Cunnington rediscovered them: 'These pieces [of bluestone and sarsen] were scattered about on the Plain before the erection of the tumuli under which they have been found. It gives higher antiquity to our British temple than many antiquaries are disposed to allow'.

Of the burial-pit, 'a fine circular cist' with a cremation, Hoare added, 'It is somewhat singular that these burned bones (a more than usual quantity) should have lain unmolested in a barrow where there were a hundred rabbit holes'. More instructively, 'we found a large piece of one of the blue stones of STONEHENGE which, with the sarsen stone, is a very similar occurrence, and decidedly proves that the adjoining temple was erected previous to the *tumulus*'. That Stonehenge was even older than the barrow was a revelation, but to Cunnington it was a contradiction. 'I confess that it has often struck me, when opening the tumuli in the vicinity of Stonehenge, how it was possible that barbarians [from the evidence of coarse pottery and stone tools] . . . could raise such a work as Stonehenge'.[13]

In May 1810 Cunnington excavated under the Slaughter Stone for the second time, 'so completely as to be able to examine the underneath side of the stone'. 'I have spent a day and a half at Stonehenge, chiefly with Sir R. Hoare. I made the men dig under the prostrate stone [Slaughter] so as to examine it thoroughly'. Hoare, Crocker and an Irish gentleman observed the work. Cunnington's belief was confirmed. The stone had stood; its base was rough. Above ground the sarsen was 'stippled like the others'.

The perceptive Stukeley had already noticed this to be true of other stones. 'The tool has only been applyd to the part above ground for that buryed in the hard chalk upon which they stand most firmly is roung [rough] & unhewn as they came of the quarry & generally 4 or 5 foot more additional length'.[14]

Beneath the Slaughter Stone were the customary antler-picks. In their place, the party put a bottle of port for future investigators. Cunnington, being abstemious, was an unlikely donor. It may have been Hoare who left the deposit, a fitting offering as port was traditionally drunk at funerals. Hawley was to find the bottle more than a hundred years later.

On 31 December 1810 William Cunnington died in his sleep at three o'clock in the afternoon. Hoare's collection of records of his colleague's work was eventually acquired by the Wiltshire Archaeological Society and the papers are now in its archives.

On behalf of a Swedish society, in 1839 an officer from Devonport, Captain Beamish – obviously unaware of what Buckingham, Stukeley and Cunnington had already done and perhaps sundry anonymous vandals before them – quarried out an area that was reputed to be of some 400cu.ft ($114m^3$) in front of the Altar Stone. This involved removing 20 tons of uninformative chalk, but that archaeological vacuum left the society's expensive curiosity about burials inside Stonehenge unsatisfied. The Stonehenge enthusiast Joseph Browne watched the digging of the futile pit and 'before the hole was filled up, I buried a bottle containing a record of the excavation'.[15]

Deterioration and restoration

In 1808 a public appeal for money to restore trilithon 57–58 raised only an inadequate £50, and the sum was spent on digging into yet more barrows on Salisbury Plain. In 1849 a further proposal to re-erect the trilithon was discussed at the Salisbury Meeting of the Archaeological Institute. The owner offered to restore stones at his own expense, providing that the meeting approved. As so often happens at Stonehenge, persuasive words were spoken, precise minutes were taken and nothing was done.

In 1880 Flinders Petrie published his *Stonehenge: Plans, Description and Theories*, in which the first two sections of the subtitle were much better than the Theories. His innovative numbering system has already been described, the circle-stones from the north-east entrance becoming 1–30 clockwise, then the survivors of the bluestone ring 31–59, the five trilithons 51–60, the remnants of the bluestone horseshoe 61–72, the Altar Stone 80, the Four Stations 91–94, and finally the Slaughter Stone 95 and Heel Stone 96. The lintels had 100 added to the number of the second of their two uprights. The fragments of a broken stone had a, b or c added to the original number. The system continues in use.

Petrie began planning in 1874, being critical of the work of Wood and Hoare, who did not 'lay any claim for accuracy greater than a few inches'. He acknowledged that no stones had gone missing since Wood's plan of 1747.[16] Dissatisfied with his own surveying chain he had improvements made and recommenced planning in June 1877. The survey took four months. Regrettably, the two published plans were so small and faint that they are almost unusable.

Petrie was impressed with the care that had been taken over

the appearance of the interior of Stonehenge, the inner faces of the sarsen ring conforming to a circle twice as neatly as the rougher, outer sides. Heights had been surprisingly well calculated. Despite the ring being on ground that sloped downwards both to north and east, the lintels along the 306ft 4in (93.4m) circumference of the great circle were no more than 4in (10.2cm) from the horizontal.[17]

In what could almost be considered heresy amongst devotees of Britain's most impressive and respected prehistoric monument, Petrie's discoveries revealed construction flaws. Stone 11 at the exact south of the circle, he noted, was only half the normal width, and a mere 8ft tall rather than the usual 14ft (2.4m, 4.3m). As the dimensions of Stones 21 and 23 also differed from the majority it demonstrated that '11 was no single freak, but was the result of not having better material'. In short, prehistoric ambition had exceeded Late Neolithic accomplishment.

It could be added that if the intended design of 30 sarsens in the circle and 10 in the trilithons depended on the builders finding a sufficient quantity of long stones to grade the trilithons in height from the lowest pairs (51–52 and 59–60) at the mouth of the horseshoe up to 55–56 at the apex, then the surveyors ought to have ensured that they had an adequate collection of 10 very long sarsens – 4 tall, 4 taller, and 2 even higher – before deciding on the lower height of stones in the outer ring. Instead, they may have started with the circle-stones and, as Petrie surmised, run out of appropriately long pillars for the trilithons. 'Is it not very probable that they had not enough to finish the circle?'[18] The outrageous suggestion that the magnificent enterprise had been abandoned, left unfinished, has received no support or mention from Stonehenge enthusiasts.

The situation of the prostrate Slaughter Stone, 'lying to one side of the axis', led Petrie to further speculation. The Heel

Stone was similarly placed east of the ring's axis. 'Were these ever paired by others forming narrow gateways in the avenue?' He would be proved correct.[19] He also decided from the very regular shape of the bank and ditch of the surrounding henge, with a centre 3ft (1m) away from that of the sarsen ring, that the earthwork predated the stones. This is still accepted.

Far less satisfactory were his theories about the midsummer sunrise and an alignment from trilithon 55–56 to the peak of Heel Stone; the calculated date of Stonehenge which was several thousand years too late; and the hypothetical units of measurements used in the construction, a so-called 'Phoenician unit' of 22.5in (57.2cm) for the earthwork and a 'Roman foot' of 11.72in (29.8cm) for the circle.[20] Neither is likely.

It was from Petrie's report that Professor Gowland in 1901 obtained the data about the inexorable tilting that Stone 56 had undergone since 1574. In 1870, just before Petrie's survey, the angle had become a perilous 66° and over the following 30 years it became 60½°. 'It is rapidly going even farther at present'. It would fall, and it would break because it was not only long but slender and had an obvious central flaw. 'It should be simply screwed and pulled back'.[21]

Stonehenge epitomizes stability. Early in the nineteenth century, George Borrow wrote *Lavengro: The Scholar, the Gypsy, the Priest*. Lavengro, an impoverished young man, meets a gypsy at Stonehenge. The stones came from Ireland, he is informed, and the ring is a temple and eternal. 'So sure as the world', said the man, 'and, as the world, they will stand as long'.[22] The image of everlastingness was an illusion. Given the state of Stonehenge it was not observation but superstition that caused the words. The entire ring resembled cricket stumps smashed by a fast ball, with sarsens backwards, sideways, prostrate; megalithic symmetry had become chaos. Lavengro himself sits on the prostrate Stone 60. In the late sixteenth century Stonehenge had been a wreck, stones lolling, flat, missing. And from 1574 to 1797 it had continued to worsen.

By 1880 bluestones 35, 64, 65 and 66 had weathered to mere stumps, and worse was to come. Public demand for more care of the popular but hazardous picnic site received nothing more than the temporary propping of unstable Stones 1, 6, 7 and 30 with ugly railway sleepers. Then, before Stone 56 could be made secure, there was further collapse. At the very end of 1899 Stone 22 and its lintel, 122, fell precisely 102 years to the day after trilithon 57–58. Sir Edmund Antrobus, owner of the unsafe circle, restricted access to what had been a monument freely open to the public.

In 1901, following a joint meeting of the Society of Antiquaries, the Wiltshire Archaeological Society and the Society for the Protection of Ancient Monuments, a letter was sent to Sir Edmund asking for his permission and assistance in restoring 56 to the perpendicular. Generously he offered to underwrite the expenses. On 12 April it was recommended that the sarsen should be lifted, that the site should be wire-fenced and that an intrusive trackway through the earthwork be closed ('a green driving road', *The Times* called it). In May the fence went up, 'not only unnecessary but highly mischievous', complained *The Times*. There was to be an admission charge of a shilling (5p).[23]

Supervision of the raising of Stone 56 was entrusted to Professor Gowland, already in his 60s, cloth-capped and heavily built with a long jowl-drooping white moustache. He was patient, skilled and punctilious, always on site before the work began, never leaving until it was finished. He was certain that unless treated, the stone would break. It 'was merely a question of time'. Examining it, he described Petrie's 'flaw', three fissures of unknown depth across the middle of its outer, broad face. Exposed to the weather the slender pillar would crack in two.

The sarsen was given a sturdy timber frame with cables attached to two powerful winches. On Monday 18 September 1901, the lifting started, no more than 2 to 3in (5 to 8cm) at a time, and at each stage larch struts were firmly propped underneath it. Four days later the towering 56 was erect, maybe for the first time in over 2,000 years. A slight inclination to one side was corrected through the use of a hydraulic jack. The stone became the first of many to be secured and stabilized by setting its base in a bed of concrete.[24]

Before Gowland, optimists uneducated in the classics had believed that the stones were set so firmly because their builders had fixed them in cement. Following the medieval belief that the sarsens were artificial, composed of 'some glewie and unctuous matter' stuck together, there was a Victorian belief that the builders of Stonehenge had cemented the uprights. While digging 'deeply for rabbits' at the undisturbed edge of the tumbled 55's stonehole, the under-gamekeeper of Sir Edmund Antrobus in October 1863, 'proved that the upright had been embedded in rough strong concrete', mistaking the almost impenetrable density of chalk undisturbed for millions of years for a man-made substance.

In reality the builders of Stonehenge had existed in complete ignorance of cement. It was a full 2,500 years before the Late Roman Republic builders of the first century BC discovered that if sandy volcanic rock (like that from Vesuvius) was added to lime mortar and glutinous substances it would form a cement, *pulvis puteolanus*. If that in turn were mixed with sand and rock a strong-setting, permanent concrete could be produced. It was good for additions to the Forum in Rome, but a score of centuries too late for the sarsens of Stonehenge.[25]

The slumping of trilithon 55–56 was unavoidable. Probably with some dismay the builders had been compelled to use a pair of sarsens completely incompatible in length that were both intended to stand 22ft (6.7m) above ground. Stone 56 was 30ft (9.1m) long and so was set in a hole 8ft (2.5m) deep. Stone 55, being only 26ft (7.9m) in length, was allowed only a poky 4ft (1.2m) pit. To compensate, the bottom of the stone was shaped into a club-foot to stabilize its base.

'A quantity of material has been removed [from its outer face]', wrote Herbert Stone, 'to give the required form to the part which would be above ground leaving a thick bulbous base to give more bulk for the foundation which was of insufficient depth'. A big sarsen was set down at its foot; other sarsens were added with mauls (stone balls) jammed into the stonehole.[26] Gowland's report of the excavation was rather unclear, but he did realize how ramshackle the means of constructing trilithon 55–56 had been. 'From the precarious nature of this packing of stones it will be evident how very easily the stone could be overthrown by any excavation made in its neighbourhood'.[27]

Gowland explored under 55a (the broken lower half), sieving the excavated soil and chalk 'so that no object, however small, might be lost'. Everything recovered was prehistoric and prosaic – tools for shaping and raising the stone; antlers used as picks in digging holes; 10 flint axes, 1 of sandstone; 23 hammerstones for scouring and smoothing surfaces; sarsen mauls for breaking off the worst protrusions. These crude balls, weighing from 36lb to half a hundredweight, might have been cased in leather slings with long straps so 'that they might be used by two or three men', whirled in great arcing loops to smash down on impervious sarsen.[28] With gangs of workers swinging and pounding together, commonsense and self-preservation were the only safeguards from a broken skull in an age lacking health and safety regulations.

Prehistoric material lay under the stone. Roman coins were 'only found in the superficial layers' at the sides of the sarsen, offering the possibility that the trilithon had stood for perhaps just a few Bronze Age centuries before winter gales howling in from the south-west tumbled the insecure setting.

A geological colleague of Gowland, Professor J.W. Judd, suggested that although sarsen was local and the bluestones were foreign, those intrusions could have arrived 'on the plain in the vicinity of Stonehenge, having been transported there by glacial drift'. He added that they were of different minerals. Some like diorite and rhyolite were hard and durable, others were 'soft, more easily broken, and at the same time [being] more susceptible to the action resulting from atmospheric changes . . . would be quite unable through a long period of years to withstand the constant alternation of rain and frost'.[29] He was confident that glaciation was the explanation for the presence of the bluestones on Salisbury Plain:

Is it conceivable that these skilful builders would have trans-ported such blocks of stone *in their rough state*, over moun-tains, hills and rivers (and possibly over seas) in order to shape them at the point of erection, when the rough-hewing of the blocks at the place where they were found would have so greatly diminished their weight and the difficulties of their transport?'[30]

It was good logic, but entirely irrelevant to prehistoric prac-tices and Late Neolithic beliefs.

The bluestones were brought to Stonehenge in the early years of the third millennium at a time when stone circles were being put up in many highland regions of Britain and Ireland.

By 2900–2800 BC there were hundreds of the rings, as far away as the Orkneys, as north-western Ireland, near Snowdonia in Wales, even at Land's End. In hardly any of these circles, wherever they stood, were the stones shaped. Except for a few whose bases were 'keeled' to facilitate erection, the pillars were left in their natural state. Because of this lack of 'improvement' the circles were still known as 'rude stone monuments' in the nineteenth century.

None of these selected stones was fashioned. To the primitive mind, living in an animistic world where all things – clouds, trees, streams, rocks – had life, it may have been that to change a stone physically was to diminish it spiritually, reducing its potency. Nature formed it. Man used it. People took what was available, finding significance in the shapes and placing them in special positions. To find that the granites of the Hurlers in Cornwall had been hammered simply stresses their exceptional treatment. Many centuries later Moses announced the same prohibition to the Israelites. 'If thou wilt make me an altar of stone, thou shalt not build it of hewn stone: for if thou lift thy tool upon it, thou hast polluted it'.[31]

One human factor did condition the choice of stones. They had to be within a mile or so of where they would stand, usually near but away from a settlement, often on higher ground with long views, but the source always had to be close. It was only when a singular block of a particular size and shape was needed such as a large recumbent stone in northeast Scotland that the rule was relaxed.

When the bluestones first arrived at Stonehenge they were left as they had been discovered, rough and unshaped like all others in stone circles. In the 'Q' and 'R' Holes in which they were first erected there were almost no fragments at the bottom of those pits. It was only much later when the 'timber' monument of Stonehenge was envisaged by the woodworking natives of Salisbury Plain (whose carpenters treated sarsen boulders as though they were oak posts, giving them mortice-and-tenon and tongue-and-groove joints, chamfers, rebates and planed surfaces) that the bluestones were 'dressed', leaving an untidy litter of bits and pieces of their chippings all over Stonehenge.

With such an understanding of prehistoric customs a source for the 'foreign' bluestones in the Preseli Mountains of south-west Wales, suggested by Thomas in 1924, and the human transportation of crude, unchanged stones are both feasible and perplexing. The illogical selection of an oddity of stones, hard and soft, good and bad, fine-grained and coarse is quite explicable if the prospectors accepted what the forces of nature had provided. To those men there was no question of logic because there was no selection, just acceptance.

Date	Description of damage
pre-Roman?	Stone 55 and lintel 156 fell. Prehistoric tools, but nothing Roman under 55a.
pre-AD1574	Stone 59 down. Many lintels missing. Only 7 remained of 30 in outer circle. 6 of 10 in the trilithons.
pre-1666	Many bluestones missing. Stone 14 leaning, Stones 8, 15 and 19 fallen and damaged.
1740	Stone 48 leaning. Stone 26 damaged.
c.1750	Stone 14 fell.
1771	Stone 48 leaning. Rabbit burrows under Slaughter Stone 95.
1797	Trilithons 57, 58 and 158 fell on 3 January.
by 1880	Bluestones 35, 64, 65 and 66 no more than stumps.
1899	Stones 22 and 122 fell on 31 December.
1963	Stone 23 fell in a gale.

Table 1: Destruction at Stonehenge.

Yet one considerable problem does remain. Unlike every other stone circle the source of the bluestones was not 'within a mile or two' of Salisbury Plain. Even as the prehistoric crow flew it was 150 miles of land, sea, river and hill. Nor can the source of the sarsens be used as an explanation for such an extravagant distance. The fact that the sarsens were brought from the Marlborough Downs 20 miles to the north only reinforces the fact that stones had to be as close as possible, because those sarsens did come from the nearest source of free-lying stone. There was nothing closer. And, as J.W. Judd added in 1902, their labourers sensibly 'left only the final dressing to be done after their transport'.[32] Moreover, there were many other stones available in Dorset, Somerset and Devon, all areas much nearer than south-west Wales. The bluestone controversy is central to the early history of Stonehenge.

Returning to the investigations at Stonehenge, after Gowland there were 18 years of neglect and decay with the Great World War intervening, and during those years the circle deteriorated. At the shabby north-eastern entrance, four stones of the outer ring (29, 30, 1 and 2) were still 'temporarily' secured by unsightly props, Stone 1 having no fewer than three of them. Stones 27 and 28 sagged, and the entire south-western sector was havoc, with more stones prostrate or ready to fall than those that stood securely. 'The site was not only a mess it was a dangerous mess'.[33]

In 1915 Sir Edmund Antrobus died and the following year Cecil Chubb bought Stonehenge at auction, later giving it and 30 adjoining acres to the nation in 1918. He was knighted. Now that Stonehenge had become a national property 'it was at once recognized by H.M. Office of Works' that the site needed urgent attention, with leaning stones made safe and fallen stones set up, 'care being taken that all appearances of restoration should be avoided'.[34] The Society of Antiquaries was given responsibility for organizing the work. By that time Gowland was too old to accept the post of supervisor and it was given to Lt.-Col. William Hawley, who would otherwise have been Gowland's assistant.

Hawley's methods were later ungraciously condemned because he published only a series of interim reports. For years after the end of the excavations he was so disregarded that, on his death, despite much good work in Wiltshire, the local archaeological society did not give him its own obituary but merely quoted an excerpt from another journal. Yet his detailed excavation notebooks from 1919 to 1926 reveal his systematic methods, acceptable in the 1920s, and their laudable results were finally acknowledged in the 1995 publication of the monumentally thorough and detailed *Stonehenge In Its Landscape*, with its compilation of data, lists and explanatory diagrams and plans. It is an indispensable Stonehenge bible.

Often in the chill of winter rain, Hawley, frequently assisted by local archaeologist Robert Newall, spent the eight years from 1919 to 1926 stripping half of the site to the east of the NE-SW axis down to the undisturbed chalk. The first undertaking was the restoration of stones, and five (1, 2, 7, 29, 30) were re-erected. Lintels 101, 102, 107 and 130 were replaced.[35] Only then did the investigation of Stonehenge begin, a systematic exploration of area after area, recovering tools, pottery, animal bones and domestic objects.

A great length of the ditch was excavated from the northeast entrance. Hawley noticed that although the result resembled a circle it was, in fact, 'an irregular polygon'. He realized that the segments of the ditch to the east had been treated differently from those to the west of the axis. 'The people they belonged to seem to have had a superstitious reason for selecting the eastern area'. For a man who did not theorize, his intention being 'to collect facts without indulging in any theory concerning them', this was perceptive.[36]

Some prehistoric societies, such as the one making Grooved Ware pottery, did distinguish one side of a monument from another through the use of contents or colour or shapes of stone. There were different colours of stone at Easter Aquorthies stone circle in Scotland. Near Stonehenge, pits at Woodhenge contained different kinds of animal bones. Consistently in the megalithic world one side was distinguished from another, by differing heights, or contrasting colour or shapes. This can easily be observed in pairs of stones, and even in avenues such as the Kennet at Avebury or at Callanish in the Outer Hebrides. The intentional contrasting of content, colour and shape was consistent in Britain and Ireland, and even in Brittany where an *allée-couverte* such as Notre-Dame-de-Lorette or a stone row like the Alignements du Moulin had tall stones of dark schist on one side, low white quartz on the other. Whether such opposites symbolized light and dark, life and death, male and female remains conjecture rather than confidence.

Megalithic tombs on the island of Arran, such as Clachaig and Giants' Graves, contain granite and sandstone slabs, even though all were not local. Very fitting for a burial-place, some slabs are as white as bones, others as red as blood. 'On Arran, however, it may be that white and red also symbolized the land itself, the white of the north and the red of the south'. The imaginative Stukeley may have felt something of this symbolism when he remarked on the noticeable differences in colour of the sarsens, the bluestones and the Altar Stone at Stonehenge.[37]

During Hawley's eight years there were unexpected discoveries, and with almost every one there came controversy. In

1923 two irregularly concentric sets of postholes, unpoetically called the Y and Z Holes, were uncovered surrounding the sarsen ring. Whether they were laid out as poor circles or as an equally imprecise spiral is debatable. It has even been suggested that because there were 30 holes in each 'ring' they could have been used as a record of the days of a lunar month.[38] Elsewhere, trowelling across the north-east causeway revealed several parallel lines of small postholes, 46 in 1922 and a further 8 in 1923 'making the total number 53'. (This is Hawley's miscalculated arithmetic.) Their purpose also is debatable – a barrier, a controlled entrance or an astronomical device are all plausible but all mutually exclusive.[39]

In plan other postholes to the south of the circle resembled the remains of a passageway, either roofed or open to the sky, leading from the south entrance but not connected to it, northwards towards the stone circle but stopping short of it at a transverse palisade at its northern end. Whether or not it had once led to a central timber setting preceding the sarsen circle is yet another enigma of Stonehenge.[40]

Holes for posts and stones occupied an area near the Heel Stone and across the Avenue. Nearby, from under the Slaughter Stone the bottle of port left by Cunnington's party in 1801 was recovered, in 1921. 'The seal was intact, but the cork had decayed and let out nearly all of the contents'. Compensation came two years later with the loveliest object ever found at Stonehenge, a beautiful perforated stone macehead with black and white stripes. Both the bottle and the macehead can be seen in the delightful displays of Salisbury Museum.[41]

Perhaps the most problematical of all the features of Stonehenge were the 56 Aubrey Holes, 5 of them detected by John Aubrey in 1666 and all of them rediscovered by Hawley and Newall in 1920. Newall fastidiously excavated 32. A simple interpretation was that they formed a cremation cemetery. They have also been identified as a Grooved Ware ritual site. Alexander Thom deduced that they had been mathematically laid out to a precise north-south alignment. Gerald Hawkins calculated that they could have been used as an eclipse predictor. More mundanely they were thought to have held stones or posts, or were just pits that had been dug into once, or twice, or even three times. Unsurprisingly, given these conflicting interpretations, the Aubrey Holes became the subject of an article entitled 'Holes in the Argument'![42]

A geological revelation was announced at the London meeting that followed the first two years of digging. H.H. Thomas, a geologist, informed the audience that the bluestones did not come from Devon or Cornwall but from south-west Wales, 'the ultimate source being in the Prescelly [sic] Mountains'. He added that the suggestion that those stones had been 'stranded on the high ground of Salisbury Plain by glacial action was contrary to all sound geological reasoning'. He has been believed ever since by the great majority of researchers. Majority, of course, implies the existence of a minority.[43]

After Hawley's final report of 1928 there followed a period of quiet stagnation for Stonehenge that endured until the end of the Second World War.

On a sunlit August weekend in 1947 the present writer, still in the Navy, saw Stonehenge for the first time, having seen Salisbury Cathedral the previous afternoon. Ignorant of all things megalithic, but enthusiastic, he was enthralled and astonished by both monuments. In this he had unknowingly experienced the same reactions of Samuel Johnson over 150 years earlier: 'Salisbury Cathedral and its neighbour, Stonehenge', he wrote to the recently widowed Mrs Hester Thrale, 'are two eminent monuments of art and rudeness, and may show the first essay, and the last perfection, in architecture'.[44]

Fig. 12: A group of eminent archaeologists in 1958 inspecting the filled pit of lost pillar 30 of the bluestone circle. On his knees, smoking, is Richard Atkinson. Bending, hands on knees, is Stuart Piggott. Behind him, pointing, is Malcolm Murray. Derek Simpson stands beside him.

It is symbolically fitting today that directly across the close from the cathedral is Salisbury's fine museum with its incomparable collection of articles from Stonehenge.

The year 1950 was the end of a long beginning. Science was

Date	Description of restoration
1901	Stone 56 raised and set in concrete.
1919–20	Stones 6 and 7 straightened and set in concrete.
1920	1, 2, 29, 30 straightened and set in concrete.
1958	Trilithon 57, 58, 158, 22, 122, re-erected and set in concrete. 19, 20, 41, 42, 69, 70 removed and replaced.
1959	Stones 4, 5, 60 straightened and set in concrete. 43, 45 removed and replaced.
1964	Stone 22 re-erected. 23, 27, 28, 53, 54 set in concrete.
Since 1964 there have been no substantial alterations to the architecture of Stonehenge.	

Table 2: Restoration at Stonehenge.

added to the pick-axe and the trowel. In 1949 Willard Libby described the process of carbon-14 dating, whereby the proportions between the stable carbon-12 and the radioactive carbon-14 contained in organic material could be used to assess how long that material had been dead. In its early years the method was far from exact, and was always expressed in ± years to indicate the upper and lower limits of a date within a 2:1 chance of being correct.

The first 'date' obtained from Stonehenge was 1848 ± 275 bc.[45] It was exciting as an innovation but almost useless as a date. The ± 275 years offers a vast period from 2123 to 1573 BC. Worse, when that is corrected to allow for the underestimated length of time inherent in the radiocarbon method, the period is enlarged to 3020 to 1520 BC, a period from the Late Neolithic to the Middle Bronze Age which is of no value at all for the time when cremated human bone was placed in an Aubrey Hole. Fortunately, radiocarbon assays have become more precise.

Other scientific methods developed, such as geo-physical prospecting where electrical impulses are sent into the ground in search of evidence of the existence or absence of material, a buried stone or a backfilled pit. The last half of the twentieth century was an exciting and informative period for Stonehenge, during which more discoveries were made and more theories propounded.

Excavation did not stop. Mesolithic postholes were located when the new car park was being laid out. The hole for a partner to the Heel Stone was found. Inspection of stones revealed unsuspected carvings on some, and because visitors walked on fallen sarsens, and children slid down those that leant, a third programme of re-erection began, following the work of Gowland and Hawley.

Stonehenge was gradually, almost reluctantly, providing answers to a few of its many mysteries that had survived the very earliest queries of Henry of Huntingdon down to those at the beginning of the twenty-first century.

The story begins with Stonehenge before Stonehenge.

CHAPTER 3:

TOMBS IN AN EMPTY LAND, 4200–3500 BC

At least some of the first farmers in Britain were colonists . . .
Boats must have been used, possibly open skin-covered boats,
but none has so far been found.

Timothy Darvill, *Prehistoric Britain* (1987), p. 49.

Neolithic settlement in Britain

It has been called the Neolithic revolution but it was not a
Neolithic invasion. Rather than a fantasia of flotillas, just a
few families arrived.

Revisionism is never content. Those tangible innovations of
pottery, cattle, pigs, wheat and barley seeds and the introduction of well-shaped stone tools have been explained away as
'essentially it was an idea'.[1] Ideas do not communicate by
themselves. They need people, not a phantom rope-line of

grain-filled pots bobbing like homing-pigeons across the Channel or herds of eagerly emigrating cows and bulls chesting the waves of the North Sea. The 'essential idea' came from living people, and during the fifth millennium the people came from the mainland of western Europe to settle in Britain. They were farmers. Some settled on the chalklands of Wiltshire where the ground could easily be tilled and planted.

In the 1940s, Gordon Childe described this migration as 'Immigrants from across the Channel [bringing], fully formed, the oldest neolithic culture recognizable in the archaeological record'.[2] But why did people cross the sea? And how did they reach this island?

There are many reasons for emigrating, such as pressure of population, exhaustion of ground, fear of conquest, desire to acquire better land, exploration for rare raw materials. Whatever their motives, respect is due to those pioneers. To peasant farmers the dangers of an unknown sea were immense, with the threats of sudden loss of visibility, uncontrollable currents, shoals of rocks and reefs, sudden gales and, near the coast, dangerous currents. 'The bones of thousands of wooden vessels have long since been digested by the sea and shifting sands'.[3]

The implication that inland farmers and their families purposefully took cargoes of household goods, precious grain and trussed cattle (even if only calves) across an ocean is facile. Boats are difficult to design and construct. They need a navigable framework, waterproofing, oars for steering, buoyancy and strength – skills that offshore fishermen develop over generations; skills that agriculturalists do not possess. An adventurous coastal society of fisher-farmers seems the more likely, using seaworthy, shallow, wicker-framed vessels lined with cowhide and made watertight with pitch. If, as DNA analysis of skulls implies, American seafarers island-hopped

7,000 miles of the Pacific to reach America 13,000 years ago, then mere cross-Channel voyages to Britain 6,000 years later need not be derided as fanciful.

The fact that the sea was crossed also suggests that there was far more and far earlier maritime activity than is usually acknowledged. Evidence for cultural contacts comes from the comparison between Severn-Cotswold tombs in southern England with similar simple passage-tombs in Brittany. In megalithic tombs near Avebury, 'the lateral chambers could be compared to passage-graves in long cairns like Barnenez in northern Brittany'. There are also architectural similarities between Breton passage-tombs and those in the Boyne Valley of Ireland. Gordon Childe wrote of 'Celtic missionaries' and 'megalithic saints'. The reality was more probably that people simply brought their burial traditions with them.

Barry Cunliffe observed that there are Early Neolithic dates from Cornwall, Devon, north-west Wales and Ireland, and concluded that there was no reason to doubt that there were long-established maritime links between Brittany and Ireland. In a relatively brief period, between 4300 BC and 3800 BC, people travelled to these islands along the Atlantic seaways, across the Channel and from the southern reaches of the North Sea: 'So rapid was the spread that there can be little doubt that the already well-developed maritime networks played an important part'.

It has been assumed that, because of the difficulty of constructing a keel sturdy enough to support a mast, the boats had no sails, but the belief that Neolithic seamen had only oars could be debated. Well-preserved woodwork in Britain and Ireland (though not from Brittany with its acidic soils) provides evidence of advanced carpentry techniques from firmly constructed, large timbered halls like Balbridie, 85ft by 43ft (26m x 13m), and planks and fashioned wood from the

Somerset Levels. However, pictorial evidence militates against the use of masts. No mast is shown in any of the carvings of questionable boats from Neolithic Brittany. Even more conclusively, nor is there a mast in any of the numerous Bronze Age rock-carvings in Scandinavia. There are keels, prows, gunnels, paddles and oars but not a single mast. Sails can be discounted for the mariners of early prehistoric Brittany.[4]

Once new land was reached, the fishing-farming communities would have settled by the sea rather than travel inland to the dry soils of Salisbury Plain. That immigration might come only generations later.

Fussell's Lodge burial mound

When the first farmers did eventually come to Salisbury Plain, they built houses, probably rectangular all-purpose structures combining a home for the family, storage for food, grain, clothing, furniture in places, tools, probably cattle and perhaps even a temporary space for the newly dead.

Remains are elusive. If there were farmsteads then their traces are almost certainly where today's villages are, in sheltered spots, near water and wood. If there were individual homes they are found almost by accident. But the postholes and bedding trenches of the few timber structures that are known reveal considerable skills in carpentry, with mortise-and-tenon joints to hold joists and purlins firmly, and planking socketed with pegs and dowels, the edges chamfered neatly together.

An example of such woodworking expertise came from the excavation, not of a house but of a burial mound, at Fussell's Lodge (Clarendon Park 4a) $7\frac{1}{2}$ miles SSE of Stonehenge. The long barrow spread over a wooden mortuary structure for the bodies of the dead.[5]

An assay of 3230±150 bc (BM-134) came from charcoal over some of the earliest burials at Fussell's Lodge, implying an erection date around 4000 BC. This needs an explanation. Until 1950, archaeologists had no means of obtaining precise dates for any object. But in that year Willard Libby introduced the concept of radiocarbon dating. All organic things, from fish to flora and fauna, breath in atmosphere which contains carbon. There are two types – C-12 which is stable and C-14 which is not. The ratio between them remains constant in life, but after death the unstable C-14 deteriorates at a constant rate over almost 4,000 years. It is possible to determine the remaining ratio of C-12 to C-14 and calculate when that object died.

By convention the assay is presented as a formula of (a) likely time of death plus (b) the degree of uncertainty and (c) the laboratory in which the calculation was made. Hence the formula above indicates that the object probably died some time between 3230 + 150 and 3230 – 150, i.e. 3380–3080, according to the British Museum laboratory (BM-134).

Unfortunately, it was later discovered that the rate of decomposition of C-14 had been underestimated and that the projected 'dates' were too late, sometimes by hundreds of years for objects from early prehistoric times. Luckily, a reliable check existed in the annual growth-rings of long-lived trees such as the Bristlecone pines of California and, more recently, oaks preserved in Irish peat-bogs. The original determinations are cited with a lower case 'bc' following the date, and the recalculated determinations are cited with an upper case BC. Thus the Fussell's Lodge date of 3230±150 bc (BM-134) is recalibrated at about 4050 BC (the 'about' indicates that there is still some spread around the date).

Fussell's Lodge was one of several well-built structures known in Britain and Ireland, whose builders appear to have used quite accurate units of body measurements such as the hand, foot and outstretched arms, and probably had counting systems of 3, 4 or 5 – facts of prehistoric engineering that are seldom considered.[6]

For a dozen people it was laborious work, digging chalk, felling and dragging trees, trimming them, elevating shaped posts into bedding-trenches. The building was well-designed. The northern side of the stockade was straighter than the south, implying that the latter had been laid out by offsets from the former. The excavator recorded that the façade was twice the width of the rear 'while the length was roughly three-and-a-half the breadth . . . it seems hard to avoid the conclusion that some reasoned system of proportion lies behind the whole concept'. He added that almost certainly a plumb-line had been used to ensure that the great timbers were exactly vertical.[7] Such techniques foreshadowed those of Stonehenge.

For 1,500 years, more than 70 generations (a crawl of centuries that would take today back to the end of Roman Britain and the pseudo-magical time of King Arthur and the Round Table), long barrows were erected. Unsurprisingly, between the beginning and the end of the Neolithic many burial customs changed, but those customs and beliefs would affect the customs and beliefs of the people who used Stonehenge.

They were a gracile people, light-limbed, short-lived, afflicted by accident and disease, and illiterate. Yet we may know some of their words from the evidence of those still used today by inhabitants of the remote Atlantic Fringe (the west coast of Brittany, Land's End and south-west Wales), particularly the commonplace words of home, work, weather, colours and landscape. The three regions were separated by miles of sea, yet culturally joined by a parochially similar tongue quite different from any Anglo-Saxon, Romance or Germanic language.

As a simple example, the word for 'black' in Latin is *niger*, in French *noir,* in German *schwartz*, in Anglo-Saxon *blaec*. But Brittany, Cornwall and Wales all share the same word, *du* – quite different from any of the others. See Appendix 1 for further examples of archaic words common to the three Atlantic Fringe languages.

The distinctions persisted into the Middle Ages and modern times. In the early twelfth century the French-speaking philosopher Abelard, recently appointed abbot of the abbey of St-Gildas-de-Rhuys in Brittany, complained that 'the countryside was wild, and the language unknown to me'. In the mid-seventeenth century John Aubrey was told by Samuel Butler that 'Mr. Camden much studied the Welch language, and kept a Welch servant to improve him in the language'. A hundred years later William Borlase said Cornishmen were indebted to Edward Lhuyd, the antiquarian, 'for his Cornish Grammar . . . without the help of Mr. Lhuyd, I think it would have been impossible at this time to attempt a language so near its last gasp'.[8] That the surviving words of these ancient vocabularies may have been used by the builders of Stonehenge is an interesting possibility. The knowledge would not, however, equip one to converse with those remote people.

Rather unexpectedly, if the people of the Atlantic Fringe were fully numerate it is not reflected in their words for numbers, all of which derived from Latin. Their 'one' was either '*un*' or '*gwym*' from the Latin *unus*, up to twelve for which their word was '*deudek*', '*daouzeg*' or '*deuddeg*' (the Latin is *duodecem*). It suggests that these early societies had only the simplest of counting systems, maybe no more than up to four or five.

Life was hard, sometimes precarious. In the dense forests there were dangers from snakes, wolves and boars. Against them was the protection of bows and flint arrowheads, and from that weaponry came prestigious personal ornaments that have survived with the dead, such as 16 perforated dogs' and wolves' teeth for a necklace at South Newton 1 bowl barrow, and 36 pierced bone points and boars' tusks from the Upton Lovell 2a barrow.[9]

But the people left no writing, no art that can be interpreted; they lived, farmed, bore children and left silence behind them. It is one of many paradoxes in early prehistory. The people may be ghosts in their lives but they come to life in death. Their bones in the long barrow cemeteries are biographies, informing us about their sex, age, stature, diet, injuries, illnesses and even family relationships.

In the mortuary house of Fussell's Lodge, over the years a family laid the bones of the dead. There were more than 50 bodies of men, women and children, the young outnumbering the adults by two to one, many of them with evidence of hardship, fractures and arthritis. Four in five children were malnourished.

The burials were contradictions. Most bones were unburnt, but some were scorched. By one of the bulky posts, skulls and longbones had been stacked, a pile of bones had been heaped tidily by another and the bones of two individuals had been assembled into a single ersatz skeleton near the entrance.

Some ribs and small bones were missing from most of the remains, and mixed amongst the bones was soil from an unknown locality. The position of an ox skull at the eastern end of the vault and bovine footbones outside its walls suggested that an oxhide, complete with hooves and skull, had been draped over the charnel-house with the horned head fixed above the entrance.

Fussell's Lodge may have been used by a dozen or more people and their descendants for a century or so, bringing the dry bones of their dead there from a separate burial-place, which explains the missing small bones, the 'foreign' soil and the weathered condition of some skulls. It is arguable that bones were carried there only after the flesh had rotted, leaving disconnected bones to be parcelled up.

In the Early Neolithic, 'burial' did not consist of immediate interment, but was a protracted ritual extending over months before the bones were taken to their final rest. Some bodies may have been exposed on a scaffold outside the entrance, safe from predatory beasts if not from scavenging birds. Others may have been buried and disinterred when the bones were fleshless. Scorching would have hastened the process of desiccation.

Treatment of the dead

In barrow after barrow excavators have commented on the disarticulated bones, their weathered condition, the absence of arm- and leg-bones and even skulls. It seems that a newly dead corpse was regarded as retaining some life, and it was only when all flesh and moisture had gone that the bones were deemed free of any lingering spirit.

On Normanton Down bodies were left in an unroofed stockade.[10] It is tempting to think of the bones of the dead being collected there and carried northwards to the Wilsford South 30 barrow and perhaps to the tiny Wilsford South 13, half a mile north-east. Two other barrows were quite close, Wilsford South 34 and the huge Lake mound, Wilsford South 41. Mortuary stockades were perhaps intended to be used by several families.

A different treatment of the dead, excarnation (the digging up of bones from a temporary grave for reburial), is also known. In the mid-nineteenth century Dr John Thurnam, of the County Asylum in Devizes, became interested in the shapes of prehistoric skulls and he dug into many mounds. Although his technique of excavation was poor, sinking ugly trenches not only into a score of long barrows but into three times as many round ones, he did leave detailed information about the crania and bones.

In 1863 he explored the Easton Down long barrow (Bishops Cannings 1) six miles NNW of Stonehenge. This huge tumulus, infested with rabbits and in the Military Danger Zone, covered eight skeletons:

> . . . the bones so mingled and so closely packed, that it was scarcely possible to regard this as the original place of burial; and it is almost certain they had experienced a prior interment, and had been removed to the spot where they were found after the decay of the soft parts and the separation of the bones.[11]

Two distinct aspects of Neolithic ritual are apparent in animal bones. The survival of ox bones 'from the fleshy parts' of the beasts seems evidence of feasting during the funerary rites, little different from modern-day wakes. An immense number of pig bones lay under the great mound of Warminster 14. Elsewhere, ribs of deer and boars' tusks littered the debris of the dead, giving the impression of leftovers from baked meats as the last acts were performed in the long, drawn-out funerary rites.

But there were also skulls of oxen near the disarticulated bones of the dead. Sometimes there were clay or stone balls, thought to be representations of testicles. It is plausible that these isolated skulls and sexual imitations were believed to give potency or protection to the dead, perhaps as totems. In view of similar discoveries at Stonehenge itself, the association of such skulls and spheres with the dead is significant, for it is from such seemingly trivial facets of Neolithic burial and belief that clues about the purpose of Stonehenge can be detected.

Perhaps nothing more clearly demonstrates the mourners' belief that death had many stages than the near absence in long barrows of objects for the dead to take with them. Once the ghost or soul had left the corpse it had no use for material things. It was while the body corrupted and retained some spirit that it had need of possessions. Only during that process of decay was anything left with it.

At Normanton Down antlers lay with the dead inside the mortuary enclosure. Elsewhere, in pits whose whereabouts were probably marked by posts, corpses were given pots or other articles, a chalk plaque, deer ribs, sherds, a complete bowl. Months after the burial, when the flesh had rotted, it was disinterred, the bones carried to the mortuary house and the unwanted articles left behind. A similar burial with possessions and a marker post was found by Hawley at the centre of Stonehenge.[12]

That the skeletons had previously been exposed was apparent, as many bones, especially the longbones, had been gnawed by rats and mice. Others, including skulls, were broken. Most breakages had been caused by flints in the barrow collapsing on to them – but not all.

Some skeletons had been buried, dug up and then apparently 'killed' by destroying the skull, maybe as an additional safeguard to ensure the total extinction of the spirit. At the Oxendean Down barrow (Warminster 6) Cunnington and Hoare found the bones of a man in a long, deep grave. He must have been defleshed before burial, because 'his skull lay chiefly upon the breast, literally beat into pieces pervious [sic] to interment, as some pieces of the jaws and skull lay more than a foot apart, yet the remainder of the limbs lay in regular order'. Similarly, in Boles Barrow, 'three of the skulls were found in an *upright* position, resting on the lower jaw . . . showing that they must have been detached from the body'.[13]

In 1864 Thurnam re-excavated Boles Barrow. Examining its skulls, he concluded that many of them had been intentionally hacked and broken after death. The 'evidence' is disputable and contradictory. There is however another, literally more sinister, explanation, one first proposed by Thurnam himself. 'From a minute examination of the fractures, I think it evident that the violence was inflicted prior to death, and in all probability during life'. One skull has been struck with great force on its left side. In their 1886 re-excavation of Boles Barrow the brothers William and Henry Cunnington, grandsons of William, saw the skulls and remarked, 'it is curious to note that, with one exception, the blows were inflicted on the *left* side of the cranium . . . Hence we may safely draw the conclusion that these old Britons were a *right-handed* race'.[14]

Following his excavation of the Old Ditch long barrow (Tilshead 2), Thurnam was more anatomically specific. 'The skull was smashed, as I thought at first by the weight of the flints, but from the peculiar character of a contused cleft near the coronal border of the left parietal, it would appear to have been purposefully cleaved before internment.'[15]

A more recent examination of crania from barrows strengthens the likelihood of intentionally heavy blows inflicted by a flint axe or club or antler and, as Thurnam and the Cunningtons surmised, by right-handed attackers. Almost one in ten of the skulls had such dentations to the left of their temples.[16] Women were not excluded. In the enormous Old Ditch barrow seven miles west of Stonehenge, Thurnam found the bones 'of a woman of small stature, the skull bearing the indisputable marks of having been violently cleft before burial'.[17]

Different injuries, such as arrows passing cleanly through a body, would leave no physical trace. Flint arrowheads have been found under or near undamaged skeletons in barrows such as the Giant's Grave (Milton Lilbourne 7) in the Vale of Pewsey where Thurnam came upon cleft skulls. Lying by one of them was 'a beautifully-chipped, leaf-shaped arrowhead'.[18] Often considered to have been offerings to the departed the arrows may, instead, have caused the departure – becoming deadly rather than dedicatory.

The Early Neolithic was not the wished-for utopia fantasized by today's neo-druids and escapists, nor some forgotten paradise despite Milton's 'Time will run back, and fetch the age of gold'. Writing six years after Milton, in 1651, Thomas Hobbes was more realistic, writing not of a golden age but of a time without writing, 'and what is worst of all, continual fear and danger of violent death; and the life of man, solitary, poor, nasty, brutish and short'.[19]

Short-lived or not, ended by peaceful death or attack and slaughter, the bodies did receive burial. The final funerary ceremonies included the digging of pits near the jumbled bones. Many pits were small, round basins containing only loose earth. Hoare commented that it was quite usual to find them near heaps of bones, describing them as 'one or more circular cists cut into the native chalk, and generally covered with a pile of stones or flints'.[20]

At Tilshead 2 there was an oval pit as neatly cut 'as if it had been done with a chissel'. Under Heytesbury 4 there was an equally well-fashioned hole, filled with black earth, stones and marl, with skeletons lying by it. Their proximity to the dead suggests that they may have received funerary libations. They have some likeness to the Aubrey Holes at Stonehenge.[21]

Filling the pits may have been the last action before the piling up of the barrow over the ageing mortuary house. Work-gangs dug two parallel ditches, each composed of short sections like grotesque bath tubs, the segments finally linked when their ends were broken down. The barrow was an inverted image of the ditches. The stripped-off turf was laid out in a thick rectangle to form the base of the mound. This turf, and the topsoil spread over it, was compressed by the weight of the overlying chalk, forming a black layer consistently noticed by the excavators of these long mounds. On to it soft, weathered chalk from the top levels of the ditches was heaped, and then harder, deeper chalk was dumped in uneven piles, giving the barrow an undulating profile like the humps of a serpent's back. When the hollows were filled in with chalk, the barrow must have stretched bleakly white against the Plain, like an enormous blanched house as pallid as the bones it covered.

It was only after five or more generations, perhaps a century, that the burials at Fussell's Lodge were sealed off. Around the ridge-roofed shelter, a trapezoidal stockade of posts was erected, wide at the east, narrower at the west, with a heavy oak log standing massively at each corner. Chalk rubble from two ditches along its sides was dumped into this enclosure, filling it and covering the mortuary house which later collapsed, fracturing many of the bones and skulls. The final barrow looked like an exaggerated Neolithic house, an imposing and conspicuous home for the dead.

Surveying the barrows on Salisbury Plain

There are over 60 of these earthen long barrows on the Plain, 16 within 3 miles of where Stonehenge would be (see fig. 13, overleaf). Except for the immediate south-east where the river

Avon curls and turns through the Amesbury valley, the site of
the future circle is surrounded by these old burial-places. Some
like Shalbourne 5, 15½ miles north-east of Stonehenge, are
ploughed and almost invisible while others, like its neighbour
Shalbourne 5a, hidden in the beeches of a dense coppice, are
excellently preserved. In summer sunshine the surrounding
countryside is a medley of beeches and butterflies.

There are monsters, open to the sky, heavy on their hillsides
like slumberous whales but twice the size, basking in a sea of
grass – Milton Lilbourne 7, the 'Giant's Grave', the Cold Kitchen
barrow (Brixton Deverill 2) with nettles, rush grass, cornflowers
and poppies growing on it, and not two miles to its east, the
beautiful elegance of the low barrow on Pertwood Down (Brixton Deverill 7) grazed by foxy-faced sheep, its eastern end pocked
and dented like a half-eaten apple by some forgotten excavation.

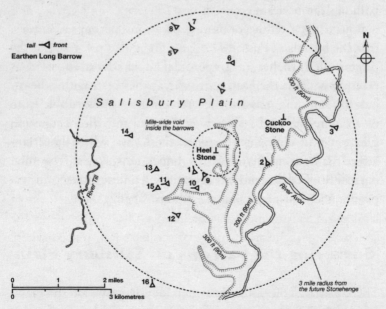

Fig. 13: The Stonehenge region in c.3700 BC, showing earthen long barrows within
three miles of the future location of Stonehenge. A mile-wide void inside the barrows
is indicated by the inner dotted circle.

Although long barrows began as sepulchres for communal family burials, slowly, over centuries, customs changed as egalitarian societies were transformed into hierarchies. Some late barrows became imposing sepulchres for one man. But it was a change concealed by the appearance of the barrow, bigger but still in the familiar shape of old.

A barrow was placed to be conspicuous. Thurnam noticed it. 'Long barrows occupy the highest points on the downs, in situations commanding extensive views over the adjoining valleys, and so as to be visible at a great distance'.[22] Bulford 2, under its old, tall beeches, was constructed at the edge of a steep drop. Tilshead 4, the White Barrow, rises at the head of a slope. Bratton has a magnificent view over the Vale of Pewsey. Two miles north-east of Stonehenge is Knighton Barrow. The Wiltshire archaeologist, Maud Cunnington, observed, 'although not of great length this is a very fine barrow, and the most conspicuously situated of any in the county, being a landmark for many miles across the Plain in every direction'.[23]

With no known settlement near these barrows, an explanation for their siting must be cautious. Possibly each of the 16 near Stonehenge had its own 'territory' of about $1\frac{1}{2}$ square miles, with the barrow on high ground and the occupation area lower down on the slopes of the Avon or the little River Till to the west. Such a territory could have supported a family, especially if the inland areas of the Plain were regarded as common land for grazing the summer herds. Some form of land organization must have existed and would explain the conspicuous position of many of the barrows, placed where their dead overlooked the homes and cultivated plots of the living.

The barrows vary greatly in bulk. A small one like Wilsford South 13, lurking in the Normanton round barrow cemetery near Stonehenge, is estimated to contain no more than

6,000cu.ft ($170m^3$) of chalk – a midget when contrasted with the enormous, overgrown and rather battered Tilshead 2, over 70 times the volume of the other, and 'probably the largest true long barrow in England'.[24] The majority of barrows, however, might be compared with Fussell's Lodge and there are reasons for believing that the bigger ones were late, when there was a growing emphasis on architectural grandeur.

What is noteworthy about the construction of these barrows is the absence of sarsen. There were few free-lying stones on Salisbury Plain, only quarries such as Chilmark, 11 miles south-west of Stonehenge, whose easily cut freestone was used for the cool austerity of Salisbury Cathedral and the soft, golden walls of Wilton House. Its finely grained sandstone is known as 'the architect's stone', for it is simple to cut into blocks.

It was not extracted by Neolithic people. If they wanted stone they took what was on the ground, glacial erratics or outcrops, neither of which was plentiful on the Plain. Only Tidcombe Down (Tidcombe & Fosbury 1) near the Vale of Pewsey and the Marlborough Downs had a sarsen-built chamber. It is in the far north of Salisbury Plain, 14 miles north-east of Stonehenge. The Tow long barrow (Grafton 5), just one mile away, had only flints. Even today the local materials are flint, timber, reeds, clay and chalk. All exist in the older houses of villages like Stratford-sub-Castle near Salisbury. Here there are half-timbered houses, flint-walled, reed-roofed houses, and walls of mud and clay with weather-proofed thatched tops. Only churches and manor houses were of expensive, imported stone.

It was chalk, earth and wood that Neolithic communities used for the majority of the great barrow mounds, although Knook 2 was composed of a cairn of flints and big marl stones lying, as Cunnington discovered in 1802, on 'a regular paved floor of flints'.[25]

The barrows still loom from the landscape, impressive in their bulk and heaviness, great mounds clamped at the very edges of steep slopes, covered in wild flowers and nettles, as ponderous today as they were 5,000 years or more ago but no longer in vivid contrast to the grassland. Once straight-sided gigantic wedges of chalk, they had been as conspicuous as white balls on the green baize of a billiard table. Whatever their condition, almost without exception, they have a feature in common. They face eastwards.

No.	Site	Grid reference	Miles from Stonehenge	Direction faced	Azimuth ± 2°	Length M.	Ft.
1	Amesbury 14	SU 115 417	½ SW	SSE	148°	13	100
2	Amesbury 42 (?)	SU 137 432	½ N	SSW	194°	81	265
3	Amesbury 104	SU 141 419	1 ESE	SSE?	145°	20?	65
4	Bulford 1	SU 163 431	2½ ESE	ESE	113°	41	133
5	Durrington 24	SU 124 444	1½ N	SE	133°	43	142
6	Figheldean 21	SU 108 458	2½ NNW	SE	138°	45	148
7	Figheldean 27	SU 127 453	2 NNE	E	93°	56	182
8	Netheravon 6	SU 114 466	3 NNW	SSE	157°	34	111
9	Netheravon 9	SU 108 466	3 NW	SE	147°	35	115
10	Wilsford South 13	SU 118 413	½ SW	NE	37°	20	65
11	Wilsford South 30	SU 114 410	1 SSW	E	80°	38	126
12	Wilsford South 34	SU 104 411	1½ SW	ENE	60°	36	117
13	Wilsford South 41	SU 108 401	1½ SSW	ESE	115°	43	140
14	Winterbourne Stoke 1	SU 100 415	1½ WSW	NE	43°	73	240
15	Winterbourne Stoke 53	SU 091 428	2½ WNW	E	87°	32	104
16	Winterbourne Stoke 71	SU 101 409	1½ SW	NE	49°	52	170
17	Woodford 2	SU 100 377	3 SSW	S?	?	20	67
			Average length of barrows:			42	135

Table 3: Earthen long barrows within three miles of Stonehenge.

'We find', wrote Sir Richard Colt Hoare, 'more generally one end of these barrows broader than the other, and that broad end pointing towards the east'.[26] It is at the eastern end that the majority of skeletons and bones were placed, a situation obviously preferred by Neolithic people. Fieldwork by the present author showed how emphatic this choice was.

The survey had problems. On the steep ridge of Collingbourne Ducis I was accosted by a farmer who suspected I was a furtive metal-detector. At Larkhill army camp, flat on my stomach, I was interrogated by military policemen who suspected I was filming secret installations rather than photographing the outline of the just visible Knighton Down long barrow (Durrington 24). Trouble with the forces continued. At the enormous mound of Old Ditch barrow (Tilshead 2), a red-brevetted brigadier-general courteously asked why I was on War Department property. Elsewhere, landowners were more encouraging when I asked permission to visit a barrow. At Cold Kitchen Hill a farmer's wife smilingly agreed that it was 'lovely air for a walk'.

Three conditions decided the situation of barrow – nearness to a settlement, visibility from that settlement and orientation. The second was the most important.

With the doubtful exception of Amesbury 42, of the 66 barrows still in good enough condition for their orientation to be determined there is only one, at the far west of the Plain, that does not face between NNE and south. Arn Hill (Warminster 1), a fine barrow darkened by beeches and weeds, faces SSW. It lies at the edge of a sharp western slope, whose ridge made it impossible for its builders to conform to a traditional axis. All other barrows have their wider, higher end between NNE and south, nine out of ten between 36° (NE) and 166° (SSE). (See table 4.)

Hawley's observation about the differences between opposing sides of a site was relevant to the orientation of the barrows. With the one exception of Arn Hill, all the others faced to the east of a north-south line. To this could also be added that the majority looked towards an arc in which the rising moon would appear. There is some indirect confirmation of this, inasmuch as those barrows which have no lunar alignment are architecturally different from those that do. This interest in a meridional line, the treatment of different sides and lunar alignments would all be included in the layout of the future Stonehenge.

Astronomical caution is needed. The weathered, sometimes ploughed-down mound of many barrows prevents an exact bearing being obtained. After making plane-table surveys of 66 barrows it became clear that the original axis could never be precisely recovered, and that it was impossible to attain an accuracy better than $\pm 2°$ – an 'alignment' of 91° at Bratton 1 means that the mound was probably oriented by its builders somewhere between 89° and 93°. One cannot be more definite.

The direction was decided before the mound was built. At Fussell's Lodge the excavator recorded that 'the mortuary house post-sockets lay exactly on the axis of the enclosure and in line with the [entrance] causeway', showing that when the people heaped up the final stockaded barrow they respected the orientation of the earlier mortuary house.[27]

There is a simple explanation for this easterly preference – it was the rising sun. It was not the direction of the prevailing wind nor was it primarily caused by the lie of the land. As well as an insistence on an easterly direction the majority of the barrows were planned to face the rising of a celestial object. It is more difficult to explain why people should want this, although the concept of the sun as a giver of light and warmth is a common one, just as the moon has often been linked with darkness, cold and death.

The problems of archaeo-astronomy, the study of astro-nomical practices in the ancient world, are many and often impossible to resolve. Fortunately, for the long barrows of Salisbury Plain matters are not intractable. At a latitude just north of 51°, sunrise in 4000 BC would have occurred around 50° (NE) at midsummer, and over the following six months would have moved steadily southwards, appearing at the east in September and at the south-east, around 130°, by midwinter.

Its precise azimuth or compass-bearing would be affected by the height of the horizon. At the Stonehenge latitude of 58.18° the midsummer sun would rise at 49.58° if the skyline were level with the place where the observer was standing. If a nearby hill were 3° higher, the rising sun would be concealed behind it, appearing only at about 54.27°. As most long barrows on the Plain occupy elevated positions, it is rare for them to be overshadowed by higher ground. The rising sun's range can be said to be between about 50° at midsummer and 130° at midwinter, but only 13 of the 66 barrows (20 per cent) are either north or south of this arc.

The range of the rising moon is wider. It rose close to 42° at its most north-easterly, and near 144° at its most south-east-erly. Although this arc covers little more than half of the eastern skyline, over nine in ten of the barrows are oriented within it. Only Wilsford South 13 faces 37° (NE) just north of it. Five others were aligned to the south of 143°. These introduce a comment about the nature of long barrows and the changing beliefs of the people who raised them over those long centuries.

Because the number of bodies in the barrows and the range of radiocarbon dates vary widely, it has been suggested that the first mounds were modest in size, no more than about 151ft long and never more than 79ft in width (46m, 24m).

Over half of them are to be seen within three miles of Stonehenge, and all were oriented within the lunar arc. It seems probable that they were intentionally aligned on the rising moon.

This would not account for those barrows facing more to the south towards places on the skyline where the moon could never have risen or set, and it is significant that these are much bigger than the others. Such mounds are gigantic, averaging 222ft long, 64ft wide and 9ft high (67.7m, 19.5m, 2.7m) – Amesbury 42, facing ±194°; Brixton Deverill 2, l49°; Grans Barrow, Hampshire, 175°; Shalbourne 5, 172°; Tidcombe & Fosbury 1, 166°; and Warminster 14, a colossus, measuring 207ft long, 56ft wide and 15ft high (63m, 17m, 4.6m). It is aligned to the SSE, 166°. All these gigantic barrows and many other outsize mounds such as Boyton 1 and the looming Milton Lilbourne 7, 315ft in length (96m), are located in marginal positions on the Plain, often in areas of poorer land. They are considered to be later than their shorter counterparts and put up at a time in the Neolithic when the population was growing.

Ritual gradually changed. So coarse is our chronology because of the paucity of radiocarbon dates that it is impossible to construct a firm framework for these changes, but it is likely that in the centuries after Fussell's Lodge was closed three major variations in burial customs developed. Fewer and fewer people were buried in the long barrows, the mounds were larger and the role of men gained greater status.

These bulking piles of earth and chalk were symbols of power in an age when a cult of ancestors was replacing the old tradition of communal burial. Some of them contain only a single, articulated skeleton, usually male. They were the final long barrows. By 2900 BC all had been sealed. No more were raised.

Direction faced	Number of barrows
NNE	4
NE	8
ENE	8
E	17
ESE	5
SE	12
SSE	7
S	3
SSW	1 + 1?

Table 4: The orientation of 66 long barrows
on Salisbury Plain.

Statistics reveal how communal burial diminished. The
average number of bodies in a long barrow is only six. In a
tomb built for a family of a dozen men, women and children
such a group could expect that number of deaths within 15 to
20 years, but it is reasonable to suppose that most barrows
were in active use for at least a century. By that time practically
50 deaths would have occurred. The disparity between the
bodies actually found and the number to be expected suggests
that the later barrows were clan structures, in which the
chosen members of only one of five or six families were given
privileged burial.

It is arguable that ageing bones were cleared out of the
mortuary houses to make room for others. Yet, as the timber
chamber of Fussell's Lodge demonstrated, it could comfortably accommodate the remains of 50 or more people. Unless the
Salisbury Plain barrows had each been open for 300 years or
longer, filled with dozens of disjointed skeletons, there would
have been no need for such clearance. Given the decaying
strength of the timbers, it is most unlikely that any chamber

could have been used for as long as three centuries. An alternative explanation has to be found for an average of only six individuals in the barrows, and a form of selective burial seems probable.

Evidence for the growing importance of men comes from the bones themselves. The number of complete male skeletons, articulated and presumably carried fully fleshed into the tomb, is small, little more than 20. This contrasts with the some 200 disarticulated remains of which a quarter are of children, a quarter of women and just over half of men. Of complete skeletons, only one child and one woman are to be set against the score of men.

These male burials are quite commonly found as the only burial, and this piece of demographic detective work has revealed a subtlety concerning children. In those barrows where a child was buried alongside an adult it was with a man five times but with a woman only once. Where the ages of the men could be determined they were between 25 and 50 years old, middle-aged in the Neolithic. That age and sex distinctions did exist in the Neolithic is shown at Fussell's Lodge, where of the heaps of bones, two were entirely of grown males and a third consisted solely of infants. A fourth collection of bones near the entrance, artfully arranged to resemble a single complete skeleton, turned out to be the re-assembled bones of two women, one of them elderly and arthritic. In front of them was an ox skull.

Outwardly nothing had altered. The new monstrous barrows had the same appearance as the old, but now they were for a single man and with him there were personal possessions that reflected the man's distinction. The moon, the pits, ox skulls and axes were all retained as part of the funerary rites as tradition required, but now they were for one person rather than the group.

Just over a mile WSW of the future site of Stonehenge, at the junction of the Winterbourne crossroads, there is a fine long barrow, its ditches still apparent and only its north-west side scarred where labourers dug out chalk in the nineteenth century. It is an almost perfect mound, 240ft long and over 10ft high (73m, 3m), facing north-east towards a long, low skyline and the most northerly rising of the moon.

Thurnam dug there in 1863. At the eastern end he came upon the skeleton of a man lying on its right side, head to the south-west, knees drawn up as though the corpse had been tied. Near the back of the skull was a pit 18in (46cm) across and as deep, 'scooped out of the chalk rock'. Close to the man's right arm was a 'bludgeon-shaped flint about 8 inches [20cm] long, and well adapted for being grasped in the hand. From one end numerous flakes had been knocked off and it had evidently constituted an object of considerable importance to its owner'. Like the chalk balls considered to be representations of testicles, it also has been interpreted sexually as a phallus.[28]

There are 17 long barrows within three miles of where Stonehenge would be, but only two closer than a mile. The sarsen circle stands at the heart of a sustained necropolis, at the centre of a ring of death six miles across. Yet it is isolated from the long and the round barrows. No mound is near it. It is also noteworthy that the innermost of the barrows are quite modest, no more than 100 to 150ft (30m to 40m) in length.[29] One supposedly longer, Amesbury 42 near the eastern end of the Stonehenge Cursus, is arguably a Late Neolithic folly.

Stonehenge has been considered a monument to be seen rather than entered. As Ann Woodward and her colleagues observed, the long barrow cemeteries around it 'lay on an imaginary *cordon sanitaire* – a zone from which the magical and illusionary monument of the dead could be viewed, and beyond which few living humans may ever have been allowed to pass'.[30] But the vacuum was an illusion. The zone was not empty. Long before Stonehenge, four posts 'inadvertently left a mark, or scar, on the landscape which was exploited several millennia later'.[31]

The story began several thousand years before Stonehenge. When its visitors' car park was extended in 1966, four large and deep postholes were found about 820ft (250m) north-west of the circle. Their positions are marked by white rings today (fig. 14). They had held posts up to 14ft (4.3m) high. To C.A. Newham (known as Peter Newham), the position and layout of the pits suggested that they had been sighting-posts 'in line with important setting phenomena of sun and moon when observed from the four Stations and Heel Stone positions . . . they align on sun and moon setting positions with an extreme accuracy'.[32]

There was a problem about these alignments. They were wrong by several thousand years. Newham noted that it was 'surprising that most of the charcoal should be pine'. Neolithic builders would have used sturdy oak for these high and exposed posts rather than soft pine. There were oak forests nearby.

The solution came with three C-14 assays. There were two early unpublished radiocarbon dates for the postholes, one of 6140 ± 140 bc (HAR-456), another of 7180 ± 180 bc (HAR-455) and the third obtained in 1988 of 6930 ± 120 bc (GU-5109). The three covered a huge range of time, between 8500–6700 BC in the Middle Stone Age, a period at least three millennia before Stonehenge when the climate was warming and when pine and hazel woodland spread across the Plain, ideal for wild ox, elk and deer and ideal for the hunters who preyed upon them. The posts could have commemorated successes in the chase.

Fig. 14: Four deep postholes were found north-west of the stone circle when the visitors' car park was extended in 1966. White painted circles mark their positions.

Michael Allen suggested anthropological parallels: 'Other hunter-gatherer communities are also known to erect such posts bearing totems or symbols, which presumably served an important ceremonial role within the complex ideology of these technologically simple communities'. Interestingly, American Indian totem-poles 'were usually of pine and represented heraldic signatures (often animals) and insignia erected as a mark of respect for past chiefs'.[33]

If it were a venerated place, then how long it remained honoured is unknown. For Stonehenge the following Mesolithic centuries are a frustrating blank, with three, perhaps four millennia of ignorance, a period that would take us back to a time when royal pyramids were still being built.

Then, late in the fourth millennium, half a mile north of where the posts had been, men dug out two extensive ditches. Stukeley was the first to notice them: 'Aug. 6. 1723. I discovrd the noble *Ippodrom* of Stoneheng . . . tis formd of two parallel lines 10000 feet 7000 cubits in length & 350 asunder going in a strait line from east to west 200 North of Stoneheng'.[34]

It was the Stonehenge Cursus, its eastern section looking towards a very old standing stone.

CHAPTER 4:

THE CURSUS – RACECOURSE OR FUNERAL PATH? c.3500–3000 BC

A stone as big as any at Stoneheng lys about 3 mile in the cornfield . . . in Durrington field.

William Stukeley (1724), p. 62.

A brief look at causewayed enclosures

Some centuries before the Cursus was laid out, quite early in the fourth millennium BC, spacious ditched-and-banked earthworks known as cause-wayed enclosures were constructed at the edges of settled land in southern England. Theirs was a brief fashion. Flourishing in 3700 BC, nearly all had been abandoned by 3300 BC. These sites, many on rounded hilltops, had no megalithic counterparts on the highlands to the northwest.[1]

The enclosures were numerous along the Thames Valley. Quite regularly spaced, about five miles apart, their purpose is contentious and presents a medley of possibilities: defensive camp, market-centre, cattle kraal, settlement, a centre for seasonal festivals, or even cemeteries. The title is to blame. Like henge and cursus, the term causewayed enclosure is used by desperate archaeologists trying to categorize sites that may be similar in appearance but possibly dissimilar in purpose.

A causewayed enclosure was an irregular circle, bounded by from one to four concentric rings of internal banks and external ditches, and covering anything from 3 to 24 acres. In the ditches of some was a litter of animal bones, flint chippings, excrement covered with soil to reduce the stench and broken sherds. Elsewhere, ditches held burials of children and tidied collections of human bones, as though from corpses exposed to rot inside the earthwork.

Autumn gatherings are likely from the discovery of hazel-nuts and crab apples. The presence of oolitic limestone and Cornish pottery in the chalk landscape of Wessex suggest that people came to sites from some distance. The cut meat-bones, domestic equipment and flints for skinning and dressing carcasses imply occupation, even if only periodically. There are sexual objects, chalk phalli, 'cups' that may be representations of vulvae, rounded balls like testicles – all indications of rituals of magic and fertility.

Many enclosures are so enormous that one must imagine both people and herds inside them. The sites clustering along the 80 miles of the central Thames Valley average about 500ft (150m) in diameter, enclosing 18 acres of shallow hillside. Such camps were almost ten times bigger than the vaguely similar single-entranced henges that succeeded them. Causewayed enclosures are some-times seen as the precursors of henges, but the two distributions do not overlap neatly, and occasionally do not coincide.

The likeliest interpretation of the Neolithic causewayed enclosure is that it was a seasonal assembly-place for scattered communities, for feasting, communal pacts, culling livestock and gathering in a temporary shanty-town whose high banks kept cattle from straying but which, centuries later, were often converted into defensive ramparts. In the long years of the Early and Middle Neolithic a causewayed enclosure reflected the complexities of an expanding social, political and commercial world.

On Salisbury Plain there was one at Robin Hood's Ball near Shrewton, almost three miles north-west of where Stonehenge would be. By 1954 it had been ploughed into extinction. Even in the early nineteenth century Hoare mourned its condition: 'We have to regret the great injury these circles have sustained by the plough, as in their original state they must have been highly curious'.[2]

It is possible that at its very beginning Stonehenge itself, with its internal bank (very unusual for a henge), was a form of causewayed enclosure.

The Curcus at Stonehenge

Just to its north there was another kind of monument. Almost exactly two miles south of Robin Hood's Ball and less than half a mile to the north of where the Mesolithic posts had been, as though to commemorate them, an immense rectangle was laid out. This was Stukeley's *cursus*, its chalk-white banks stretching over a mile across the undulating landscape. On its alignment, half a mile to the WNW, was a great sarsen 18ft (5.5m) tall, standing like a signpost towards the river Avon. The Cursus had a counterpart, the Lesser Cursus – begun, added to, but left unfinished – half a mile to the north-west.

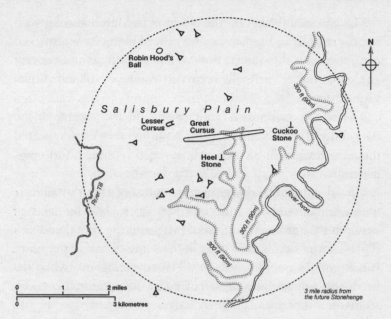

Fig. 15: The Stonehenge region in *c*.3500 BC. The Great Cursus now stretches north of the mile-wide void inside the barrows.

In 1909 Sir Norman Lockyer suggested that the Stonehenge Cursus was 'a processional road, a *via sacra*, to watch the rising of the Pleiades' in 1950 BC. It seems too late. In 3500 BC, Alcyone (a *Tauri*), the brightest of that lovely cluster of stars, was rising a long way from the alignment of the Cursus.

John North thought that a medley of cross-Cursus sightings – from the centre of the 265ft (81m) long Amesbury 42 long barrow to two worn-down round barrows inside the western terminal, and in reverse to Amesbury 24 itself – were linked to various risings and settings of the stars Arcturus, Pollux, Rigel and Antares, their declinations clustering in a not improbable set of dates from 3420 to 3240 BC. He added that probably the Cursus had been 'built in a short period of time – perhaps as little as a year or so'. Darvill observed that the arrangement of the Cursus meant 'that on the equinox in March and September the sunrise and sunset can be viewed along its length', but continued that the observation was irrelevant, as the concept of the equinox 'is generally regarded as a recent observational phenomenon'.

The equinoctial sun is an elusive and inconstant object. Alexander Thom stressed this, pointing out how essential modern equipment is for precise calculations. Obviously, prehistoric observers lacked such facilities. For this reason any precise equinoctial alignment propounded for a megalithic monument should be scrutinized very critically. The 'interval between the autumnal equinox ($180°$) and the vernal equinox ($0°$) is shorter by $7\frac{1}{2}$ days than in the summer half of the year'. It has not always been so. 'In 4040 BC perihelion [when the earth was nearest the sun] occurred at the autumnal equinox so that the winter and summer halves of the year were equal'. But by 3000 BC this was no longer true, and because of the varying heights of the skyline 'without instruments we cannot determine this instant'. As the Stonehenge Cursus is between $5°$ and $7°$ away from true east ($0°$), any claim for its equinoctial alignment betrays astronomical carelessness.[3]

Rather than constellations, single stars, elusive equinoxes or any other astronomical target, the Cursus may have been sighted on a very old standing stone. Darvill notes that 'The cursus is not straight but sub-divisible into three straight segments, set slightly offline to one another'. Thus the eastern end seems likely to be primary, set out towards the isolated sarsen.[4]

The Stonehenge Cursus is one of more than a hundred of these linear settings, just over half of them in England. They vary. Some, like the six miles of the Dorset cursus, are extremely long. Others are so short that a child could throw a ball from end to end. Some had open ends. Others had straight or curved terminals. The only common features were two parallel banks and ditches, and even they are not invariably parallel, one side unwavering, the other a wobble of uncertainty. It is probable that many consisted of additions that joined together once separate sections.

As with the causewayed enclosure, 'cursus' is a catch-all term used to classify what may be unclassifiable. In a similar manner one might use 'tube' as a definition of a hollow pipe with or without a lid. The term is treacherous, encompassing tubular objects as different as a pillar-box, a soup tin, a factory chimney or the Leaning Tower of Pisa. 'Cursus' is as inexact, accounting for a medley of earthen lines of banks and ditches – not only in the lowland zones of Britain but in Ireland's Co. Meath, near the famous sites of Newgrange and Tara, and even in France, in Calvados and the Paris Basin. Widespread in time, space and layout, they almost certainly were widespread in function.[5]

How old these linear chameleons are is less unclear. An antler recovered from the Stonehenge Cursus in 1947 gave a C-14 assay of 1950 ± 105 bc (OxA-1403), between 2910 and 2480 BC in real years. It is probably too late, and the antler may have been left there long after the Cursus had been constructed. That may not be true of the 'piece of foreign bluestone' found in the ditch. Whether any Welsh stones were on Salisbury Plain before 2700 BC is a matter of sharp, geological argument.

In the first phase of the Lesser Cursus, two radiocarbon assays from antlers suggested that it could have begun around 3300 BC. Radiocarbon assays from other cursuses indicate a general period of building from the middle to the end of the fourth millennium BC, perhaps from 3640 to 2920 BC – a span of time as short as 200 or as long as 650 years. Well before 3000 BC is the best that can be offered for the Stonehenge

Cursus. Excavations at the Cursus, of necessity limited in scope, have added little to the understanding of it.[6]

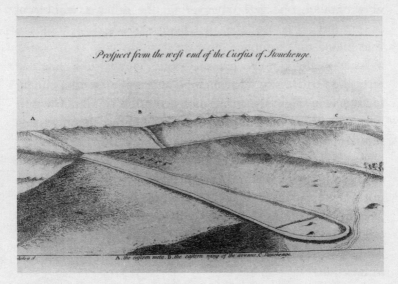

Prospect from the west end of the Cursus of Stonehenge.

A. the eastern meta. B. the eastern wing of the avenue. C Stonehenge

Fig. 16: William Stukeley's 1740 drawing of the Cursus. The curved end is incorrect. Above it are round barrows of the Cursus group, and beyond them (at 'C') is Stonehenge.

The purpose of these linear settings has puzzled archaeologists ever since William Stukeley detected the faint outlines of one at Stonehenge. He concluded that it had been a course for chariot- and horse-racing, 'for nothing els can I suppose it. tis formd of two parallel lines 10000 feet 7000 cubits in length and 350 [3km, 107m] asunder going in a strait line from east to west, 200 [2,000ft?] north of Stoneheng. the vallum [bank] is inward of both.' He added: 'at the west end of this Ippodrom are two barrows'. He also mentioned two banks, 'which seem the Starting places of the horses . . . this spot of ground for the horses and chariot races declines a little'. For *[h]ippodrom* (racecourse), he substituted the shorter Latin *cursus,* which became 'course' in English. To add conviction to his theory he falsified the shape of the terminals, drawing them not flattened but rounded (fig. 16). Had he discovered the Lesser Cursus he would have been delighted to see that in its beginning it had curved ends.

In 2003, substituting male athletes for Stukeley's horses, the idea of a racetrack was renewed. 'Could such sites have served instead as proving grounds for young men, where the main focus was on a race from one end to the other?'[7] It is feasible, but beyond proof. And, as will be seen, there are more persuasive alternatives.

Stukeley had been mistaken. With its squared corners the Stonehenge Cursus, like many of its counterparts, was unsuitable for chariot-racing. Nor are wheeled vehicles known from this period in Britain. Despite the presence of horse-bones in southern tombs such as West Kennet and Winterbourne Stoke, it is unlikely that the animals were used for riding or traction. People walked. Life was slow and four miles was a long hour across the countryside, something which makes the three-and-a-half mile long perimeter of the Stonehenge Cursus all the more astonishing.

The enclosure was like a monstrous pathway, a mile and three-quarters long from end to end and over 330ft (100m) wide, but uneven, falling 39ft (21m) to its centre in the muddy valley of Stonehenge Bottom, then rising 56ft (17m) eastwards.

The elongated interior covered 70 acres, big enough to accommodate three-dozen football pitches laid end to end. Although it would have been hypothetically possible for a few fanatical families to have dug out 250,000cu.ft ($7,100m^3$) of solid chalk, it would have taken them years. Forty thousand man-hours or more were needed for the construction of this incredible structure. Its completion demonstrates the cohesion of a society prepared to undertake such a project. Calculation suggests that a hundred men could have dug the Cursus in four-and-a-half months. Their efforts were probably sporadic, with stretches leading to the terminals completed first and the space between added to barricade it from humanity. The Cursus may have begun as two processional ways. It ended as a partition between one world and another.

The result was spectacular. The chalk-white lines of its banks stood starkly against the greenness of the Plain, sweeping up and down across the landscape like the ski-tracks of a giant. Now eroded, with ditches choked, today the banks are almost imperceptible. From Stonehenge their outline is hardly visible, but they lead eastwards from the trees of Fargo Plantation, first downhill and then rising gradually to a coppice (where the imitation long barrow mentioned in this book's introduction lies buried under a footpath).

The Cursus followed the contours of the landscape like Avebury's Kennet Avenue between Waden Hill and the Ridgeway. So did the Neolithic Thornborough henges by the river Ure near Ripon in Yorkshire. The Roman road to the east, Ermine Street, later the Great North Road (the A1), observed the same NNW-SSE contours. It was natural and easy. Prehistoric societies respected the land in which they lived and frequently represented it in their monuments. The laboriously dug, unstraight Cursus created a template for both its outlying stone and the environment.

A noticeable feature of many cursuses is their association with water, often directed towards a river or associated with a river-valley. Francis Pryor commented, 'If cursuses are indeed involved with the movement of people through a ritual landscape, then in these instances their journey was deliberately towards wet places'.[8] The Stonehenge Cursus did have a connection with water. It was also involved, albeit spuriously, with death, a collusion that intentionally joined the past to the present. Its extremities were transformed into imitations of long barrows.

Beyond its flat end, lying obliquely at the west, a 125m long, curved and segmented extension was added, terminating in a very deep, straight ditch, reminiscent of those trenches that had been quarries for the great barrow mounds. While the similarity between the deep ditch at the western end and those of Neolithic long barrows was too striking to be ignored, it was later found to be an illusion.[9]

At the other end of the Cursus the imitation was so successful that, despite the unusual north-south axis of the 'barrow', it deceived Stukeley, Hoare, Thurnam and modern archaeologists. Thurnam dug there in 1868, finding only a late interment of a woman and child and another infant slightly below them. Significantly, there was no human burial at the bottom, just leg-bones, pelvis and skulls of oxen set there when the Cursus end was 'changed' into a long barrow. The late long barrow of about 3110 BC at Beckhampton near Avebury also had no human bones but three skulls of oxen lay along its axis.

For years the Stonehenge Cursus 'barrow' was accepted as genuine, known as Amesbury 42, until excavation in 1983 revealed the truth – that it was an imitation, a 'burial-place' intended by the builders of the Cursus to enhance the enclosure. Today what had been a farm track covering it has been transformed into a path that passes over the hardly perceptible mound. Few visitors notice it.

Its construction, centuries after the Cursus, was a statement that tradition had not been abandoned. By the time it was built the oldest barrows were so eroded and rounded by weather that they resembled the backs of basking whales, green with algae. More recent mounds were already blotchy with vegetation and crumbling. But Amesbury 42, sharp-sided, was a spectacle of glaring white.

A passer-by would have thought that the Cursus had been laid out between two well-separated long mounds. Such prehistoric 'follies' show how determined the living were to maintain bonds between their ancestors and the spirit-world by means of the Cursus. It was both a barrier and a link between the living and the ancient dead. Even today the landscape contains evidence of it.

Superficially cursuses appear to be the earthen counterparts of the avenues of standing stones leading to stone circles, but the likeness is deceptive. The avenues are later, perhaps fashionable between about 2600 and 2000 BC. They have open ends and they have a target, the circle to which processions approached. They were pathways. It is arguable that this was almost exactly the opposite of what cursuses were. Rather than providing access they were barriers, separating one world from another.[10]

J. Harding commented: 'The enclosing ditch and bank perimeters may well have symbolized a distinction between those who had access to their inner sacred areas and those who were deliberately excluded from these defined spaces; and, the linearity of these sites would perhaps divide the landscape and present an obstacle to free movement'.[11]

Walking along the Stonehenge Cursus reveals starkly how it split one world from another. To its north are long barrows. For a long way to the south there are none. The modest Amesbury 14 to the south-west – in which Thurnam found three skeletons, two with 'killed' skulls – was closest, and it was almost a mile away. Eight others were a mile or more to the south. And the east end of the Cursus is different from the west. To reach it one must cross water.

Observant fieldworkers have quite recently walked the length of the Cursus from west to east:

All the way down the western sector of the Cursus, the
monument lies 'tilted' on a steep slope, forcing one to look
north . . . The general feeling generated by this effect, the
visibility of Robin's Hood's Ball, the King Barrow Ridge
and Coneybury Hill – all probably important locales since
mesolithic times, and the prominence of the key long barrows,
is one of an 'old world', the lands of ancient ancestors and
primeval origins. To the south there is no view out.

At the end of the long downward slope one comes to Stonehenge Bottom, 'still marshy and full of nettles'. This is the wet
place, 'a transition place where you cross water'. This 'lowest
point is in an area of virtually nil visibility'. Then, uphill,
eastwards, the landscape changes. 'One has left the old world
and is entering a new one . . . A new world has been reached, a
world which looks away from the Plain . . . and the "real"
long barrows, and across to the south'.[12] It looks to where
Stonehenge would stand.

This could have been the purpose of the Stonehenge Cursus.
It formed the northern side of a rectangle some two miles wide
and two-thirds of a mile deep. No long barrow lay inside it.
There were six within two miles to its north, five to its west,
one to its east and four to its south, but its interior was a void.
It was a land for the living. Stonehenge would stand close to its
heart. For centuries, along its northern side families from
scattered farms had carried the bodies of their dead for burial
in the long barrows beyond the sterile zone.

Over the centuries beliefs changed. By the Early Bronze Age
the vacuum had become a graveyard, not of just a few burials
but of whole cemeteries of round barrows nestling around the
Cursus, testifying to its long association with death. The Old
and New King Barrows were to its east. Mounds, now
ploughed-down, lay along its northern edge. Others can be

seen to the north on Durrington Down. The conspicuous Cursus group, dug into by Stukeley and Lord Pembroke, hump near its western terminal. Two round barrows were built inside the Cursus itself, one of them covering the skeleton of a man, head to the north. By it was a 'curious pebble' that Hoare described as kidney-shaped, striped and with little white dots all over it: 'After dipping it in water, it assumed a sea green colour'.[13] To its owner it may have seemed magical. But all this was more than a thousand years after the Cursus.

The orientation of that Cursus is another of the many challenges of Stonehenge, having defied every conscientious astronomer by its complete indifference to the sky. Laid out as it was, 263° – 83°, it had no good solar or lunar rising or setting alignment, and it was several degrees from any equinoctial line. But it did look eastwards across the river Avon and beyond Bulford to the distant landmarks of Beacon Hill and a neighbouring rise. In outline the pair resemble a woman's breasts.

'The past', observed L.P. Hartley, 'is a foreign country', and the prehistorian enters it with the most inadequate of sketch-maps.[14] Given the shape of those far-off hills it is possible that the Stonehenge Cursus, like some other Late Neolithic monuments, was connected not only with water but with a prehistoric belief in a protectress of the land. To liken the Bulford hills to breasts might be no more than romantic escapism into a wished-for utopian world that never was, were it not that Loveday noticed a similar phenomenon in which the Dorchester-on-Thames cursus was aligned on the dominant shape of the 'two curious hills' of Sinodun near Wallingford. Cautiously, he mentioned a 'deity'.[15]

To prehistoric people in their landscape in which everything – man, river, boulder, hill – had existence, the juxtaposition of hills, feminine in shape, may have been perceived as the personification of a guardian of the land. Terms such as 'Mother Goddess' are too evocative in their implications of a fecund being. Instead, the concept of a protectress of the dead certainly existed in Neolithic Brittany, where 'her' presence was carved onto slabs inside tombs, portraying her head, arms and breasts, and holding an axe or a dagger to guard the bodies interred there.[16]

In Britain such representational art does not exist, but place-names hint at related womanly associations, particularly with hills. Tuck has commented on the 'outrageously suggestive peaks', like monstrous breasts, of the twin Paps of Anu in Ireland. In Scotland there are similar 'female' hills, such as the Paps of Jura or the Maiden Paps near Hermitage.[17]

As well as such physical likenesses, there are informative folk-stories, medieval and later, but whose roots may be millennia older. They link women with the dead. 'Old Hags', *cailleachs*, are air-borne with bundles of stones that slip from their aprons to become megalithic dolmens and chambered tombs. In Shropshire the Stiperstones cairn was formed of boulders being carried by an aged crone, only for her apron-strings to be cut by the Devil. The same Devil appears to have supplanted both the old women and Merlin at Stonehenge when he hurled Irish stones at an insulting friar.[18] But the imagery is the same, of a protectress, even though in England she was rarely portrayed in art.

One clear instance of the prehistoric belief in a defending spirit was discovered in the Somerset Fens, 40 miles west of Stonehenge. Corduroyed paths had been laid across danger-ously marshy land. Beneath the planking of the Bell Trackway, a little ashwood carving was found, apparently set there to defend the track from sinking. The hermaphroditic effigy had a head, breasts and an erect penis. Two radiocarbon assays from trackway stumps of 2890 ± 100 bc (GaK-1600) and 2025 ± 90 bc (BM-354) allow the possibility that the figurine was contemporaneous with the Stonehenge Cursus of around 3000 BC and with the first phase of Stonehenge itself.[19] The Cursus, therefore, was associated with water and, more hypothetically, with a potent defender of the landscape. Less obviously, but more definitely, it was also in line with a great sarsen standing half a mile to the ENE.

Standing stones on the Harroway

Just beyond Amesbury 42 the land rises slightly and then, at the head of the brief ridge, there is a long, gradual fall towards the Avon. Behind a little wood in a field before the river there is a battered sarsen. It is known as the Cuckoo Stone. Today it is much broken, a stumpy block of about 6ft (2m) long, rough and thick, but it may once have been used by builders of the Cursus to become a venerated pointer to the river. When Stukeley saw it, it was prostrate but 'it was as big as any at Stonehenge', and would probably have measured about 18ft (5.5m) in length.[20]

It is one of the most disregarded of all the sarsens of Stonehenge, only ever mentioned in reference to some other site, whether the Cursus or Woodhenge, yet it was individually important. It was one of those venerable standing stones marking the route of the Harroway. Earlier writers guessed as much. In 1901 the Rev. C.S. Ruddle described it as 'a huge sarsen stone . . . on a line from the river to the avenue of Stonehenge'. Stukeley had already realized that as there were comparable stones in the vicinity 'one would rather guess they were sett there for guides to the Britons when they came hither'.

E. Barclay sketched the Cuckoo Stone in 1895, noting that it had a 'cleavage or ridge running its length in the direction of the Cursus 3,210ft [978m] away'. He added that another stone was 'within sight of the last-mentioned stone, and lies on the opposite bank of the Avon, on the open down above the village of Bulford; it evidently once stood erect, and has fallen southwards'.[21] ('Avon' is another of the suspected prehistoric words, quite different from the Latin *fluvius*, or French *rivière* or German *fluss*. In Breton, Cornish and Welsh respectively, *aven, avon* and *afon* suggest a common and long-established term for 'river'.)

Stones in the neighbourhood of the Cuckoo Stone had legends of the incompetent and re-sexed Devil. Predictably, the fiend had dropped them on his way to Stonehenge. One that he lost in the river near Bulford had an iron ring inserted later, presumably for mooring a boat. It was bewitched. A straining team of oxen could not shift it. Alarmingly, if ever it was turned over it always righted itself. Finally, with huge reluctance, labourers did raise it. It was not sarsen but oolitic limestone. 'It is not a little curious that it is in line with, and almost exactly equidistant from, its neighbours in Durrington Field and on Bulford Down'.[22]

The Cuckoo Stone had nothing to do with the Devil. It had a different folk-story, engendered by late nineteenth-century enthusiasm for the summer solstice and Stonehenge. The whimsy claimed that a cuckoo perched on the sarsen on Midsummer Day but, prosaically (though perhaps just as romantically), in 1740 the sarsen was known as the Cuckhold Stone, hinting that midsummer might be right, but late evening rather than dawn, and a different form of enthusiasm. Similar optimism claimed that another bird had alighted on the Heel Stone on 21 June 'and flown away a moment before the sun rose over the stone'. No other bird, and at no other time of the year, ever landed there.[23]

The Cuckoo Stone did provide a link between the Cursus and the river. It was also part of a series of standing stones set along the easiest gradients and at the best places to cross marshes and water. Of necessity visible from one to the other, acting as signposts, they were also precariously isolated as convenient sources of building material. Some were taken in entirety. Others were fragmented. The sarsen in the river was reduced to a small block just heavy enough to secure a boat against the current. In the 1920s Herbert Stone waded nearly up to his waist to inspect it.[24]

Others, taken away over the centuries, left wide gaps along the old trackway. The Cuckoo Stone, although hacked as a useful quarry, survived, and it remained between the Bulford stone on the far side of the river and another far more well-known pillar a mile-and-a-half to its south-west – the Heel Stone. That famous pillar enters this chapter with an almost heretical statement of 200 years ago. An antiquarian had the temerity to affirm that it was standing on Salisbury Plain long before Stonehenge. In a letter of November 1809 to William Cunnington, the Rev. James Douglas, author of the acclaimed 1793 *Nenia Britannica* (Funeral Dirges of Britain), wrote, 'I have ventured to hazard an opinion that the *Bethyl* or stone of adoration situated [outside the] grass circle, was the primary erection, to which the circle was dedicated'.[25]

If so, it was not alone. Initially, in remote antiquity, menhirs (*meini hirion*, 'standing stones') had been erected to guide travellers or to inform seafarers of safe landing-places but, years later, were often re-used as outliers or else surrounded as respected pillars by megalithic rings. A navigational marker by the coast on the Isle of Lewis was transformed into the tall centre stone of the Callanish circle. A trackway marker near Penrith became the outlier to the Long Meg & Her Daughters stone circle. The gigantic menhir of the Grand Menhir Brisé in

Brittany, once at the head of a row of smaller stones, was converted into an *'indicateur'* pointing to the monstrous Carnac mound of Er-Grah.[26]

Similarly, the Heel Stone, once one of a series of antique signposts on the Harroway, was integrated into the Stonehenge complex. Its name is only one of a medley of mistakes about it. Indeed, it is doubtful whether any other prehistoric pillar has experienced as many changes of name and interpretation, all of them wrong. There were two major errors in a statement by Barclay: 'The *Friar's Heel, the Heel-stone, Sunstone, or Index-stone* – By means of this huge unwrought rock the temple is set to the rising sun at the summer solstice'.[27] The names are wrong and so is the astronomy.

The outlier is an eroded block of sarsen about 254ft (77.3m) from the centre of the sarsen circle. It leans towards the south-west at an angle of almost 27°. Crudely cylindrical, with a tapering top, the stone weighs well over 35 tons and would have demanded the strength of more than a hundred men to haul it upright. The description is prosaic but the appearance of the stone is not. Like all 'drab' sarsens it changes colour with the weather and the seasons, sometimes appearing dark-blue, dull grey or brown, or moss-green, even glowing golden in the sunlight. Its name, situation and significance also changed.

Which of the Stonehenge sarsens was meant by Friar's Heel remains a matter of conjecture. From John Aubrey's description it was not the Heel Stone. Aubrey distinguished between the nameless Heel Stone, which stood to the north-east outside Stonehenge, and the Friar's Heel which lay inside the circle. It was not the upstanding outlier:

One of the great Stones that lies downe, on the west side, hath a cavity something resembling the print of a mans foot; concerning which, the Shepherds and countrey people have a

Tradition (wch many of them doe stedfastly believe) that when Merlin conveyed these Stones from Ireland by Art Magick, the Devill hitt him in the heele with that stone, and so left the print there.

Precisely which of the sarsens it was has never been agreed. It was probably either Stone 12 or 14, both in the south-west quadrant as Aubrey stated. Surprisingly, given the increasing seventeenth-century interest in Stonehenge, the Heel Stone was unmentioned before Aubrey. Despite visiting Stonehenge and digging inside the circle, Inigo Jones completely ignored the outlier.[28]

Stukeley never discussed either a Heel Stone or a Friar's Heel. In 1724 he surmised that an un-named outlier was a surviving portal, then in 1740 it became 'a *crwm leche* still standing in its original position and place in the avenue . . . The use of it I can't certainly tell'.[29]

A few years later, as we have seen, John Wood made the first accurate plan of Stonehenge. Like Stukeley he did not think of the Heel Stone and the Friar's Heel as the same sarsen, although he referred to the outlier, his Stone R, many times. There were two obvious reasons for his omission. In 1747 the stone had not been linked with the sun, and no such term as the 'Heel Stone' existed.

Wood did include the Devil who had tricked an old woman into accepting devalued Irish coins which, remembering Geoffrey of Monmouth's fantasy of Merlin and Ireland, explains the origin of that garbled folk-tale. Wood, however, changed Geoffrey's Merlin into a holy friar running for his life, having insulted the Devil. He did not get far. Satan furiously flung a stone, hitting him in the heel. But to Wood it was not the Heel Stone because the projectile rested inside Stonehenge.[30]

It was John Smith in 1771, unaware of Aubrey's unpublished manuscript, who confused everybody. From Wood he knew that the frightened monk was scurrying away and, intelligently but mistakenly, Smith deduced that the missile had to be outside Stonehenge. Hence it was the Heel Stone:

> I suspected the Stone, called the Friar's Heel, to be the Index that would disclose the uses of this Structure . . . This stone stands in a right line with the centre of the Temple, pointing to the north-east . . . The stone number 1, in the middle of the grand avenue of the Temple is the Key or Gnomon.

An arch-druid at the centre of Stonehenge, looking over the Slaughter and Heel stones 'at the summer solstice . . . sees the sun rise from behind the hill . . . the apex of Stone number 1 points directly to the place'. Smith has been unfairly maligned, accused of 'the greatest archaeo-astronomical fallacy of prehistoric Europe'. This is unjust. Smith was entirely correct, although for the wrong reason.[31]

It is noteworthy that he called the solar outlier the Heel Stone but never the Greek *heol* or 'sun' stone. That was to be a later solecism, but it shows the insidious deceptions lurking behind any hopeful study of long-forgotten languages. Unlike the Latin *sol*, French *soleil* or German *sonne*, is the quite different Greek ηγιοξ (*helios*) related to the Breton *howl*, Cornish *hewl* and Welsh *haul*? Perhaps. Despite the likelihood of prehistoric long-distance voyages, it is most improbable that the linguistic inhabitants of the Atlantic Fringe were conversant with archaic Greek. But one wonders.

Funerary customs had changed. For their final burial, skeletal bones (and the occasional corpse) were no longer taken from isolated farmsteads. Instead, late in the fourth millennium BC as long barrows declined in use, the remains of the dead may have been carried past the Cuckoo Stone and along the side of the Cursus from a communal mortuary centre a mile to the east.

There, lines of postholes and hollows, Middle Neolithic bowls, flints and three C-14 assays show the site had been occupied around 3200 BC. Several centuries later, the open settlement was enclosed in an enormous bank and ditch that later became known as Durrington Walls.[32]

The circle comes into being

For a time, perhaps centuries, the Heel Stone stood alone on the slope above the Cursus, perhaps a mere 300 paces from where the Mesolithic posts had been. Then there was catastrophe. Towards the end of the fourth millennium BC there were decades, perhaps centuries, when a collapse in established ways of life resulted in a loss of faith. Traditional customs were set aside. A steep decline in the number of radiocarbon dates between 2500 bc and 2300 bc (about 3200 to 2900 BC) indicates a time of crisis. In previously cultivated areas, scrub and weeds spread across deserted fields. Forests regenerated. Long barrows were blocked and abandoned.

Open settlements were converted into stockaded villages with heavy gateways. They were attacked. At Carn Brea in Cornwall, Hambledon Hill in Dorset and Crickley Hill in Gloucestershire, burnt-down entrances and bombardments of flint arrowheads are evidence of savage conflict. Explanations have been many – overuse of land, failure of crops, famine, plague or an expanding population too large for the available food. A more insidious agent was the worsening of the weather. Annual growth-rings in ancient Irish oaks show a sudden contraction around 3190 BC caused by colder, wetter weather.

Around the same time, 3250 ± 80 bc, acid rain from volcanic eruptions in Iceland created miasmic clouds, almost eliminating sunlight in northern Europe. The growth of pines declined in Scotland.

With water-logged, poorly drained soils, the effects for farmers were disastrous. In western Ireland peat smothered fields. 'We have to envisage the possibility of failed harvests, famine – and no doubt plague and pestilence as well . . . vast tracts of land rendered uninhabitable. In such circumstances the survivors would have been those who were more warlike than their neighbours'.[33]

As the stricken world of a people betrayed by hallowed customs and safeguards slowly recovered, there was change, even in the shapes of things. Men turned to new faiths, to the open sky. Rectangular houses, long barrows, mortuary enclosures, even cursuses were no longer constructed. By 3000 BC the circle was predominant.

Where there was no stone, men dug out large earthen rings – henges – some of them early like Arminghall in Norfolk and Llandegai in north-west Wales, both before 3000 BC. Where there was stone, men erected circles of standing stones such as the splendid site of Castlerigg near Keswick in the Lake District. Where the lowland and highland zones met down the central spine of England, men combined earth and stone into majestic circle-henges from Long Meg & Her Daughters in northern England, Arbor Low in the Midlands, down to the Stripple Stones in the far south-west.[34] When completed, Stonehenge would become another.

CHAPTER 5:

THE BEGINNINGS OF STONEHENGE, c.3000 BC

Death hath a thousand doors to let out life.
Philip Massinger, *A Very Woman* (1655), Act V, Scene 4.

Proposed phases of development

The beginning of Stonehenge is an introduction to confusion. It is a kaleidoscope of shifting images, of which only one can be correct. The later sarsen Stonehenge is a masterpiece of make-shift engineering. The early site is as insubstantial as a garden cobweb after rain, shimmeringly attractive but broken with holes and torn threads.

There are so many interlocking, sometimes incompatible, elements that one begins confidently with what is clearly understood, then exercises judgement and discrimination with more difficult questions and, ultimately, descends to wary guesswork where there are few helpful clues. Despair should be ignored. But even with these caveats there remains the peril of changing articles of faith into matters of fact.

The components of this early phase consist of an almost unique form of henge with a substantial inner bank and shallower outer one; a central timber structure; postholes at the north-eastern entrance and near the Heel Stone; the Aubrey Holes; the cardinal points of south and north; and the moon, perhaps even the sun. All these exist. It is the sequence that is controversial.

For the various phases of Stonehenge, Richard Atkinson proposed four stages: (i) the henge, the Aubrey Holes and the Heel Stone; (ii) widening of the north-east entrance, beginning of the Avenue and the Q and R Holes; (iii) several developments including the sarsen circle and trilithons, the Slaughter Stone, the Y and Z Holes, and various formations of the bluestones; (iv) the circle and horseshoe settings.[1]

Sixteen years later in 1995 Rosamund Cleal, her two editorial colleagues and a score of contributors produced a volume that is a model of scholarship, meticulously researched. Where matters are clear-cut its statements are positive. Where questions remain debatable there are reservations. With much more material available, the suggested sequence of development was rather different from Atkinson's. Phase 1, c.3000 BC, comprised the henge and the Aubrey Holes. Phase 2, 2900–2550 BC, brought together some backfilling of the ditch, postholes at the north-eastern entrance and a timber structure with façade and passageway at the middle of the earthwork. The final phase, Phase 3, 2550–1600 BC, comprised the Q and R Holes, the sarsen ring and trilithons, the changing settings of the bluestones, the Y and Z Holes, and the Avenue.[2]

The writer would only debate the time of the wooden structure and the associated postholes, all of which could be seen as primary for reasons connected with the long rectangle of the Cursus and the mile-wide void to its south. One must ask why that space existed. And then wonder if there was something at the heart of the apparently empty ring, something connected with death. There is also the question of possible lunar and solar sightlines. This was a subject outside the range of the 1995 report, which was to present the results of excavations at Stonehenge and discuss their implications. Astronomy was not part of that brief. Heavenly alignments of avenues are considered briefly.[3] Neither moon nor sun is referred to in the index.

In discussions of this earliest period of Stonehenge, death is a central issue. Between the closing of the long barrows and the raising of the round ones several centuries later, there is a Dark Age on Salisbury Plain, an almost complete ignorance of what happened to the dead bodies of important men, let alone of other men and all the women and children. Despite assiduous research and arduous excavation, archaeological knowledge has hardly moved from the blackest of nights to the foggiest of dawns. Whether the bodies were buried (individually or in groups), cremated, exposed to scavenging animals or thrown into rivers, little is known.

It is tempting to believe that the position of the Stonehenge Cursus is the clue, that to its south there was a surviving memory of that long-vanished Mesolithic setting of tall posts which in some manner had been connected with the dead, just as the long barrows preceding the Cursus had been. Pryor commented that the Cursus would have provided:

a special or ceremonial route for the dead to pass through the dangerous no man's land or liminal zone occupied by timber and chalk Stonehenge, between the two domains of the ancestors and the living . . . The domain of the living surrounds the ritual landscape, but especially towards the river Avon, where the land was richest and where barrows don't occur so frequently.[4]

Atkinson thought so, writing of a timber building within the henge, 'a *sanctum sanctorum* in which resided the numinous principle of the place'. It should be immediately stated that Cleal disagreed, expressing the opinion that any wooden structure was more likely to belong to the succeeding period 2900–2500 BC. 'There are powerful arguments for placing the timber features of the interior, the southern "passageway" and the north-eastern entrance in Phase 2'.[5]

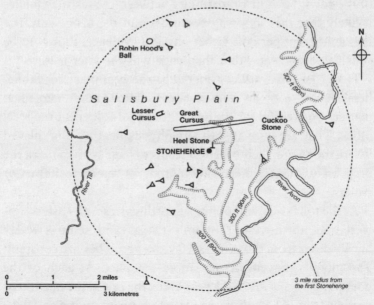

Fig. 17: The Stonehenge region in *c.*3000 BC, showing the situation of the first Stonehenge.

The dilemma is one of stratification. There are three independent groups of postholes: some across the north-eastern entrance, a line of four to the west of the Heel Stone, and several incomplete sub-circular rings with a 'passage' and façade placed centrally. It remains debatable whether these existed before, or contemporary to, or even later than, the henge. The only overlap between the holes and the earthwork is with the causeway postholes and the causeway flanking them, and this presents a problem for the reasonable interpretation that the arrangement of posts created a controlled approach to the interior of the henge.

For this to be so, it could be expected that the body of postholes and the area of the entrance would coincide. They do not. Two complete lines of holes lie north of the gap, and the gap itself continues southwards a full 16ft (5m) beyond the last of the rows. Such incompatibility between the features makes it likely that the causeway postholes and the henge entrance are of different periods. Other physical evidence, shortly to be considered, indicates that the henge was the later feature.

Here, the posts are considered as the beginnings of Stonehenge because of an almost unconsidered, never explained matter – the reason for the line of four postholes near the Heel Stone. They are unrelated to any physical feature. But, placed where they were, their function seems to have been to mark the progress of the northern moon from its minor to its major risings.

At the four collateral points of north-east, south-east, southwest and north-west, the sun's risings and settings today hardly differ from those of 5,000 years ago. They are constant. The moon's movements are more complex. At each of the points it moves in an 18.61 year cycle, the one at the north-east veering from 41.8° at its major rising to its minor at 59.6°, ENE, nine years later. Then just as slowly and steadily it returns like a celestial metronome, backwards and forwards, major to minor to major over an infinity of years. Poets knew it: 'But how strange the change from major to minor', 'Behold the wandering moon' and 'the inconstant moon'.[6] It is said that it was only considering the lunar oscillations and perturbations that gave the eighteenth-century genius Isaac Newton a headache.

There is evidence that prehistoric observers were aware of these lunar fluctuations. It was in 1924 that, 83ft (25m) beyond the north-east entrance, Hawley discovered the line of four great postholes. They were so deep that 'the first hole, owing to its depth (3ft 7in) [1.1m], had given the person who made it some difficulty in removing the soil, and to facilitate this an indentation at the side had to be made, thoroughly spoiling the shape of a hole symmetrically round like the others'.[7] With depths varying from west to east of 3ft 7in, 2ft 11in and 2ft 8in (1.1m, 0.9m and 0.8m), the posts were probably graded in height, westwards, rising from 8ft to 10ft (2.4m to 3.3m). The depth of a posthole multiplied by three is considered a reliable rule of thumb to estimate the height of a post above ground.

Spaced tidily 6ft (1.8m) apart, the four holes had supported thick, heavy posts as much as 11ft (3.3m) high. They may have served as lunar sighting-devices as guides to the moon's progress along the skyline. If the henge's 6ft (2m) high bank had existed, it might have blocked that view to people of relatively small stature.

When the moon rose in the gap between the eastern or right-hand post and its partner, it was a quarter of the way between the midpoint of its cycle and its north-eastern extreme. When it rose between the second and third posts it was one-third of the distance, each post indicating a stage in its movements. Such signalling markers enabled watchers to estimate how long it would be before the full moon reached its major position. Yet there is a paradox. Observers obviously needed a post to define that extreme rising, and had two more equally spaced uprights been added to the left of the four, the sixth would have indicated the major moonrise. There is no such marker.

Inspection of Hawley's plan shows why. Not appreciating its significance, he stopped excavating just where the fifth posthole would have been uncovered. And even if he had located that one, he would not have found the sixth and most tell-tale hole of all, because when the ditch of the later avenue was dug the posthole would have been destroyed.

These markers were never very accurate. Spaces about 1° wide between the four (or six) posts allowed only an approximation of where the moon was on its journey, but to Neolithic people that may have been all they required. J.E. Wood observed, 'In spite of their limitations, the sightlines to the A-posts would have sufficed for discovering the 18.6-year cycle and for identifying where the moon was in its cycle at any time'.[8]

Although it is rarely appreciated, there is an interesting coda to this astronomical excursion. The Heel Stone stood almost exactly midway between these lunar major and minor extremes.

The 'A' posts, as they are unpoetically termed, had adjacent counterparts. In 1922 Hawley uncovered the holes of 46 posts arranged in 6 parallel lines across the north-east entrance.[9] From their layout the late 'Peter' Newham calculated that people had laid out an orientation towards the moon. The posts in the causeway, he thought, had acted as temporary sighting devices for recording the moon's northerly risings from minor to major, and back over its 18.61 year cycle:

Their arrangements are similar to what could be expected if the 'Stonehenge Astronomers' planted poles aligned on successive midwinter full moon risings . . . The number of such moon risings in a cycle of 18.61 years in this half of the Sector would usually be nine. Apparently some are missing probably due to occasions when the rising moon could not be seen because of cloud or mist.[10]

Newham's theory has been criticized. Heggie thought the explanation poor, 'for it would imply that the holes should be more thickly distributed on the left, near the standstill position, than on the right, whereas they are not'. Cleal believed that 'the postholes form a very restricted entrance to the monument, possibly consisting of two narrow corridors barely 1m wide and flanked by at least two lines on each other side and by three in the middle'.[11]

Hawley, however, had already provided plausible and independent confirmation of Newham's idea – which, paradoxically, was correct for the wrong reason – when he found the four postholes near the Heel Stone. Those 'A' Holes were twice as broad as those across the causeway, on the same alignment and parallel with them. He thought the two sets contemporary. 'They resembled those on the causeway and were evidently of early date, as the Avenue bank passed over the first and partly over the second'.[12]

For that reason it is arguable that the posts were earlier than the henge and its north-eastern entrance, whose sides also corresponded with the moon's arc from midpoint to its major rising. If the earthwork and the sides of its bank framing the moon's passage were earlier than the 'A' posts, there would have been no need for the posts. But later they would be a useful calendar for the users of the henge.

How, when and why the observations were made can be

deduced. To record where the moon had risen required no more than someone watching from the middle of an intended structure, whether it was of wood or earth. The viewer would have to be near enough to where an intended sighting-post would stand, perhaps no more than about 155ft (50m) away, to ensure that in moonlight he would know exactly where to have it erected.

The time would be in midwinter when the moon would be opposite the sun in the south and there are bright moonlit hours each night.[13] The moon is notoriously fickle; so is British weather. Often the moon rises almost invisibly during the day. The first sighting might be possible only days after it reached the midpoint of its cycle. During a prolonged spell of cloud, rain or mist attempted sightings might have to be abandoned.

Because of such hindrances, years of observations were needed. The first of the series may be the farthest row of posts recording the movements from midpoint to major position, the second line of the slow return eastwards year by year – three entire cycles, six sets of posts, fifty long years, two or three brief generations – before it was known conclusively that the moon rose no further north than where the final post stood. Then the six 'A' posts could be erected as semi-permanent lunar timekeepers.

The causeway postholes were the instrument. The 'A' Holes were the culmination. That the two edges of the henge's north-eastern entrance were also in line with the lunar midswing and major rising demonstrates no more than that the causeway was a successor to the posts. Without recorded sighting-posts it would have been almost impossible to know exactly where to place the entrance.

The two angles of some 50° and 42° could not have been fortuitous. With 360° of the horizon to choose from, for observers to select alignments within 1° or 2° of precision, the location of the alignments produces a statistical probability of almost 100:1 in favour of the points being intentionally selected.

The reason why this tedious process was undertaken is easy to answer. The choice of the moon as a target simply reaffirmed a continuation of the old beliefs from long barrows and death into the creation of a new structure also associated with death. That the new structure also contained a cardinal orientation to the south is yet more evidence of how the present never relinquished the past.

In 1923 and 1924, at the centre of what would become the henge, Hawley began the excavation of a minor woodland of postholes, some in orderly angular arrangements, others in incomplete and untidy circles. Cleal's book states, 'It can be seen that many of these features occur in groups, and may represent deliberate settings of one form or another'.[14] Many of the holes, despite erosion, were wide enough and deep enough to support an arrangement of high oak posts. 'I should think it was contemporary with the causeway at the main entrance and places where similar postholes occurred, as they are all identical in method of making, and in appearance'.[15] At first there seemed to be no pattern to them, but eventually Hawley came upon two parallel trenches containing a series of postholes leading northwards towards the centre.

Construction of a well-built wooden setting would have given little difficulty to the Late Neolithic inhabitants of Salisbury Plain. With more than a thousand years of accumulated experience in carpentry, the techniques of estimating stresses, of jointing beams together and making them stable would have been well understood. Only 40 miles to the west, in the Somerset fens, other people were selecting specific woods for particular tasks, easily split oak for planks, hazel for lightweight posts, hazel or alder for the pegs and dowels.

Woodworkers chipped out mortise-and-tenon joints with flint chisels. A mallet made of yew, a tough and heavy wood, was found preserved in the peat.[16]

In Hawley's trenches there were regularly spaced postholes which he thought were the remains of a fenced, probably roofed passage about 13ft (4m) wide and 8 or 9 paces long. It began well away from the ditch, but 'the ground between was devoid of anything relating to the place and was very flinty and hard from traffic over it', as though the area had been subjected to constant trampling.[17]

This was an entrance rather than an exit, because there was no direct access to what manifestly had been a secretive place. Five posts had stood diagonally across the entrance, which itself was at an angle to the central structure, making it impossible for anyone outside to peer down the gloomy corridor into the interior. At its far end it was crossed by a long façade of nine posts, three to its west, three at its end like gateposts, and three to the east. It would have blocked the view to an intended central ring from any distant spectator.

Passing through a gap, visitors followed what was an intentionally devious route. Turning left and then right the fenced, perhaps screened, way led to a second passage as long as the first. As some of its postholes had been cut into by the Y and Z Holes of the Middle Bronze Age, they were obviously older than those pits.

At the end of the passage was what had promised to be a group of concentric rings of posts but which, in reality, resembled an abandoned building-site. 'If a circular structure existed, it was not of the regularity and complexity of, for instance, the phase 2 timber circles at Durrington Walls'. There may have been as many as four or five potential circles and 'there is a very strong temptation in considering the postholes in the interior to "join the dots", but a large number of circles were generated . . . and no plausible circular structures have been identified'. As Hawley himself sighed, 'The more one digs the more the mystery appears to deepen'.[18]

There may have been as many as five rings, of differing sizes but with much the same centre. The variations hint at changes of mind, as though the results were unsatisfactory. Whether this was the outcome of a succession of rings to observe lunar risings is imagination rather than deduction. With all the 'circles' lacking a central pole none could have been roofed, a bitter disadvantage during midwinter nights.

Inside, the ground was a honeycomb of pits, some cut by later stoneholes, others riddled by rabbits. Some may have been for scaffolding when the stone circles were put up, others for the market-stalls and fun-fairs of more modern times, but these would not have been so big nor so tidily refilled as many of Hawley's were. Yet, as Hawley recorded, the whole of this disturbed area coincided exactly with the direction taken by the postholes on the outside of the circle. It is of considerable interest that what may have been the largest of these possibly unfinished structures was about 98ft (30m) in diameter, almost exactly that of the sarsen circle five centuries later. It is speculation. There are too few postholes of this theoretical ring to make a firm claim for its existence.[19]

Shabby and weathered as they are today, such fragments of antiquity show that people had the skill and the workforce to erect a designed approach and central setting. The mutilated plan of the postholes points to its former existence. There is, as Atkinson observed, no reason to doubt the likelihood of a timber building, the surviving postholes offering positive evidence in its favour. But there are contrary comments about its period. 'A timber circle pre-dating the Ditch would be earlier than almost every other datable ring in the British Isles'. Yet, 'Gibson's work demonstrates that it is not impossible that there should have been a timber circle at Stonehenge at around 3000–2900 BC'.[20]

That it was a place of death is a matter of conjecture. The people who raised the posts and laid out the zigzag of tortuous passages to shield the centre clearly wished to have their ceremonies concealed from the outside world. Allen has suggested that if the winding approach from the south was 'to create a sense of mystery or anticipation about what lay ahead, then an enclosed passageway with substantial screens on either side would seem a very effective means of achieving these ends'.[21]

Rites of initiation are possible. But the undeniable association with the Stonehenge Cursus and the situation at the heart of the zone of exclusion make it feasible that before burial, funerary rituals were performed inside the ring, perhaps at the times of significant lunar events.

It is puzzling that the entry to the setting should have been from the south, unless it was intended also to return in that direction. The south was very accurately defined. In times when there were no compass or theodolite, and when there would be no helping Pole Star near the north for a further three millennia, it would appear impossible for the surveyors to have achieved such precision.

For some years the present writer believed with the Thoms that they were the first to demonstrate how competently prehistoric societies overcame this cardinal challenge. To determine exact south all that was needed was merely to observe where the midwinter sun rose at the south-east and set at the south-west, and bisect the two positions. With a level skyline that midpoint would be to the precise south. Pride precedes contrition. The ever-percipient Stukeley had anticipated the method by well over two centuries. Our ancestors, he explained, found the meridian or north-south line 'by observing the rising and setting of the Sun so taking the medium between'.[22]

From the evidence of the unfinished rings of posts it is possible that their construction was abandoned. Discontinuation of projects, even deliberate destruction of existing monuments, was commonplace in prehistory. Despite escapists who wilfully ignore facts, there was no Golden Age of tranquillity in prehistory. Nor were people always hardworking, competent and peace-loving. They had all seven sins. Many plans were abandoned halfway through as too demanding. Others were botched. Antagonism and vandalism are not modern phenomena.

The planned stone circle of Wildshaw Burn in Lanarkshire was either left unfinished or destroyed in antiquity. In the Outer Hebrides the megalithic mongrel of Callanish was never completed. Only one side of each of three intended avenues was put up. Later, people of another cult despoiled the ring by inserting a minuscule chambered tomb inside it. Half the pillars of Cultoon on Islay were left lying by their stoneholes. At the sarsen ring of Stonehenge itself Petrie wondered why the uncharacteristically small Stone 11 had been selected. He mused, 'If the builders ran so short as to have to use such a stone as 11, it is not very probable that they had not enough to finish the circle?'[23] Heresy did not vanish with the intrusive tomb at Callanish.

The ring of posts is replaced by a ring of earth and chalk

Change followed. The great posts were dismantled. In their place, but sharing the identical centre, came a more prestigious earthwork, a so-called henge but whose design owed more to antiquity than to contemporary architecture. With unusual inner and outer ditches and entrances at north-east and south, it was built at a chronological and architectural watershed between the ending of causewayed enclosures and the onset of henges. Again, its directions repeated the traditions of the abandoned long barrows.

During the closing centuries of the fourth millennium BC large free-standing earthen enclosures, henges, were raised in the easily worked soils of eastern Britain. From region to region there were clear-cut distinctions amongst the design of henges. In the south of Britain material for the ditch was used to heap up an outer bank. In the north-east of England two shallower ditches were preferred, with one heavy bank between them. In Ireland, around the Boyne Valley, henges had no ditch. Instead, for the bank the interior of the henge was scooped out around its edge leaving a convex arena like an upturned saucer. Mayburgh near Penrith was similar, and its people may have had trading contacts with the north of Ireland.

The blueprint for the three divisions was broad but blurred. No two henges were identical. There were always minor mutations but in southern England, with its norm of a single inner ditch and outer bank, Stonehenge, ever the maverick, did not conform. It had an internal bank, outer ditch and, still visible, a low outer bank of turves stripped off at the onset of the work. Although the result is called a henge, with its external ditch it more closely resembled a traditional cause-wayed enclosure, reassuringly joining what had gone before with what was new. A comment in Cunliffe's volume is pertinent here: 'Whatever lay in the centre of Stonehenge . . . visitors had to pass a familiar external ditch, and move through a zone given to the dead and ancestral practices'.[24]

Radiocarbon assays proved that there had also been a

deliberate deception. Objects of great age were deliberately buried in the ditch at both entrances. It infused the brand-new with the wrinkled evidence of antiquity, converting the earth-work into an ancient monument. A similar deception to the 'long barrow' of the Cursus, this was one more instance of merging the present with the past.

The ditch and bank of the Stonehenge earthwork were constructed around 3000 BC. Antlers at the very bottom of the ditch provided nine radiocarbon assays, the earliest 2480 ± 18 bc (UB-3789), the latest 2341 ± 18 bc (UB-3788), at the very onset of the fourth millennium BC.[25] Quite in-tentionally, the henge contained articles 200 years older. 'Both terminals for the north-east gap had fires in, and abundant antlers. The south entrance had cattle jaw bones on either side'.[26]

A rare example of jargon unexpectedly appears in the pleasingly orthodox *Stonehenge In Its Landscape*. 'The date of the skull and pair of mandibles strongly suggest[s] that these had deliberately been curated', and, 'provide a strong argu-ment for the curation of these special objects before the deliberate act of placing them at strategic points at the base of the ditch'.[27] (In a paper about Stonehenge Andrew Lawson expressed his reservations with this usage by putting 'curation' in inverted commas.[28] The commonplace 'preservation' can be its substitute.)

In a pit on the east side of the south entrance was the right jawbone of an ox. Carbon-14 analysis dated it to 2510 ± 45 bc (OxA-4834). On the other side of the causeway a similar bone had an assay of 2885 ± 40 bc (OxA-4835). In the terminals of the same entrance there was an ox skull of 2570 ± 100 bc (OxA-4842) and the leg-bone of a red deer, 2600 ± 60 bc (OxA-4833) – an accumulated assemblage of around 3200 BC, long before the henge was thought of.

In a less well-defined position, because the ground had been disturbed, a cattle leg-bone was found in the later stonehole of sarsen Stone 27 at the north of the earthwork. Its 'date' of 3400 ± 80 bc (OxA-4902) was accepted as reliable, but it appears to be no later than an astonishing 3900 BC.[29] Such relics may have been pillaged from long barrows as hallowed remnants of an ancestral past, procuring rather than 'curating'. Both ends of the north-eastern entrance were also specially treated. Hawley described them as 'craters'. The west terminal held a 'stack' of antlers charred by fire. The east had animal bones and flint flakes.[30]

Deeply buried and hidden from sight, the objects would have meant nothing to people passing through the entrances. The intention must have been to persuade the earthwork, through the possession of the bones, of its own great age, that it was an ancient and animate monument with an independent existence. Everything had life.

The symbolism of such deposits is not beyond modern speculation, but it is beyond modern certainty. Ancient alphabets, even Linear 'A' and Etruscan, can eventually be deciphered. The arcane beliefs and spiritual values of prehistoric societies will always be incomprehensible to our scientifically conditioned minds. Even in recent centuries, when western anthropologists asked Maoris to explain their word 'mana', the best occidental translation was 'a mysterious supernatural power or magic associated with persons and things', which explains nothing. For the early Stonehenge facts can be presented. Beliefs cannot.

From miles around men, perhaps also women, came straggling from their lonely farmsteads in the sheltered dells, carrying their tools of wood, antler, animal bones and flint (fig. 18). These were the people who dug out the beginnings of the world's most famous prehistoric monument. From Petrie's survey of 1877 the dimensions of the henge are known. A circle for the inner side of the ditch, some 340ft (104m) in diameter, was scribed out with a low outer bank and a wider, higher inner one.

To believers in prehistoric ignorance, there is an engineering surprise. There was a subtlety to the layout of the trenches from which chalk was to be excavated. They did not follow the circumference of the circle. Instead, the trenches were a polygon of about 60 straight-sided segments. This had been a practice since the time of causewayed enclosures. The rectangular sections at Stonehenge are blurred, but are very evident at smaller henges like Gorsey Bigbury and Knowlton Centre.

With the exposure of the chalk below the grass, the task of digging out the great ditch began. Working outwards from its inward rim, pairs of diggers with antler-picks hacked out pits deep enough to stand in and then levered away the jagged lumps of chalk to make elongated hollows like foxholes, steep-sided and flat-bottomed. Pit after pit was quarried by the gangs, and from the air the site would have looked like a child's model railway to which more and more trucks were added, an ever-growing chaplet of holes.

A couple of men accustomed to digging in their fields and holdings could have shifted half a ton of rubble in an hour. This was shouldered in woven panniers and leather sacks by other labourers up to the bank that they were building along the inner edge of the ditch. When finished it was 20ft (6m) wide and 6ft (2m) high, broken only by two causewayed entrances, a wide one at the north-east, the other, one-third of the width, at the south. Both respected the widths of the former causeway post-holes and the south-facing direction of the timbered passage.

The bank itself was a considerable barrier. On it, from the discovery of postholes in the sections that have been excavated, there may have been a fence preventing outsiders from seeing inside the enclosure.

Fig. 18: Neolithic tools in a wicker basket – on the left is an antler-pick and in the centre is an ox shoulder-blade, used for scraping up loose chalk.

Up to 25 ditch segments, from each of which came 50 tons of chalk, may have been dug at the same time. Digging and carrying 8 hours a day, 4 men could have completed a section in a fortnight before smashing down the crude ends between it and its neighbours and moving on to the next part to be opened.

The earthwork was a secret place. Concealing it from the north was a long and high barrier lying south-west/north-east and extending for at least 900m. With posts some 16ft (5m) high it masked Stonehenge from processions approaching from the Cursus until they reached a gap near the henge's north-eastern entrance.[31]

The people that Tacitus dismissed as 'barbarians' and that Charles Dickens described as 'poor savages, going almost naked, or only dressed in the rough skins of beasts'[32] introduced delicate religious grace-notes into the layout of their earthwork. The north-east entrance contained an alignment, its northern edge looking towards the westernmost of the row of six posts near the Heel Stone. It stood in line with the most northerly rising of the midwinter moon.

There may also have been a second lunar orientation. In 1924 Hawley uncovered a pit, the largest posthole yet found at the south-east, some 14 or 15 paces from the bank. Two smaller posts had stood behind it. With a bearing of 142° from the centre of the henge it could have acted as a foresight to the major rising of the midsummer moon.[33]

The chosen site was very uneven. A puzzled visitor approaching the circle from east or west would notice that the ring stands on a slope falling steadily to the north. On the site itself he could also see that the henge lay on land declining towards the muddy hollow of Stonehenge Bottom. Whoever selected the situation deliberately rejected the flatter, higher ground nearby, despite the difficulties. The cause appears to have been the Cursus.

It will never be possible to enter the minds and understand the motives of a society that existed 5,000 years ago, but two hypotheses about the location of the henge can be tested. The people who dug it may have wished it both to be conspicuous and to overlook the Cursus. If those conditions were to be fulfilled, together with a third to be considered shortly, then there was only one place for the structure.

The earthwork can be seen from the east, west and north, but it is from the south that its position is critical. Were it to lie farther down the slope it would have been concealed from the Lake cemetery, a mile-and-a-half to the south. Its modest long barrow was described by Hoare as 'very unproductive of articles of curiosity'.[34]

Conversely, were it to be higher much of the Cursus would have been obscured. All of the Cursus can be seen from the centre of the henge, but with just a few paces to the south entrance much of the western sector is hidden by the curve of the hillside. It is likely that the henge was situated as high as possible to be observable from the surrounding countryside without losing the prospect of the Cursus.

It might still be asked why it was not constructed a few hundred steps to the west where the ground was more level, where the Cursus was still in full view and where the site was still visible all around. The answer may rest with the third of the builders' requirements, the existence of the Heel Stone, Sidbury Hill and the summer solstice. It could also be asked why, despite the plans of earlier investigators such as Aubrey in 1666, Stukeley in 1723 and John Wood in 1740, that it was not until 1770 that the Heel Stone was claimed to be an astronomical marker for the midsummer sunrise. It was John Smith who introduced the idea.[35]

Aubrey knew that Midsummer Day was 24 June, the birthday and Feast Day of St John the Baptist. But as mentioned in an earlier chapter, 24 June was not one of the four days of the midsummer solstice in Aubrey's time because Britain was still using the Julian calendar of 46 BC, which had been losing a day every 163 years since its inception. Aubrey's 24 June was actually 14 June, when the sun was rising over 4° east of the Heel Stone, well away from the solstice.

That was not the cause of Stukeley's oversight. He had talked about Stonehenge with several astronomers and had a fair understanding of its alignments there. His 1721–24 manuscript contains an undated note, 'The Entrance of Stoneh. is 4° E. from the true NE loc. that is the suns utmost elongation in Somer Solstice'. He had reliable solar data and could have been expected to notice how close the Heel Stone stood to the midsummer alignment. But his compass was faulty with a misdirection of about 3°, probably because the compass pivot was worn or rusty.[36] Neither Aubrey nor Stukeley was as wrong as William Shakespeare. A dozen years after Catholic countries changed their calendar he arbitrarily shifted Midsummer's Day from June to May in his *A Midsummer Night's Dream*.[37]

Smith's was the first solar interpretation, and it had been accepted by the majority of writers about Stonehenge, such as Wansey in 1796: 'On the top of that stone the Sun is supposed to make its first appearance on the longest day of the year', and others agreed, among them Duke (1846), Herbert (1849) and Stevens (1882).[38] The first surveyor to disagree was the astronomer, Sir Norman Lockyer in 1901: 'It is placed at some distance . . . to the south of the axis so that the Sun must have completely risen before it was vertically over the summit of the stone'. Others emphasized that Wansey had been mistaken about the sun rising at the top of the Heel Stone. Stone wrote in 1924 that the sun 'will not do so until more than 1000 years have passed away'; Atkinson wrote in 1956, 'Actually, it does nothing of the sort'.[39]

Despite the 'evidence' of the famous photograph by Dr Georg Gerster – showing the midsummer sun at the tip of the Heel Stone – Lockyer, Stone and Atkinson were correct but, like Newham, for the wrong reason. The picture is a deceit. Chippindale explained:

> The many photographs . . . which seem to show half the sun's disc sitting neatly on top of the Heel Stone are all 'adjusted': as the sun begins to come up the photographer moves to one side – a foot or two is ample – to align the sun over the Heel Stone, and stands up straighter or crouches a little to get them exactly into the vertical relation he wants.[40]

It is always assumed that it was from the centre of the sarsen circle that the observations were made, but from that position, as pointed out in 1975, 'the sun ought to rise to the right of the top of the Heel Stone on the morning of June 21 in our time. But it does not: it rises about a foot and a half to the left'.[41]

The seminal question and the solution to the dilemma depend on which of Stonehenge's three centres was the relevant one – that of the henge, the Aubrey Holes or the ring of sarsens. From the middle of that ring the Aubrey Holes' centre is 3ft 6in (1m) to the SSW, and that of the earthwork almost the same distance to the WSW. It was from that unconsidered place that the midsummer sun rose above the Heel Stone.[42]

Beyond it, eight miles away, was the height of Sidbury Hill, and the merging of a man-made object and one of nature may have been significant to the animistic minds of a prehistoric society. There are many stone circles and henges, even standing stones, where the existence of a conspicuous hill or mountain appears to have determined the choice of site.[43]

It is just possible that the henge contained a dedicatory burial marked by a standing post. In 1926 Hawley came upon a very disturbed grave about 20ft (6m) north-east of the centre. There were many human bones 'in a disordered mass', where greedy Georgian marauders had dug up the remains, throwing the useless bits of skeleton away amongst a litter of broken pottery, coins and items of many periods ('like an odd lot in an auctioneer's catalogue', wrote Atkinson imaginatively).

It was a shallow pit about 8ft (2.4m) long, lying across the SW-NE axis of the henge with the skull at the north-west end of the grave. To Gibson it 'recalls the child sacrifice at Woodhenge, marked by a cairn, in the centre of the monument and aligned on the main axis'.[44] Mixed with the bones were a few prehistoric sherds but none so distinctive as to indicate a specific period. The associated post did, however, suggest that the burial occurred before any obtrusive stones distracted attention.

Stonehenge was never still. A stride or two from the inner edge of the bank a wide ring of pits, the Aubrey Holes, was dug.

CHAPTER 6:

AUBREY HOLES AND GROOVED WARE, c.2800 BC AND BEYOND

I dug a pit . . . And poured libations to the countless ghosts.
Homer, *The Odyssey*, XI, pp 25–26.

Investigating the Aubrey Holes

In 1666, while making his survey of Stonehenge for Charles II, John Aubrey noticed five faint depressions irregularly spaced around the inner edge of the bank. On his plan he marked 'b b b & c little cavities in the ground, from whence one may well conjecture the stones c c were taken', adding (in what is today an ironical foretaste of another of the current controversies about Stonehenge, what the contents of the holes were intended to be), 'that they did hold stones round within the Trench, ornamentally, as at Aubury'.[1]

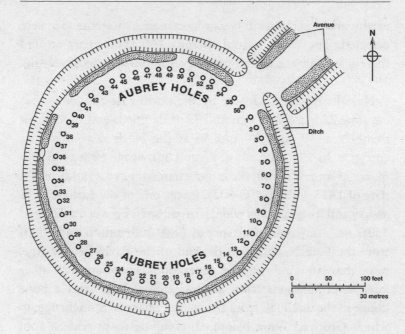

Fig. 19: Diagram showing the circle of 56 pits known as the Aubrey Holes.

Sceptics have doubted that Aubrey could have detected the tops of ancient, grass-covered pits. But as mentioned in chapter one, 1665 and 1666 were not only the years of the Fire of London and the Great Plague, they were also exceptionally hot summers. As Leasor wrote, 'the sun shone with Italian fierceness, roads crumbled into dust . . . dunghills steamed'. Prayers were uttered daily for rain.[2] At Stonehenge, in contrast to the feeble grass on the parched chalk of the interior, the richer, greener turf over the moist, earth-filled pits would have stood out, especially to the eyes of an observant fieldworker like Aubrey.

In 1920, after inspecting Aubrey's manuscript in Oxford's Bodleian Library, Hawley and Newall searched with a steel bar for the 'cavities'. After locating one of them, 'and subsequently more, all apparently at regular intervals round the earthwork',[3] excavation began in earnest. Altogether 56 were detected. They were spaced roughly 16ft (5m) apart around the circle, and resembled an unevenly beaded necklace (fig. 19).

Newall started clockwise by the north-east causeway, excavating 23 in the first year and 32 in all, north-east to SSW for numbers 1–30, and 55 and 56 at the NNE near the main entrance. In 1950 Atkinson, Piggott and Stone excavated two more, 31 and 32. From the latter, charcoal gave a radiocarbon date of 1848 ± 275 bc (C-602). It was one of the earliest C-14 assays and its range was wide, a broad span between 3020 and 1520 BC – an unhelpful spread of a millennium-and-a-half from the Late Neolithic to the end of the Early Bronze Age, more than 50 uninformative generations. Fortunately, 8 other later determinations from antlers, animal bone and a bone gouge in the ditch (all from the second phase of Stonehenge, to which Grooved Ware belonged) combine to provide a converted date of 2860 BC. A date around 2800 BC is feasible, a time before any stones were erected. Bluestone fragments, sarsen and other material from later phases lay only at the tops of the holes. Newall also pointed out that it was possible to draw an exact circle through the holes, something impossible once the obstructive sarsen ring was standing.[4]

Despite this symmetry, there was little that was geometrical about the pits. Lying on the circumference of a ring with an average radius of 141ft 6in (43m), they were anything from 30 to 70in (0.8 to 1.8m) wide, sub-circular or misshapen, and from 24 to 45in (0.6 to 1.1m) deep. Nor were they evenly spaced, varying by as much as a foot (30cm) between their centres. They lay neatly on a circle some 19ft (5.8m) inside the bank, but of haphazard shapes and depths as though dug by unsupervised work-gangs. Whatever the reason for the pits, it had not been obligatory to make them identical.

Many objections can be made to some slipshod theories about the Aubrey Holes. Their ragged spacing and the latitude allowed in their width and depth warns that their diggers were not concerned with geometrical precision. One question, however, that has arisen and which is not susceptible to accusations of ramshackle thinking is whether the actual number of Aubrey Holes mattered.

It was suggested that Neolithic people, long aware of the moon's movements and realizing that 56 was a significant lunar number, laid out that number of pits to use them for eclipse-prediction.[5] Asking why the people had not simply bisected quadrants of the henge, Gerald Hawkins hypothesized that the pits had 'provided a system for counting the years, one hole for each year, to aid in predicting the movement of the Moon' over its 18.61 year cycle.[6] Although close to 18.61, the multiples of numbers such as 19 (19 x 3 = 57) or 18 (18 x 3 = 54) would soon have resulted in errors. 'The smallest time unit that would have remained accurate for many years would be the triple-interval measure, 19 + 19 + 18', a total of 56 years.[7]

If three black and three white stones had been placed on holes spaced 9, 9, 10, and then a further 9, 9, 10 holes apart and moved sideways anti-clockwise one hole each year, they could have foretold lunar eclipses. 'This simple operation will predict accurately every important lunar event for hundreds of years', claimed Hawkins. Three holes were critical – numbers 51, 56 and 5. Whenever a stone arrived at Hole 56 on the major axis of the earthwork, that would be the year of a solar or lunar eclipse occurring within 15 days of midwinter. It was also the year of an eclipse of the summer moon. Equinoctial eclipses would happen whenever a white stone reached Holes 5 or 51. Critics pointed out that, astronomically, 47 would have been a more workable number than 56 for eclipse prediction.

No.	Site	No. of pits	Diameter		Spacing		Miles from Stonehenge	Contents of pits	Posts
			M	Ft	M	Ft			
1	Cairnpapple. West Lothian	7	17.1	56	7.6	25	330	cremations, bone pins, long bone	no
2	Llandegai A, Gwynedd	5	7.6	25	4.9	16	170	cremations, Grooved Ware	no
3	Maxey A, Northants	10	13.4	44	4.3	14	125	cremations	?
4	Maxey B, Northants	10	9.5	31	3.1	10	125	cremations, incised antler	no
5	Dorchester I, Oxfordshire	13	6.4	21	1.5	5	45	bone pins, Grooved Ware flints, antlers	?
6	Dorchester IV, Oxfordshire	8	6.1	20	2.4	8	45	cremations, antlers	no
7	Dorchester V, Oxfordshire	13	10.4	34	2.4	8	45	cremations, Peterbor'gh ware	no
8	Dorchester VI, Oxfordshire	12	11.9	39	3.1	10	45	cremations, late neo' ware	no
9	Dorchester XI, Oxfordshire	14	12.2	36	2.7	9	45	cremations, antlers	no
10	Maumbury Rings, Dorset	44–45	51.5	169	3.7	12	45	Grooved Ware, carved bone	no
11	Stonehenge, Wiltshire	56	86.6	284	4.9	16	–	cremations, bone pins	?

Table 5: Henges with Aubrey Holes.

Against the eclipse prediction theory is the fact that there are several other henges with 'Aubrey Holes', some of which held posts, most of them with cremations like those at Stonehenge, a few also with Grooved Ware pottery, but not one with the critical eclipse number of 56 (see table 5).[8]

In 1973 Alexander Thom made a survey of the holes and demonstrated how the diggers had respected the cardinal positions of their forebears:

Since the position of the first Aubrey Hole is 3° 7' [3.12°] from geographical north and the mean spacing is 6°.429, the north point is very nearly midway between two holes, and since there are 8 x 7 holes then all the cardinal points and the four intermediate [collateral] points (NE, SE etc) lie midway between holes.[9]

This could explain how the holes were set out. Pairs of holes were first dug astride the long-favoured cardinal points of north, south, east and west. Then each of the intervening arcs was filled with 12 more holes along the perimeter of the planned circle. If this is what did happen, then the number 56 was entirely fortuitous, no more than the unconsidered total of (4 x 2 = 8) + (4 x 12 = 48), a chance combination of 56 arrived at by semi-numerate people with no thought of eclipse prediction.

There was, however, little evidence of precise measurements. Thom believed that prehistoric people in Britain and Brittany had devised a yardstick of 2.72ft (0.829m) long, his 'Megalithic Yard' (MY), which was sometimes multiplied by $2\frac{1}{2}$ to make a staff of 6.8ft (2.07m), his 'Megalithic Rod' (MR). He calculated that the circumference of the Aubrey Hole circle was exactly 131MR or 891ft (272m).

The radius (of which he had said 'the holes were placed more accurately' than they were along the circumference[10]), however, was an unconvincing 20.8MR, 141ft 6in (43.1m), despite it having been the template for laying out the ring, and the holes were some 2.4MR, 16ft 3in (5m) apart, an error of nearly 10 per cent if the intended spacing had been 2.5MR. It is possible, instead, that a local measure of about 2ft 11in (just under 1m) was used but not, as Stukeley said, with 'a mathematical exactness'; perhaps in multiples of 4 to make rods of 11ft 10in (3.7m) of which 12 would be required for the radius.

It is an article of faith that the holes contained posts. In several recent books faith has been transformed into fact, yet this 'fact' was not considered indisputable. With characteristic open-mindedness, in *Stonehenge In Its Landscape* Cleal and Walker noted that 'such is the disturbance to the fills of these features that no clear postpipes have been recognized', and concluded: 'Although the evidence is inconclusive and will no doubt be the subject of continued debate, the authors are inclined to support the view that the Aubrey Holes held posts which were removed, rather than burnt *in situ* or left to decay'. The present writer hesitantly accepts this cautious opinion, despite a similar pit-circle, actually a 'squashed ellipse' of some 200ft (60m) with Grooved Ware, being found in 2004 on Boscombe Down 3 miles east of Stonehenge. Only 4 of its 32 pits held posts.[11]

The evidence, or more precisely its absence, is equivocal. As Cleal and Walker stated, there is nothing to support or deny the presence of posts. Hawley at first thought the pits had held stones. Later, perhaps after visiting the 1926–27 excavations by the Cunningtons at Woodhenge two miles away, he changed his mind. The holes, he said, are 'now thought to have held the posts of a timber circle'.[12]

Some archaeologists who have not excavated an Aubrey Hole are insistent that he was right. Richard Atkinson, Stuart Piggott and J.F.S. 'Marcus' Stone (who did excavate two, Holes 31 and 32) were as insistent that the critics were wrong. Stonehenge's bowl-shaped pits were quite different from the round-topped, straight-sided, flat-bottomed, indisputable postholes at Woodhenge. Buttressing their objections were undisputed realities, the first being that they had previously found similar post-less hollows elsewhere, Atkinson at Dorchester-on-Thames, Piggott at Cairnpapple in West Lothian. Secondly, Newall, the man who had examined many in 1921, agreed with them. 'The writers had the advantage of Mr. R.S. Newall's presence and advice throughout the work and are authorized to state that he concurs in the conclusions reached'.[13] This seemed conclusive.

Incontrovertible facts are luxuries in prehistoric research. In 1929 Newall had written an article about Stonehenge in which he said that the cremations discovered in the pits may have been additions rather than primary fillings, and 'at the present time one can only presume that the holes, whether they originally held anything or nothing, had some ritual significance'. In 1950, the year when Holes 31 and 32 were examined, Newall was writing a guidebook about Stonehenge. He recalled that the majority of the cremations were not in compact masses deep in the holes, but had been placed quite shallowly at the sides of the holes and had 'dribbled down to the bottom'. This was explainable. 'If . . . a wooden post stood there, its gradual decay would cause the cremation to dribble down, and stones and earth at the top would fall in and generally reproduce the description of the holes given above'.[14] The evidence is equivocal. But the judgement of *Stonehenge In Its Landscape* remains persuasive. For a time, long before the cremations, 56 posts had probably stood in a wide ring at Stonehenge.

Changing customs and the appearance of Grooved Ware

Then there was change. The crest of the henge's bank was toppled into the ditch, smothering its life. The arena was abandoned. As long ago as 1921, Hawley suspected that something unusual had happened: 'At some time in the history of Stonehenge, and perhaps for a long period, there must have been a considerable amount of vegetation covering the site. I conclude this from the great amount of small snail-shells occurring throughout the excavations'.[15] These were tiny specimens, very restricted in mobility and just as sensitive to their habitat.

The presence of the carnivorous snail *Ceciloides acicula* in long barrows implies that corpses rather than skeletons had been buried there. Similarly, shells of *Oxychilus cellarius* lay in Wayland's Smithy barrow, 'where it was attracted by the rotting flesh of bodies'.[16] Other snail-types provide information about their prehistoric environment, some liking daylight, others dark, some warmth, some cold, others damp or dry conditions. Their shells are a barometer of the local landscape at the time they died.

In 1978 a cutting through the bank and ditch recovered hundreds. Dug just west of the north-east causeway, it exposed ten distinct layers from the modern turf down to the bedrock of the ditch. Above it was evidence of the partial backfilling. There were few snail-shells at the bottom of this thrown-back chalk, suggesting that for a while the rubble had remained dry and grassless before, gradually, some weeds and vegetation grew, inhabited by a snail, *Vallonia costata*, that preferred open-air conditions. The phase was followed by an abundance of light-loving snails, *Zontidiae*, common in grassland and in the shade of woodland leaves. Around Stonehenge there were still clearings and open spaces, but 'nevertheless, on a local scale, it seems clear that this episode reflects human abandonment of the site'.[17]

During that time, around 2900 BC, trees and scrubby undergrowth spread across the Plain, and where there had been agricultural land there was a wilderness. The earthwork was deserted to wind and rain, the posts sagging in slow decay, as untidy as a huddle of javelins. Within the eroding bank were trees and bushes. Hawley found their cavities, quite different from man-made holes. Thickets overshadowed the ditch. Stonehenge was shabby in neglect.

Just over a mile to the ESE a small henge was erected in a woodland clearing on the low Coneybury Hill. As always, it was an imitation of an old form but with a new purpose. It was to be an accepted ritual centre. Old cults had been rejected. A new cult replaced them. Within sight of the derelict Stonehenge and close to a deep pit against which animal butchery and feasting had occurred a thousand years earlier, near 3800 BC, the enclosure at Coneybury ('rabbit warrens') had been almost levelled by medieval ridge-and-furrow ploughing, but extensive excavation in 1980 showed it to have had a single entrance at ENE. Lining the inner edge of the ditch was a ring of posts, and in the interior at least seven rows of sharpened stakes had radiated from south-east to north-west like an unfinished wheel of a cart with half the spokes missing. The reason for such triangular bays is unknown.

From Coneybury's ditch came sherds of native ware and an alien style of pottery, Grooved Ware. There were also the bones of a dog and of a white-tailed sea eagle, a *rara avis* for Salisbury Plain. A C-14 assay of 2250 ± 110 bc (OxA-1408) 'suggests that the ditch was dug in around 2750 BC'.[18]

It has to be asked who raised the monument, why Stonehenge had been discarded, and who those leaders were. Were they natives, rather than invaders of whom there is no sign? The simplest, most cogent answer is the appeal of a novel cult, a cult connected with Grooved Ware. It brought the most mystical of all phases to Stonehenge.

Unlike the finely made beakers that appeared in Britain centuries later, Grooved Ware was a phenomenon with few individual associations. The flower-pot shaped vessels are found with local articles. They were not connected with a particular type of barrow or settlement, they were not associated with a special form of burial; no unique assemblage of tools, weapons or ornaments has been discovered with them.

No physically distinctive people used them. It is likely that the pots were part of an attractive cult rather than the property of an intrusive people. In this they were different from beakers.

Where the cult was born is not certain, although from the symbols that were reproduced on the sides of Grooved Ware, such as the spiral, the Boyne Valley of Ireland is a strong candidate (the spiral is carved on its passage-tombs). The vessels were the first to have flat bases that were functional, and had walls decorated by panels and bands of incised lines. They have been found as far north as the Orkneys, in mainland Scotland, in Yorkshire and in much of lowland Britain.[19]

The eventual combination of pottery shapes and decoration developed, however, in the Orkneys at the far north of the long-established Atlantic sea-route. Early dates between 3400 BC and 3100 BC confirm this, with the fashion becoming established in southern England only many generations later, around 2800 BC. It was at the little settlement of Rinyo, near the east coast of Rousay, that Grooved Ware was proved to be earlier than beakers. Like its counterpart of Skara Brae on Orkney mainland, the walls of houses in the village were 'surrounded by mounds of well-rotted middens, which appear to have been curated for the purpose'.[20]

In an excavation of 1938, Gordon Childe recorded the stratified divisions that showed the ware to precede beakers. Stuart Piggott noticed its similarity to vessels discovered at Clacton in East Anglia, and throughout the 1950s and 1960s the pots were known as Rinyo-Clacton ware.[21] Further research showed that there were four definite regional types that varied from north to south, two of them on Salisbury Plain (the Durrington and Woodlands styles). At Stonehenge Hawley found both, although only in small sherds and very few in number; perhaps the remnants of two complete pots.[22]

Grooved Ware tub-, barrel- and bucket-shapes were lump-ish and heavy (more 'thing' than Ming). Yet they are the mundane products of an ethereal mystique, the everyday objects of a society converted to a new faith that cremated its dead, used the sun and the moon in its rites, possessed aesthetic objects, often of rare material, and placed dissimilar objects together, contrasting darkness and light, life and death. It is an elusive cult. Almost symbolically, Childe's co-ordinates for Rinyo were so inadequate that over the years the houses became lost, buried under drifting sand, like a ghost town for spectral people as tantalizing as phantoms in a mist.

At Rinyo the villagers had subsisted on seafood – cod, coalfish, crabs and shellfish, such as limpets. It was a marine connection that would persist in the location of Grooved Ware sites in the south with a pronounced coastal and riverine distribution, particularly near the upper reaches of rivers. Stukeley had realized this. 'I observe most of our Druid temples are set near rivers'. It has been suggested that the frequent 'lozenge-lattice' motif on the pots was a type of leitmotif, an indication of an arcane connection with fishing nets.[23]

Grooved Ware adherents were illiterate poets, not me-chanics. They were mystics searching for safeguards that would protect their existence, fashioning methods of contact-ing the hidden world of natural forces to control disasters that could ruin their lives. And, like poets, they worked in similes and metaphors.

Of homes on Salisbury Plain almost nothing is known. Isolated farms are discovered only by chance. Finds of pottery prove this. Merely a third of local Peterborough ware has been found on domestic sites. Other sherds have been stray finds from ploughed fields, rabbit burrows and the banks of streams.[24]

Medleys of postholes are more suggestive of temporary camps than of permanent homes. Lightweight shelters were detected as scattered stakeholes under round barrows in the cemetery at Snail Down, just north of Stonehenge. They are best interpreted as the remains of flimsy tents abandoned before the barrows were heaped up. These could not be seen as normal homes unless their people had lived semi-nomadic lives, wandering with their herds and flocks, restlessly moving across the open downs. It is more often Beaker pottery rather than Grooved Ware that is associated with them.[25]

Grooved Ware is not impressive. The often poorly fired pots were far inferior to native Mortlake bowls. It was the ritualistic associations of Grooved Ware, the beautiful objects that could be worn or paraded ostentatiously, the arcane symbols and the votive rituals that were different. The fact that Grooved Ware has been recovered from early stone circles and henges demonstrates that the vessels were elements of a new cult that was rapidly adopted. The one strong association with the pottery – maceheads of antler or stone – confirms this. These implements, made of material chosen for its attractive appearance and sometimes decorated with coiled spirals, were ceremonial, the symbols of a cult that left little behind it.

When Hawley was excavating in the ditch alongside the south causeway, he unearthed half a dozen sherds from a little pit dug 10in (25cm) into the silt that had accumulated there. Four were badly eroded but two could be joined together, and on them was a typical Grooved Ware motif, a rough chevron pattern. They lay very close to the causeway, indicating the special attention these people gave to the entrances and alignments of their ceremonial monuments.[26]

The importance of the entrances was also stressed by other deposits, but not by the use of pottery. Those already mentioned were the only sherds to come from this early phase.

They indicate the re-use of the enclosure during the shadowy Late Neolithic period, a time when the site retained its old associations with the dead but in a changed way, by receiving cremations.

We shall never know the ethos of this cult. Hints come from the manner in which its devotees deposited apparently disparate things together. The apparent 'rubbish' has been reassessed as the intentional conjoining of unrelated articles. It appears a belief that such juxtapositions were acts of sympathetic magic, like sticking pins into wax effigies, to guarantee the well-being of the community.

Of the three aspects of this cult – the objects, the symbols and the rites – it is the objects that are most easily understood. These were prestigious items, such as maceheads of antler or exquisite stone chosen for its bands and swirls of colour, and then polished and perforated to receive the wooden shaft on which it could be displayed, and finely chipped flint arrowheads shaped like the blade of a guillotine for slicing through the hide of hunted game.

There were also flat plaques of chalk, often holed, the size of a postcard and incised with grooves and lines whose meaning eludes the modern mind. They were probably figuratively sexual, like the chalk balls and phalli that have been discovered with them. They were the handiwork of skilled craftsmen.

Taboos were attached to the deposits. No pot was placed with a burial. Nor was any axe or carved stone ball. Maceheads, to the contrary, have been found on settlements and in graves as articles permissible to take into death, perhaps to ensure that the role of its possessor would not be diminished in the Other-World. Some have been discovered as offerings, buried or thrown into rivers, given to the gods.

A macehead of lustrous red antler was dredged from the river at Garboldisham in 1964. It was incised with what may have been the most potent of all Grooved Ware symbols, the spiral, an Irish motif carved on chambered tombs, on pottery and on maceheads, including a superb one of multi-coloured flint from the Knowth passage-tomb in the valley of the Boyne.[27] There has been speculation that the spiral represented two aspects of the sun, arranged clockwise in narrow coils to show how the sun's shadow would be cast day after day as it moved from midsummer to midwinter, whereas it would make wider anti-clockwise rings from midwinter back to midsummer.[28]

Other symbols, such as the meander, lozenge, small dots and lines, although common to the passage-tombs and Grooved Ware, have no resemblance to anything, although to their society they must all have had a ritual significance. Of Grooved Ware rites, knowledge is meagre. The burial of objects, including sherds, in postholes and pits was widespread. So was the custom of demarcating zones in which only selected things could be deposited. At Durrington Walls several of these zones have been detected.[29] There were concentrations of decorated sherds, flint tools, scores of antler-picks and the meat-bones of pigs, the relics of feasting on this succulent animal. The ox was still a beast of importance for traction, for its hide and for everyday work, but it was pork, not beef, that was preferred by the elite, as the proportion of animal remains inside the earthwork shows.

Nearby at Woodhenge (another ritual site that came before beakers), inside an oval ditch and bank there had been six concentric rings of posts. When the 56 postholes were investigated in 1929, deposits were found in only 5, all in the outer 3 ellipses. They were in significant positions and all contained special deposits. Three marked cardinal positions. At the exact north was the only cremation. A chalk 'cup', probably female sexual imagery, and a piece of worked chalk lay with the bones. At the east another chalk 'cup' and incised chalk had been buried. At the south was a chalk axe and more worked chalk.

Two deposits were solar. Midsummer sunrise was defined by another chalk axe and a piece of chalk incised with indecipherable motifs. At the south-east a posthole in line with the midwinter sunrise held a chalk 'cup' and one more chalk plaque. It was as though Woodhenge had been endorsed by a Grooved Ware ceremony.[30]

The selected contents of ritual pits suggest that this was material deliberately placed in magical combinations that would generate power and protection. There is an opaque vision of a secret society engaging in ceremonies that has left few traces. In every region the cult merged with native customs in different ways, so that we have no more than a blurred picture. In the vicinity of Stonehenge, offerings were buried in Grooved Ware pits in a profligacy very different from the austere emptiness of the Aubrey Holes.

A quarter of a mile south of Durrington Walls, by the modern road to Amesbury, four pits were found, carefully dug and then filled with basketloads of almost perfect flint tools. With them was a Welsh stone axe, another of flint, sharp-edged arrowheads, bones of ox, pig, roe deer and fox, nutshells and, astonishingly, marine food brought by people from the coast over 30 miles away – jaws of chub, shells of scallops, mussels and oysters, sea-fare reminiscent of Rinyo unimaginable miles to the north and signs of good living almost five millennia ago. Amongst these enticing gifts to the gods were three large flint balls with little or no signs of use.[31]

At Ratfyn, a mile from Durrington, two pits held exceptionally large cattle bones, bones of a brown bear, flint arrowheads and flakes, and fire-crackled pot-boilers. The esoteric melange was not refuse. The brown bear, an immensely strong creature of the forest, and the very heavy cattle may have symbolized strength just as oxen had done centuries before. Another pit contained footbones of young pigs, a selection unlikely to be the leftovers of feasts – unless of trotters!

A further pit in Stonehenge Bottom was even more informative.[32] In a small, shallow basin, a broken antler and a sheep's shoulderblade lay side-by-side near the top. Below them were Grooved Ware sherds and animal bones. Deposited at the very bottom were two thin plaques of chalk about 64mm ($2\frac{1}{2}$ in) square, with designs of lozenges, chevrons and triangles carved on them. The designs had been executed with care and, resting where they did, it is clear that they had a powerful meaning. Their motifs were Irish. They were also like carved stones in the Neolithic village of Skara Brae on Orkney, of the same period but over 500 miles (800km) to the north. Such far-off links display the ubiquity and strength of the Grooved Ware cult.

It was a restless time. Great field-systems were developing in Ireland. Ageing axe-factories in Cornwall, Wales and Cumbria continued to produce stone axes, but fresh sites were exploited as people prospected for new sources of hard stone that could be perforated for hafts and handles. Gradually over the centuries, in the phase named Mount Pleasant after the immense Dorset stockaded site, gigantic earthworks were erected in Wessex at Knowlton, Marden, Avebury and Durrington Walls, the last three having almost identical 'territories' of about 14 miles (22km) across, some 150 square miles (390 km²), each with an earthwork enclosure at its centre.

Burial practices changed. During the early third millennium BC, cremating the dead, a custom long practised in the east of Britain, was gradually adopted in the south. It was a more certain method of drying dead bones and driving out any lurking malicious spirit than the protracted technique of allowing the flesh to decay naturally. For celebrants of the Grooved Ware cult, who may have revered the sun and whose rituals were embedded in the belief of associations between different symbols, the link between fire and the sun may have been so strong that cremation, with its heaped fires and flames, replaced the burial of entire bodies or skeletons. It was the burnt bones of the dead that were put into the Aubrey Holes against the rotting remains of the posts.

With remains of more than 200 burnt bodies buried in the ring, Stonehenge was the largest enclosed cremation cemetery in prehistoric Britain.

The first cremations were messy, with large splinters of charred bone and lumps of wood-ash bundled together and packed into hollows between the edge of the pit and the post. Little was found with these first interments, but at some time the posts were withdrawn and many holes were re-used to receive a neater, more ritualized offering of tiny bone fragments from which the ash had been washed. With some of these later cremations there were characteristic Grooved Ware objects.

At Stonehenge Hawley often remarked on the compacted state of the secondary cremations, speculating that they had been buried in a container of skin or fabric. Such meticulous preparation of the bones was in contrast to the first grubby deposits, and it was a difference reflected also in the grave goods. Only in one pit was anything discovered with a primary cremation.[33] Here, in Aubrey Hole 55, two antlers rested under a thick layer of ash and bone and, significantly, these exceptional offerings were in the pit alongside the north-east axis of the earthwork, perhaps deliberately put there to add vitality to the entrance. Elsewhere, it was with the secondary cremations that objects were found – long bone pins, flints, a chalk ball, antlers and animal bones. It is clear that people had paired items in ceremonies of fetishism, believing that the objects would combine to animate the magical powers of the Other-World. It was the evocation of supernatural spirits by association and exclusion. A chalk ball could be placed with antler and animal bone; flint flakes could not be grouped with anything else; bone pins could lie with antler, with animal bone and with finely made flint fabricators.

In the context of a cult in which combination and situation were so vital, Aubrey Holes 5 and 21, at the east and south of the henge respectively, each had a rich assortment of articles, antlers, animal bones and long bone pins, as though to enhance two of the cardinal points that had been so fundamental to the beliefs of the people who had built the henge.

There is uncertainty about the bone pins. Found in the Orkneys, eastern Ireland, Yorkshire and Wessex, made of whalebone, antler or walrus tusk and from 4in (10cm) to 10in (24cm) long, they are usually found with burials. The idea that they were skewers for securing the tops of leather bags in which the cremations were parcelled is weakened by the fact that the pins were charred from the pyre. Other pins with carved heads were so unevenly balanced that they are unlikely to have been nose decorations. Although it is possible that they were for tying back the hair, some in Yorkshire, over 5in (14cm) long, were found with infants, making this interpretation debatable. Many pins are plain but some have a perforated end for a thong and others have poppy- or mushroom-shaped heads, apparently to prevent them slipping through an eyelet. It is feasible that in the days before weaving they were fasteners for leather cloaks or tunics, symbols of distinction worn by the well-to-do.[34]

Contents of the Aubrey Holes differed. One on the eastern side of the north-east causeway had only chalk in it. Hole 19

by the south causeway held 'a mass of white flint flakes . . .
discarded by an implement-maker', who had squatted there,
skilfully striking 'thin and delicate implements' from a block of
flints whose core and waste flakes were buried under the chalk
rubble filling the hole. Some pieces fitted together. It may have
been this craftsman's industry that created the 'elegant long
flint blades', found by Hawley, 'so clean and sharp that they
could be used to cut the bread at picnic lunches'.[35] Reputedly,
they are lost.

Everything had purpose. Every offering and every action
was conditioned by the demands of the cult, everything was
ordered by association and exclusion.

> All things counter, original, spare, strange,
> Whatever is fickle, freckled (who knows how?),
> With swift, slow; sweet, sour; adazzle, dim . . .
> Gerard Manley Hopkins, 'Pied Beauty', *Poems* (1918).

Even the burials were kept apart. The Aubrey Holes and
their contents have frequently been described as a cemetery,
but that is mistaken. These were ritual offerings. Finally, chalk
was rammed back into the pits, sealing the evanescent offerings. For decades the tops of these entries to the Other-World
were kept clean of grass; as exposed white chalk they main-
tained the power of the magical ring inside the spoiled bank.

Less well known are the other cremations, in the ditch and
along the inner edge of the bank, cremations different from
those in the Aubrey Holes but just as punctiliously positioned,
mostly in the ditch at the east and south-east to the causeway.
Whether in the ditch or just under the turf of the henge itself,
the majority of these pockets of bone were so small that
Hawley believed them to be the remains of children. Hardly
any ash or anything else lay with them, just one or two bone

pins and some blackened antlers. They seemed so insignificant that they have generally been disregarded. Yet in some respects they are more informative than the famous cremations in the Aubrey Holes. It is possible that it was the bones of men that were buried in the holes. Women and children might have merited less prestigious parts of the enclosure. Even so, inside the henge the situation of their interments was no less carefully planned, not for the benefit of the dead but to the advantage of the living.

At the exact east, two cremations lay side-by-side in the ditch. Also in the ditch, alongside both entrances, there were arrangements of an adult, a child and animal bones, one group just west of the north-east causeway, another by the south entrance where two adult cremations were accompanied by the smaller limbs and teeth of a child lying by a long bone pin. Nearby was a minute collection of burnt bone, no more than 5oz (142gm), mixed with animal bones. Hawley remarked that 'this is the third instance of human and animal bones occurring together'.[36] Another adult, probably a woman, and a child were buried in the ditch at the south-east.

Hawley also noticed that, unlike the Aubrey Hole burials, there was not one example in the ditch or by the bank of a cremation west of a line drawn north–south through the middle of the henge, even though he had cleared out 150ft (46m) of the ditch west of the south entrance. 'Perhaps they may some day be met with beyond that spot, but probably not far beyond it, as the people they belonged to seem to have had a superstitious reason for selecting the eastern area.'[37] For a man who professedly would not speculate, this was imaginative and it was right. It was the easterly rising, not the western setting, of the moon and sun that dominated people's vision of the world. The west, as the orientations of the long barrows had showed, was a direction to be avoided.

The cremations in the ditch were small but those along the inner edge of the bank were slighter, mere handfuls of bone set in hollows often no deeper than a saucer. Yet with the cult's obsession with arrangement it is noteworthy that no fewer than nine of the cremations were cramped together at the ESE. That the position was important is emphasized by the fact that it was here that Hawley came upon the loveliest object ever to be found at Stonehenge.

In a shallow hole only 7in (18cm) deep was a beautiful macehead, shaped like a doll's cushion and small enough for a young child's hand. It was of black and striped gneiss, highly polished, as smoothly hard as planed teak, with a perfect hourglass perforation. It was foreign. The nearest and most likely locality was Brittany, another possibility being Scotland. 'The trueness of the boring is quite wonderful when it is remembered that there was only sand and a revolving cutter of wood or bone held in a bow-drill for making it'.[38] It is now displayed in Salisbury Museum.

Maceheads were vital to the cult. They were often made of attractive stone or gleaming antler, with one of red pottery from Longtown in Cumbria. The excellent quality of many of them suggests they were 'the products of a specialized crafts- man or a small number of skilled workers'.[39] One of Cornish greenstone tumbled from the earth of a round barrow that Cunnington and Hoare were digging at Winterbourne Stoke, barely a mile from Stonehenge:

We found a perforated pebble-stone, about 2 inches [5cm] long, and very neatly polished, it has one corner broken off, and some cracks as if it had been burned . . . the Britons seem to have attached particular qualities to certain stones; and this, probably, may have been suspended as an amulet front the neck.

Hoare was probably correct that they were fetishes or talismans.[40]

An unrecognized lunar alignment may have belonged to this period, marked by a heavy post. In 1924 Hawley recorded 'the largest posthole yet found', 2ft 6in deep and 2ft wide (0.8m, 0.6m), probably once 8ft (2.4m) high, that had stood near the edge of the bank, and not far north of the nine cremations. Two smaller postholes were found near it.[41] 100ft (30m) south-east of the centre of the henge, it was positioned some degrees south of south-east at 144°, in line with the rising moon at midsummer. The three postholes marked that orientation from the centre of Stonehenge.

It was a crucial orientation, the old creed in a new form. It elaborated a lunar tradition established centuries before with the midwinter postholes of the north-east causeway. The sun might be honoured, but the lines to the moon were made stronger. Symbolic objects were brought to the earthwork. Rough stone balls were buried in the ditch, even in the Aubrey Holes, balls like others, often in pairs, in the passage-tombs of the Boyne Valley. In the Norfolk flint-mine of Grimes Graves, comparable balls were associated with a chalk phallus. At Skara Brae they had delicate spirals incised on their polished stone surfaces. At Tara in Ireland, 30 such balls lay in a tomb alongside a phallic granite pillar.

Balls like these, often found with the dead and with carvings of male and female sexual organs alongside them, can plausibly be interpreted as testicles, symbols of rebirth, of an awakening from the dead. So may the flat chalk disc in the ditch near the entrance. It had a hole through it; nearby was a roughly cut chalk ball. A similar but more perfect chalk ball came from Aubrey Hole 9. Similar discs have been recovered

near corpses in megalithic tombs. The position of the perforated disc at Stonehenge close to a chalk ball, and their
association with phalli, can be seen, like the so-called 'cups',
as female sexual symbolism, vaginas to accompany the mascu-
line symbols.

There were also imitations of different objects, such as the
object discovered by Hawley in the loose earth around the
tallest stone of the sarsen circle, lost there when the stonehole
was dug. It had been cut into the shape of a stone axe, but it
was made of chalk, useless materially but powerful as the
representation of an axe cult whose origins reached far back
into the Neolithic. Near it was an even cruder axe of rhyolite,
and some pieces of antler. Similar chalk axes came from two
postholes at the neighbouring Woodhenge – both of them were
found in astronomical locations.

In Brittany, tiny axes of prettily coloured stone were
perforated for hanging around the neck like a crucifix.
They were amulets, miniatures of the axe known to be
carried by the female protectress of the dead. Real axes
were often buried with the dead. And, like the 'figurines' of
the 'goddess' carved at the entrances and in the passages of
Breton megalithic tombs, they were also placed in front of
other burial places, personifying the spirit of the watchful
deity.[42]

The chalk axe at Stonehenge presumably belonged to the
same system of beliefs, repeating that – throughout its many
changes – the themes of death, burial and rebirth survived on
Salisbury Plain.

Looking back over almost five millennia the Grooved Ware
cult seems almost an interlude, perhaps of no more than a
century or two in which it flourished, reacted to tension and
collapsed. It disappeared, leaving evidence as enigmatic and
vague as a tantalus of phantoms in a mist.

Today signs of the mysterious period are physically obscure and, very sadly, ignored. People can see the places where the Aubrey Holes were dug. Hoop-sized concrete discs mark the positions of those magical pits. The writer has never seen a visitor looking at them.

CHAPTER 7:

BLUESTONES AND QUESTIONS OF THE UNLIKELY, c.2550 BC

Those that approve a private opinion, call it opinion; but they that dislike it, heresy; and yet heresy signifies no more than private opinion.

Thomas Hobbes, *Leviathan* (1660), vol. I, p. 11.

Testing theories of origin

The previous chapter was concerned with a mystery. This one confronts a controversy, one that began with words written in archaeological ignorance 900 years ago: ' "If you want to grace the burial-place of those men with some lasting monument", replied Merlin, "send for the Giants' Ring which is on Mount Killaurus in Ireland" '.[1]

The sentence remained unconsidered until 1921. Then its

nonsense caused a disruption in Stonehenge studies, because it resulted in a popular but uncritical belief that the first stones at Stonehenge had come not from Ireland but from Wales. It remains the most contentious of all the Stonehenge uncertainties.

Fig. 20: The grooved bluestone 68, seen in front of the sarsens.

Around 2550 BC, stones were erected inside the earthwork. They were not native to Salisbury Plain. Where they came from, how they reached the Plain and what was to have been their intended arrangement became questions of strong, occasionally antagonistic, debate. They were the bluestones, set out in two concentric half-circles entitled 'Q' and 'R'.

The holes of Q deviated more from the line of a perfect curve, and it is probable that its holes had been offset from R which, being the innermost, was set up first. They were called 'Q' and 'R' after the *'Quaere quot'* that often appeared in John Aubrey's manuscripts when he wanted to query the number of stones or posts or measurements of a monument: *'Quaere* Mr Robinson the Minister there, about the Giants bone and Body'.[2] (This example refers to the stone circle of Long Meg & Her Daughters, Penrith.)

Both Stukeley and Cunnington had puzzled over the origin of the stones, but it was not until 1921 at a meeting of the Society of Antiquaries of London that H.H. Thomas, a petrographer for HM Geological Survey, stated that the stones came from a range of hills in south-west Wales. 'The occurrence of such felspathic spots was highly characteristic of, and as far as he was aware, confined to the diabase sills of the Prescelly Mountains of Pembrokeshire'. The president of the Society added percipiently, 'How the bluestones reached the site was likely to remain an unsolved problem'. Thomas's findings were published in 1923.[3]

The following year E.H. Stone, having accepted the analysis[4] and remembering Geoffrey of Monmouth's chronicle, decided that Geoffrey's description was a half-remembered folk-story of prospectors for gold returning from Ireland, landing in Wales and taking the potent bluestones to Salisbury Plain to build a stone circle. He was wrong.

The twelfth-century monk had not mentioned bluestones.

He did not mention the Preselis nor even mention Wales. He did mention Merlin, and stated that 'the stones are enormous and there is no one alive strong enough to move them', which even to the most unimaginative geologist meant that Geoffrey was thinking of the sarsens, not the very much smaller and six times lighter bluestones.

It can be claimed that Geoffrey, credulous and uncritical, had been misled by stories he had heard. The crucial question is why he had referred to Ireland. The answer is simple. It begins with the location of Mount Killaurus where the Giant's Ring had stood. Early writers thought the site to be in Co. Kildare.

It is noteworthy that near the town of Kildare there was the Hill of Allen, famous in Irish legend for its links with the Other-World. In the seventeenth century John Aubrey remembered that 'Mr . . . Gethin of the Middle Temple London, told me, that at Killian-hill (or a name like it) ['the church of Allen'] in Ireland, is a monument of Stones like those at Stone-heng: and from whence the old Tradition is that Merlin brought them to Stoneheng by Conjuration'. In Latin, he added that the pillars were 'located on the plain, not far from Naas' in Co. Kildare.[5]

Churchmen would have known the region. There was a rich monastery at Kildare, founded by St Brigid in the fifth century, and often visited by English and Welsh clerics. Anglo-Norman priests had been travelling to Ireland since the late eleventh century. In the opposite direction Irish priests went to Canterbury or Winchester to be consecrated as archbishops. The Irish Sea became a busy monastic thoroughfare. In England other clerics followed the Harroway, passing the monstrous ruin of Stonehenge, astonished by it. But it was the towering bulk of the sarsens that impressed them, not the insignificant lintels and poky bluestones, blocks no bigger than those the travellers knew well in their own monasteries and churches.

The natural port for travellers from Britain to Kildare was Dublin, 30 miles from the monastery. From there wayfarers skirted the Wicklow mountains and passed through Naas, 10 miles from Kildare. In Geoffrey of Monmouth's time it had several monasteries.

When he visited Ireland with Prince John in 1185 another churchman, Gerald of Wales (Giraldus Cambrensis), saw many megaliths:

> In Ireland, in ancient times, there was a collection of stones called the Giants' Dance, that demanded admiration . . . and on the plains of Kildare, not far from Naas [giants] set them up as much by skill as by strength. Moreover, stones just like them, and raised in the same way, are to be seen there to the present day.[6]

Many of these stones are still standing. They are the well-known pillars of Wicklow granite, not sarsen, and are amongst the tallest stones in these islands, concentrated in the counties of Carlow and Kildare. The highest are close to Naas – Craddockstown West, over 14ft (4.4m) tall; Longstone, a slender needle, its top more than 23ft (5.3m) above the ground; and the Punchestown pillar, the second tallest menhir after Rudston in Yorkshire. It stands a soaring 26ft 5in (8m) in height and weighed over nine tons. The dimensions of these great stones compare well with the average 17ft 6in (5.3m) height of a Stonehenge sarsen.

These scattered stones around Naas were the huge pillars commented on by medieval scholars. They imagined that those lofty menhirs, so similar in size and appearance to the sarsens of Stonehenge, were the remnants of a vast stone circle, the work of giants, the majority of whose stones had been taken to Salisbury Plain – to be erected in another ring of exceptionally big uprights, as Geoffrey of Monmouth described: 'Merlin . . . put the stones up in a circle . . . in exactly the same way as they had been arranged on Mount Killaurus in Ireland, thus proving that his artistry was worth more than any brute strength'.[7]

Geoffrey's Stonehenge story is not a relic of folk memory but an early twelfth-century attempt, blemished by geological incompetence, to explain how the ponderous sarsens had been erected. The legend is no more than a monkish mixture of Merlin, magic and imagination. It has nothing to do with the bluestones, but by geographical misfortune the Preselis happened to lie midway between Kildare and Salisbury Plain. Archaeological gullibility did the rest.

The bluestone seafaring saga from Wales to Wessex would have been a form of seafaring suicide. Perils and obstacles confronted the seamen. Contrasted with entirely feasible voyages for metal prospectors, with a manageable cargo of ores and travelling in easily beached canoes, the endeavours of crews attempting to manoeuvre a heavily laden, clumsy raft along the seas of the Welsh coast would have been commitments to calamity.

On a floating platform (probably without sails), with propulsion dependent on paddles and poles, with little control over steering and affected by every capricious current of the Bristol Channel, the crews would have faced daunting hazards, the vicissitudes of weather and a recurring series of threats – strong tides, undertows, treacherous sandbanks. Added to these difficulties is the fact that natives of land-locked Salisbury Plain were not experienced seamen. To cope with the treacheries of the southern Welsh coastline, with the second highest tidal range in the world, as well as the swirling waves of the Irish Sea, they would have needed the assistance of local fishermen knowledgeable about the currents and the signs of suitable weather, maybe having to change boats frequently – unloading and reloading from craft to craft.

Even towards the end of the voyage, challenges remained. When the unpredictable Severn Estuary was reached, with the rushing current racing up to about 20 mph (30kmh), the vessel would have had to be abandoned and the stone transferred to something more suited to the Bristol Avon river (the Atlantic Fringe '*afn*'). After many miles upstream it would have been removed for an arduous overland portage along exhausting slopes, until it could be put onto another craft for an upriver crawl along the river Wylye (the 'tricky or treacherous stream'), then northwards up the Christchurch Avon to Salisbury Plain and Stonehenge. This unparalleled undertaking would have had to be repeated almost 80 times, possibly for as many years.

The improbability of such an enterprise was underlined by a recent attempt to reproduce the journey. As a scientific experiment it was flawed, compromised by economies, precautions and shortcuts. A bluestone a ton lighter than any at Stonehenge was chosen. Lacking sufficient volunteers to haul the sledge, instead a lorry took the load up steeper slopes. On more level but rough ground it was dragged along mesh-covered trackways. Once at the coast, the stone was lashed on a cradle between two lightweight curraghs or coracles instead of a well-constructed raft. At the end of the intended voyage it was planned to avoid the challenge of rivers and an arduous cross-country haul by floating the cargo on a barge along the Kennet & Avon canal to Stonehenge. Yet even with these senseless adaptations the mission ended abruptly four miles out to sea, when the poorly secured stone slipped, fell into the water and sank 60ft (18m) to the muddy bottom of Freshwater Bay. The spurious 'reconstruction' was an ill-researched, ill-prepared fiasco. But its failure does emphasize how difficult and dangerous a genuine venture would have been.

Any belief that men transported the stones is without foundation – the people are missing, the Preselis are missing and the bluestones have vanished. The one near-probability, but not certainty, is that stones from south-west Wales were used in the construction of a semi-circular setting on Salisbury Plain. Exactly when the so-called bluestones arrived on the Plain can be conjectured. Four later radiocarbon assays, one for the ensuing sarsen circle, three for its trilithons, do not provide 'a coherent and obviously contemporary group', but the circle was clearly early, around 2450 BC, and the trilithons were unlikely to be later. From the assays it was possible for the circle and the trilithons to have been built at about the same time, around 2450 BC.

The Q and R Holes were earlier. In several places, holes for the sarsens damaged pits where bluestones had stood – Q4 was cut by sarsen 3, R37, and R38 by sarsen 49. As some Q and R Holes had disturbed the earlier Aubrey Holes they were later than those, but earlier than the arrival of the sarsens, perhaps dating from around 2550 BC (fig. 21).[8]

The place where men found these stones remains debatable, but the stones themselves offer an explanation. They are not identical. The majority are dolerite, spotted or plain, but there are others of rhyolite, of volcanic and calcareous ash, and there is sandstone. All may have come from the Preselis, but rhyolitic tuff did not. Nor did they occur in the chalk of Salisbury Plain. The Snowdonia area of north Wales, however, is rich in rocks of this type.[9]

If men did transport the stones hundreds of miles, it must be asked why they did not first roughly shape them, in order to remove unnecessary weight. They would, moreover, have chosen the hardest, most durable of the rocks rather than an indiscriminate mixture, some of which would rapidly weather and crumble. Many of the bluestones were 'too soft or fissile to have been of any value as building material. The inference is plain . . . Glacial action is the only reasonable solution'.

It is arguable that the bluestones were transported during the Pliocene glaciation rather than the favoured, much later Pleistocene glaciation. The ice-sheet would have flowed down a large palaeovalley, probably along the Monnow–Little Avon fracture zone. Kellaway's favoured resting place for these Stonehenge boulders was 'in the vicinity of the Cursus'.[10]

Amongst that petrological clutter was the Altar Stone, Petrie's Stone 80. It was not a bluestone. It was a greenish, glittering sandstone that did not come from the Cosheston Beds near Milford Haven. Being highly micaceous (having a high content of mica, a glittering silicate mineral), its source could have been the Brecon Beacons, a hundred miles to the east of the Preselis.[11]

Another and almost unmentioned stone argues against human transportation. A gritty and unglittering sandstone was found by Hawley on 29 April 1920, deep in Aubrey Hole 1, earlier than the bluestones. It came from neither Wessex nor the Cosheston Beds. Known as OU9, the awkward piece mutates in *Stonehenge In Its Landscape*. On page 99 it is a bluestone, on page 377 a Cosheston Beds sandstone, and on page 394 a silicified rock. It is sandstone – but not from the Cosheston Beds. It is an awkward but indisputable fact of which most geologists seem unaware.[12] 'Thus the height of Antiquity ends in Fable; and the depth of Ignorance discends to Credulity', wrote John Aubrey in *The Naturall History of Wiltshire* (1656–91).

The significance of the Q and R Holes was realized when, following Hawley's work in 1926, part of the interior of

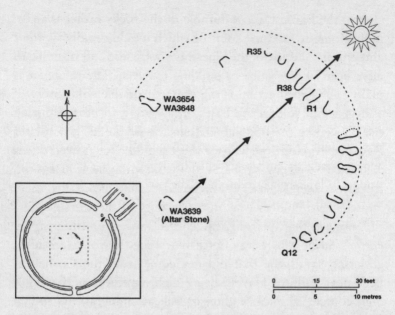

Fig. 21: Diagram showing the Q and R Holes, c.2550 BC.

Stonehenge was re-examined by Atkinson, Piggott and Stone between 1954 and 1956.[13] They found a concentric semi-circle. Each hole consisted of a central trench about 10ft (3m) long and with a deep cavity at either end, as though a great dumb-bell had been pressed into the chalk. The trench contained clean chalk rubble but the holes had dirtier chalk, caused by falling earth when the stones were withdrawn. Chippings of bluestone in some of the holes proved that they had held stones.

The 'dumb-bells' were set across the circumference of the arcs of a semi-circle with a SW-NE axis and about 82ft (25m) across and 53ft (16.2m) deep. Not knowing at first how many 'dumb-bells' there had been, it was assumed that there had been 38 stones in each arc. Later reassessment has reduced this to about 22.

The evidence of the stoneholes is so fragmentary that what was planned is beyond certainty. The intention 'may loosely have been a semi-circle, or even a three-sided, open rectangular form with rather rounded sides . . . There is no need to see this setting as unfinished'. Fortunately the symmetry and the perfect curve makes the interpretation of a half-circle the most likely. At the south-east terminal was Q12. Northwards the eastern half of the setting was fairly complete, but at the west, where much ground had been disturbed by the later sarsens and even later treasure-hunters, there was a wide gap of some 52ft (16m) from Q35/R35 at the NNW to a feature of two adjacent holes, WA3654 and WA3648, that could be identified as a probable Q/R Hole at the north-west.[14]

The majority of the holes had held one stone each. At the north-eastern apex Q37/R37 and Q2/R2 had three. Straddling a slightly altered axis, Q38/R38 and Q1/R1 had five, apparently forming an entrance on an amended alignment of 48.35°.[15]

There had also been a free-standing stone at the south-west, some 21ft 4in (6.5m) from the base of the semi-circle and the old north-eastern entrance beyond. There, to the south-west but midway between the ends of the arcs, Hawley discovered an enormous stonehole, WA3639. In it, like a dedicatory offering, was a worn-down Neolithic Group I greenstone axe. It was not from Cumbria, like those of the Grooved Ware cult, but was Cornish, the type used by natives.

The existence of such a pit and such an object hinted that its stone had been important. The pit probably held a single bluestone of exceptional size, only 8ft 6in (2.6m) from where the great trilithon 55–56 was to stand, and the ramp for the gigantic sarsen 56 had to be dug from the north-western side to avoid the stone as it was so bulky and respected.[16]

The hole was far too big for an average bluestone, and it is probable that the big column later known as the Altar Stone had stood there as a backsight for the new axis. From it, looking through the 'avenue' of five bluestones, there was a sightline to the midsummer sunrise at 50°, with sunlight pouring down a thin tunnel of stone onto the upright pillar, a dramatic change from the orientation to the northern side of the entrance and the major midwinter moonrise. There was a further alteration.

In 1979 an unexpected stonehole was found just north-west of the Heel Stone. With no surviving stone it should have been allocated the letter 'F' after Petrie's system, but British archaeology termed it Stone 97. Together it and the Heel formed a gap about 3ft (1m) wide, a perfect foresight for the observation of the midsummer sunrise, acting like a gunsight to the solstice rising, changing the monument's major alignment from the rising of the moon from one to the sun.[17]

A megalithic and mathematical grace-note must be added. In 1923, digging in the avenue, Hawley came upon two more holes for stones, in a line between the western side of the bluestone 'avenue' and the pit of Stone 97. Both stones had gone but, unlike Stone 97, were called B and C following Petrie. The distances between the centres of the three ragged holes are intriguing. From C to B is about 27ft 7in (8.4m), B to 97, 26ft 11in (8.2m). There may once have been an intervening stone with its hole in the disturbed area of the six lines of postholes across the henge's north-east entrance.

One might imagine a row of standing stones towards Stone 97 in a line 108ft 7in (33.1m) long. Quite unexpectedly to this writer, this is almost exactly 40 of Thom's Megalithic Yards of 2.72ft (0.829m), a length of 108.8ft (33.16m), with the stones spaced 10MY apart. If the gap between them was 2.5m, this would be 3MY. The width and depth of the semi-circles also correspond quite well to 30 and 20 Megalithic Yards. The apparent counting bases of 3 and 5 in these measurements accord with the 30 stones of the later sarsen circle and the 5 trilithons inside the ring. Such conclusions must be tentative, but may be evidence of the use of a measuring-rod.[18]

How the medley of 40 or 50 bluestones reached Salisbury Plain remains unclear. Three possibilities have been postulated. Prospectors returning from Ireland, and regarding the spectacular Preselis as the home of the gods, undertook the awesome but spiritually rewarding task of taking the holy stones to Wessex. Alternatively, 'the ancient men of Dyfed, realizing that the centre of neolithic society had moved from the West to Salisbury Plain, were taking with them the stone of their native land, or perhaps even stone circles that had already existed in fourth millennium Dyfed', with 'a liking for the blue-grey rock which bordered on insanity'.[19]

A third, more convincing, solution is glaciation. If men really did transport the stones hundreds of miles they would not casually collect an indiscriminate mixture of stones, some of which would weather and crumble quickly. People living around the Preselis were knowledgeable about local material. There are stone circles around the Preselis, Gors-Fawr and Meini-Gwyr among them. They are built, like all stone circles, of the most suitable local stone, in this case hard-wearing dolerite, not the softer, weather-worn calcareous and volcanic ashes.[20]

Similarly, intrusive groups of explorers from Salisbury Plain were quite competent to recognize a stone's quality. Centuries of selecting tuffs and greenstones for their axes gave them experienced eyes. Yet, in 1880, a few inches below the turf at Stonehenge, Henry Cunnington (grandson of William) found the base of an overgrown and worn-down schist between bluestones 32 and 33, 'foreign to the county of Wilts', weathered into a mere stump: 'Fragments of this stone have been continually turning up at Stonehenge, and in the neighbourhood'.[21]

It is hard to believe that prehistoric people would choose soft stones when so much good material was available. More probably, on the chalky, almost stoneless Salisbury Plain, men chanced upon a litter of bluestones and others, some from the Preselis, 'but probably fetched proximally from a site, as yet undiscovered, in West Wiltshire,' in a clutter of rocks and boulders of which only a limited number were of the ideal shape and texture.[22] It should be added that there is no other stone circle, cromlech or Breton *fer-à-cheval* ('horseshoe'), among the more than 1,300 known in Britain, Ireland and Brittany, to which stones have been dragged from more than 5 or 6 miles away.

There are many objections to the idea of human transportation. Geoffrey of Monmouth has been misinterpreted. No other stone circle was given such exceptional treatment. Men competent to recognize the difference between good and bad stone would not have chosen a ragbag of dolerite, spotted dolerite, rhyolite, volcanic and calcareous ash, welded tuffs and sandstone. Geologists consistently assert that there is no evidence for glaciation around Stonehenge, despite conscientious and methodical searches.[23] Absence of evidence, however, is not evidence of absence. Residues of earlier glaciations could have been eliminated by later incursions. And, never explained by geologists, is the large block of dolerite found 12 miles from Stonehenge in an earthen long barrow by William Cunnington in July 1801.[24]

There have been almost desperate attempts to dismiss this awkward discovery. It has been suggested that the stone was too small to be significant. It was not. It weighed two-thirds of a ton. Some say it was not a bluestone. It was. It was a block of spotted dolerite. Petrie's methodical survey disproves the theory that it had been taken from Stonehenge. A suggestion that it was lost en route to Stonehenge is geographically unlikely – the men sledging it must have been wandering in a dense fog to leave the stone more than 13 miles from where it was taken ashore from the Christchurch Avon river. Likewise, the theory that Saxons buried it in the long barrow alongside a victim they had executed does not explain why the ponderous block would have been carried so far from Stonehenge. In *Hamlet* one of the prince's officers asked, 'is this not something more than fantasy?' When exponents of the bluestone extravaganza ask the same question the answer is 'No!'[25]

The reality was much less complicated. The past had been forgotten. The Cursus mouldered in neglect. Bushes, grasses and weeds camouflaged long barrows that had been blocked and abandoned centuries earlier, long before Stonehenge's earthwork was dug. Yet deep in the mound of one of those barrows was a large bluestone, left there amongst heavy sarsens as much as a thousand years before the Q & R Holes were thought of. William Cunnington recognized it in Boles Barrow (Heytesbury 1), $11\frac{1}{2}$ miles from Stonehenge. Appositely, if regrettably for geologists, the mound was quite near Breakheart Bottom.

In a letter of 18 July 1801 to his friend H.P. Wyndham, M.P., Cunnington complains of the dangerously 'large stones continually rolling down upon the labourers', adding that the heavy boulders were 'of the same species as the very large stones at Stonehenge, which the Country people call Sarcens'. They weighed up to 200lb. In a postscript he added, 'Since writing the above I discovered amongst them the Blue hard Stone, ye same as the upright Stones in ye inner Circle at Stonehenge'.

He was so taken with the massive stones and their mixture in the barrow that he told Wyndham, 'I have brought away Ten to my house . . .' The distinctive blocks were arranged in a circle around a tree on the lawn outside his home. Some time before 1860, Cunnington's 'Blue hard Stone' was, according to the Hon. Mrs Hammersley, 'removed from the late Mr. Wm. Cunnington's garden at Heytesbury to its present site at Heytesbury House . . . It was called the "Stonehenge Stone"'. Years later, in 1934, the stone was given to the Salisbury & South Wiltshire Museum by Siegfried Sassoon.[26] The block was substantial. It measured 2ft 6in by 2ft 2in by 1ft 4in (76cm x 67cm x 41cm). In 1990, museum scales proved its weight to be 12.04cwt.

Cunnington's bluestone came from Boles Barrow, not from Stonehenge, and it is the block in the museum. Of Cunnington's ten stones taken to his home it was the one selected by Sassoon to be given to the museum. To deny this is to contradict Flinders Petrie. Following his punctilious survey of Stonehenge in 1877 in which 'no distinction is made . . . between perfect stones and mere stumps of which the upper part is removed', he was able to assert entirely confidently that 'No stones are missing since Wood's plan in 1747'. Cunnington, therefore, could not have removed it in 1801.

John Wood had made the first really accurate plan of Stonehenge. As befitted an architect he was fastidious in his recording of the size and position of every stone. His survey of August 1740 was so detailed that by hatching, cross-hatching and dotting he distinguished between 'the erect Stones in the Body of the Work, together with those in a Leaning Position, and such as are buried in the Ground from those that lye flat on the Surface of the Earth, or on the Surface of other Stones'.[27] He is unlikely to have left a largish bluestone, more than half a ton of it, unplanned, especially as he had gone to the extent of plotting Stone 32 at the east of the bluestone circle, a stump no bigger than Cunnington's. (It is still there.) Flinders Petrie was equally conscientious, checking Wood's plans minutely, and in 1877 he was just as unlikely to have overlooked the absence of Cunnington's bluestone from Wood's plan. Scrutiny of the two plans shows that Petrie was right, no stone is missing. As Cunnington found his bluestone in 1801 it could not have come from Stonehenge.[28]

The construction of the bluestone setting is often attributed to the users of 'Wessex/Middle Rhine' (W/MR) beakers, but the revised C-14 dates for the sarsen ring of about 2500–2450 BC do not accord with the presence of W/MR people being on Salisbury Plain at that time.

When David Clarke published his *opus magnum* on beakers in 1970, the sarsen circle of Stonehenge was considered to be an Early Bronze Age monument of about 2000 BC. He could comfortably introduce the W/MR chieftains into Britain around 1800–1700 BC, which, when calibrated, became *c.*2200–2100 BC, a century or two before the great stone circle.[29] He wrote:

> It is at least possible that these powerful chieftains directing the trade and exploitation of Southern Ireland, by way of the Bristol Channel and South Welsh coast, may have had the Prescelly [sic] stones brought along the copper/gold route to Wiltshire and Stonehenge, remembering that Prescelly Top, at 1760 feet [537m], is every sailor's landmark on the shortest crossing from the gold bearing hills of Wexford – a veritable Welsh Olympus.[30]

More recent studies have revised the Beaker chronology, with the earliest (the 'European' and the 'All-Over-Corded' ware) not reaching Britain much before 2600 BC. W/MR beakers came later, several centuries after the Q and R bluestones which were standing before the sarsens of 2450 BC.[31] The 'prospectors' are chronologically non-existent, well over a hundred years too late. It should also be noted that an organized archaeological search for evidence of early prospecting in the Preselis was unsuccessful. 'The field survey [of 1987] has therefore not provided any direct evidence that the Stonehenge "bluestones" were quarried or collected from the Preseli Mountains in the 3rd or 2nd millennia BC'.[32] Subsequent fieldwork has not resolved the question.

Glaciation remains the most plausible explanation. It is a view that is strongly supported, indeed virtually confirmed, by the 2006 petrographical examination of the Altar Stone and of some sandstone fragments from the Aubrey Holes, published in *WAM*. The Altar Stone came 'most probably' from the Senni Beds, 'far from the Preseli Hills and Milford Haven'. The authors continue: 'None of the five sandstone samples have [sic] an origin within the Old Red Sandstone lithologies around Milford Haven. Therefore they cannot be cited as evidence for Milford Haven being the exit port for the bluestones'. There was no human transportation.[33] It is a geological certainty that agrees with several quite independent facts.

Examining the semi-circle

Another question about the Stonehenge bluestones would be to ask why such an unusual setting was employed (a concentric semi-circle unlike any other ring in Britain or Ireland). It is a question never asked, and yet the answer is critical to an understanding not only of this phase but the entire succeeding history of Stonehenge.[34]

It could be optimistically argued that Breton seafarers – men familiar with megalithic cromlechs and horseshoe-settings in Brittany, having voyaged from Ushant to Scilly – went on to Cornwall's Padstow Bay near Bodmin Moor. Enterprising explorers then ventured 50 miles northwards to south-west Wales and the harbour of Milford Haven. There is no need to doubt their ability. People had been crossing the Channel and the North Sea from the Early Neolithic, centuries before any Breton incursion into Britain. They had followed the 'Atlantic Route' that early voyagers followed, protected from the turbulence of the ocean itself, northwards between Britain and Ireland and then between the Outer Hebrides and the Scottish mainland. It was a long-known, much travelled seaway.

The landmark of the Preselis guided them, mountains that on a clear day are visible from the Wicklow Mountains in eastern Ireland, from Snowdon in north Wales and from Dunkery Beacon in north-east Exmoor. The theory could be that, to those daring crews, such a magical range, rising like an enticing goddess, would have seemed the embodiment of powerful stone, potent material ideal for a Breton sanctuary on Salisbury Plain. So they exploited the deserted earthwork of Stonehenge, setting up a double *fer-à-cheval* of bluestones (two semi-circles, one inside the other), with the sandstone pillar of the future Altar Stone erected like a phallic statement at their mouth.

It is a commendable theory with one enormous benefit. The undertaking would occur at the right time, unlike the favoured candidates for the unlikely feat, the W/MR Beaker people.[35] Dates establish that those copper and gold prospectors were exploring Ireland two centuries too late for the Stonehenge bluestones. Nor were there native rivals.

Unlike those Beaker wraiths beloved by romantics, bearing disembodied bluestones across the waves and through the woodlands of a never-never wonderland, Breton seamen could be identified as the heroes of that prehistoric triumph, paddling, rowing, even sailing, tons of stones across the sea, along the south coast of England to the Christchurch Avon river and Salisbury Plain. Sea-going had for generations been part of a Breton way of life. Mesolithic hunter-gatherers fished off the Morbihan coast. Carvings that may represent boats exist in Neolithic *dolmens à couloir* and later *allées-couvertes*.[36] 'Perhaps these alleged ships were ceremonial vessels carrying away the souls of the dead'. Centuries later, the Iron Age Veneti of southern Brittany were experienced mariners whose heavy, leather-sailed vessels rode the Atlantic waves.

There was no sudden irruption of overseas sightseers when the sarsens of Stonehenge were erected. Contacts between Brittany and Britain had existed for centuries before that megalithic astonishment, and continued long afterwards, from the earliest of New Stone Age tombs to Early Bronze Age stones, in arrangements unlike anything known in these islands. There was cross-Channel interaction for over a thousand years.

At the onset of the Neolithic there were stylistic affinities between the single-celled Severn-Cotswold tombs of the Marlborough Downs and the *dolmens à couloir avec chambre simple* of Brittany.[37] A thousand years later, in the Late Neolithic, there was a comparable similarity between the long-chambered Breton *allées-couvertes* and a monument inside Avebury that John Aubrey described.

It is a commendable theory and has one enormous benefit of being persuasive. The chronology is perfect. It explains why geologists have discovered no trace of doleritic deposits in Wiltshire, and although the theory contains no comforting leyline it does have sex in accord with current thinking about prehistoric societies and stone circles. There is one discordant note. 'We speak from facts, not theory', stated Hoare. 'Such is the motto I adopt, and to the text I shall most strictly adhere'.[38] The present writer is at one with Hoare. I do not believe in one Breton boatload of this maritime fairy tale. But those who do wish to adopt it will have to accept that Stonehenge was partly a production from Brittany. But they will also have to explain the Boles Barrow bluestone.

From the fabulous waters of romance it is reassuring to find the firm ground of reality. Those who oppose the idea of glaciation must face three facts about Cunnington's bluestone. He found a boulder of hard, spotted dolerite and bits of the same stone 12 miles from Stonehenge in a long barrow that had been blocked two or three centuries before the bluestones were brought to the circle. The durable block was only 2ft 6in (76cm) long, far too short ever to have been chosen as a pillar to stand inside the ring. It was discovered 13 miles from the supposed landing-place of the bluestones by the river Avon, and much farther from any other place on that fictitious route.

The likelihood is that the bluestones of Stonehenge lay near the ring. Within 20 miles there were several alternative sources of stone – to the north on the Marlborough Downs there were hundreds of sarsens, big and small; to the west around Bradford-on-Avon there was masses of oolitic limestone on the valley sides of the Bristol Avon river, the same pass through which the bluestones were thought to have been ferried. Probably the Welsh rocks were much closer, perhaps on the slopes above the river Wylye near Boles Barrow and a dozen miles from Stonehenge. Who transported them remains unknown. Their work did not last. The motley of 'bluestones' was removed to allow the erection of the gigantic sarsen ring. Before that circle was begun it was preceded by four stones known as the Four Stations.

If their builders were natives of Salisbury Plain then it is perplexing that the alien shape of the bluestone horseshoe should be followed by an equally alien setting, a rectangle almost unknown in Britain and Ireland but, like the semi-circle, a design commonplace in Brittany.

CHAPTER 8:

THE FOUR STATIONS STONES – SYMBOLISM, NOT SCIENCE, c.2500 BC

I observ'd two remarkable places, which plainly have a conformity with the two stones set upon the vallum; which stones puzzle all enquirers.

William Stukeley, *Stonehenge* (1740), p. 14.

Dating the Four Stations

Four sarsens once stood at the corners of a spacious and exceptionally accurate rectangle, its long sides aligned ESE-WNW (see fig. 22, overleaf). Clockwise from the north-east the stones are numbered 91 to 94. Two, 92 and 94, have gone, their places shown near the centres of small sub-circular ditches. A third, 93, although erect, is a stump. Stone 91 lies by the bank. Inconspicuous, ignored by visitors, the stones are a vital introduction to a new phase of Stonehenge. Until recently there was almost no debate about the strange oblong.

Whether the bluestones had been removed from the henge before the arrival of the sarsens is unlikely. The little physical evidence indicates that the Altar Stone was still standing at the time that the Great Trilithon was erected, suggesting that the Four Stations had been arranged around an undisturbed blue-stone semi-circle.

In 1872 Fergusson termed such megalithic sites 'rude stone monuments', and 40 years later Peet was no more compli-mentary with 'rough'.[1] The only roughness or rudeness about the Four Stations was that they had not been smoothed. But the four sarsens formed a model of elegance.

Inigo Jones never mentioned the sarsens. John Aubrey noticed the two stones, thinking that they had been part of the Aubrey Holes ring, 'from whence one may well conjecture the stones c c were taken'.[2] In the early eighteenth century, Stone 91 still stood, although leaning slightly. Stukeley saw the semi-circular hollows from which Stones 92 and 94 had been withdrawn. He considered them the places where great vases for 'water to be us'd in the sacrifices' had stood. Stones 91 and 93 between the vases had been altars 'for some particular rites, which we don't take upon ourselves to explain'. Untypically he mistakenly deduced that the two stones 'form an equilateral triangle with the inside of the grand entrance'.[3] They do not.

In 1740 John Wood described the same holes, 'one with a simple Bank of Earth about it; another with a double Bank separated by a Ditch', perhaps the result of rubble being spaded out during the removal of the stones. Thirty years later John Smith agreed: 'Directly north and south of the temple just within the vallum of the ditch, is the appearance of two circular holes encompassed with the earth, that was thrown out of them; but they are almost effaced by time.'[4]

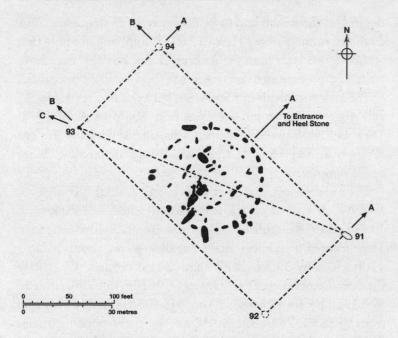

Fig. 22: Diagram showing the location of the Four Stations (2 missing, 1 standing, 1 recumbent), c.2500 BC. 'A' indicates midsummer sunrise; 'B' indicates major northern moonset; and 'C' indicates the Beltane (early May) sunset.

The untidy mounds or 'barrows' inside the ditches around 92 and 94 reported by early antiquarians, and still recognizable today, were no more than earth thrown up by diggers and trampled down by animals and visitors, perhaps also upcast from the excavations made by Hoare.[5]

Hoare and Cunnington described 91 and 93 as 'rough and unhewn'. They also dug into both 'barrows' of 92 and 94, finding a 'simple interment of burnt bones' in 94 where they had unknowingly cut into Aubrey Hole 46. They recovered nothing from 92. Hawley re-excavated 92 in 1921. A large stone had stood there. Around its pit was a ditch similar to one around the Heel Stone, its trench interrupting the edge of Aubrey Hole 19, something unanticipated by the prehistoric diggers 'as the trench had to be deepened in consequence'. The ditch ran round Aubrey Holes 17 to 19, implying not only that Stone 92 was later than the Aubrey Holes, but also that those holes had become so overgrown that they were unnoticeable.[6]

The hole for the absent Stone 94, between Aubrey Holes 45 and 46, was found by Atkinson and Thom in April 1978. Their 6ft (2m) square excavation was limited but probably cut through Aubrey Hole 46, the one already affected by Hoare and Cunnington.[7]

The geometrical reason for such an unusual rectangle of four widely spaced stones was seldom asked, but surveys in 1973 and 1978 established the precise distances between them. They formed an almost exact parallelogram, about 262ft x 110ft (80m by 33.5m) with right-angled corners. Clockwise the distance between 91 to 92 was 112ft 10in (34.7m); from 92 to 93, 262ft 3in (79.9m); 93 to 94, 107ft 4ins (32.7m) and from 94 to 91, 263ft 3in (80.38m). The corresponding angles for the corners were 89.5°, 89.5°, 91.1°, 91.1°.[8]

There are many questions about the four stones – concerning their date, why they formed a rectangle, whether they contained astronomical alignments and, most important, what their purpose was. Possible answers are many. Possible solutions are like handfuls of snow.

The Stations were later than the Aubrey Holes, but had to be earlier than the sarsen circle of Stonehenge because its high, wide stones would have blocked any sighting across the ring. R.S. Newall, who often dug with Hawley, was the first to realize this. He wrote: 'Since [the diagonals] cannot be seen from each other, their careful planning diametrically opposite each other suggests that they were earlier than the [sarsen] monument'.[9] Conversely, it would have been easy to see over, even between, the lower and thinner bluestones of the half-circle.

An examination of the geometry

Why the Four Stations stood in such a rectangle is seldom asked, but a plausible interpretation is that they created a template whose intersecting diagonals established a centre for the forthcoming sarsen ring that the world knows as Stonehenge. If so, it might seem no more than prehistoric idleness that failed to withdraw them when the circle was completed. Richard Atkinson, however, had an equally plausible explanation:

> One need not suppose, of course, that the existing Station Stones, or their vanished fellows, were actually used as surveyor's reference points, for which purpose they are far too large and imprecise; but rather that they form permanent and symbolic memorials of an operation of field-geometry which if it were repeated today, would tax the skill of many a professional surveyor.[10]

Such a change from neat pole to bulbously commemorative stone would explain the slight discrepancies between the relative lengths of the widths and depths of the two sides of the rectangle. If sarsens such as Stone 91 – 9ft (2.6m) in girth with a crudely pointed base – replaced slender sighting-posts, it needed only minor errors in the centres of the stoneholes to affect the measurements of the sides of the oblong.

The name 'Stations' was given to them by E.H. Stone in 1923, but it derived from observations made by the Rev. Edward Duke of Lake House. He was a contemporary of Sir Richard Colt Hoare and William Cunnington, and dug with them occasionally. He also delved into many barrows himself in the Lake cemetery a few miles south of Stonehenge, but was not as punctilious as his colleagues in recording his discoveries. Many were preserved in his museum at Lake House. Cunnington complained that much of the amber was 'in a state of decay'.[11]

Barrow-plundering appears to have been a family obsession. It may have been Duke's grandfather who told Stukeley that 'in a barrow between Woodford and Lake was a Scull so large that it was kept in Wilford [Wilsford] church upon the bier for many years as a sight'.[12]

Astronomical alignments

In 1846 Duke claimed that Stones 91 and 93 were 'astronomic gnomons', like the pin of a sun-dial, to which a priest looked from the observing-platform or 'station' of the mounds at 92 and 94. Standing at Stone 92 he would have seen the mid-summer sun rise over the formerly erect 91. Six months later, standing on 94's station, the astronomer would have observed 'at the winter solstice, the setting sun descend at the south-west exactly behind [Stone 93]', a theory 'very obligingly tested by the ingenious Rev. L. Tomlinson of Salisbury, author of *Recreations in Astronomy*, ably assisted by Mr. Browne of Amesbury'.[13]

Victorian enthusiasts offered optimistic refinements, such as 13 alignments to a pot-pourri of stars and an earthbound imitation of the heavenly Plough. The majority of their un-critical theories were as ephemeral as rainbows. Some were not. It is arguable that there was an alignment not only to the sun but also to the moon. In 1964, returning to his computer, Gerald Hawkins calculated that the long sides of the Four Stations rectangle were in line with important lunar events – Stone 91 to 94 towards the major northern moonset, with a declination of +29°; and, in reverse, 93 to 92 to the major southern moonrise, -29°. 'I believe that the standing stones formed a unique figure:- historically, geometrically, ritualistically and astronomically. They were immensely significant'.[14]

The astronomy was unarguable, but the implication that men had intended it was treacherous. It could have been a celestial coincidence. Because the major northern moonset, on which the long sides of the rectangle were aligned, happened to occur at right-angles to the midsummer sunrise, the short sides of the rectangle had to point towards that event and, in reverse, rather imprecisely to the midwinter sunset. Because the Four Stations stood at the corners of a rectangle, its diagonals inevitably also formed two Pythagorean triangles – even though the Greek mathematician would not be born for another 2,000 years.

By an unrealized chance, the site of Stonehenge stood on the latitude at which the midsummer sunrise and the major northern setting of the moon occurred almost exactly at right-angles to each other. The precise latitude is about 40 miles away at sea off the south coast, but to the unaided eye the difference is indiscernible. Because of this and the right-angled setting of the Four Stations, the combination of solar and lunar lines could be accidental. But the significance of the rectangle's diagonals was not.

At the beginning of the twentieth century Sir Norman Lockyer made a special study of Stonehenge. Amongst other considerations he suggested that, from the centre of the circle, sunset during the first week in May would have been seen over Stone 93 and the early November sunrise over Stone 91, respectively the dates of the Celtic festivals of Beltane ('bright fire') and Samain ('end of warmth, onset of cold').[15]

He could have been correct for the wrong reason. The centre of the sarsen ring was the centre of the Four Stations rectangle where its diagonals intersected. If Lockyer's observation was valid, then originally it could have been from Stone 92 to Stone 94 that the stones had been aligned on Beltane, and from 93 to 91 on the ominous 'festival' of Samain when the dead rose from their graves. In addition, the alignments in reverse between the four sarsens would have marked two other important festivals, Imbolc in February and Lughnasa in August.

The alignments were not accurate, the declination to Beltane being close to +16° rather than slightly larger. As Clive Ruggles properly observed:

> The question of why the station stones were placed in a rectangle and not a square has given rise in the past to the tentative suggestion that the WNW-ESE diagonal might have astronomical significance; however its declination -16°, has no obvious explanation in terms of the sun or moon and in any case the diagonal passed across the centre of the site where it might have been partially obscured by the bluestones, and certainly would have been obscured by the later sarsens.[16]

The length of the rectangle's shorter sides is the clue. Because of them, the long sides pass 4ft (over 1m) to north and south from the circumference of the planned sarsen circle. Should the sides have been longer or shorter, the diagonals would have formed different angles.

Ruggles was correct. Yet the comparative crudity of the Beltane and the other festival lines is explicable celestially. The solar positions of the summer and winter solstices, and the risings and settings of the moon, are virtually unchanging. The Quarter Days of early February, May, August and November are not. No constant solar or lunar 'standstill' occurred as a target at those times. The dates could only be calculated, if calculated at all, by the movements of the inconstant monthly moons. To prehistoric societies a calendrical 'error' of a few days may have been of no importance. It is arguable that Lockyer did discover sightlines towards the times of Late Neolithic festivals, occasions that are usually thought to be Iron Age.

There is a final point to be made about the astronomy of the Four Stations. It might seem perplexing that Duke's proposed orientations towards the sun should have been formed by the short rather than the longer, more emphatic, sides of the rectangle. There is no conflict. To have designed long solar sides would have turned the setting through 90° and altered the diagonals by the same amount. It is almost, if not complete, proof that the Quarter Day alignments were intended by their architects. They were not astronomers attempting to predict eclipses, but men and women engaged in rituals of life and death in which the sun and moon were essential.

It was a time of transition. From the Late Neolithic onwards, orientations towards the rising of celestial bodies, once commonplace in chambered tombs and earthen long barrows of previous centuries, slowly gave way to alignments towards their settings, and ceremonies were held not in the light of dawn but in the darkening night, lit by the flames of burning torches. The mixture of sightlines in the Four Stations is an example of the gradual metamorphosis.

In Britain and Ireland rectangles of stone are uncommon. Only four are certainly known (one, of course, being the Four Stations). There were two in Scotland. The third, King Arthur's Hall on Bodmin Moor, is an earth-banked oblong, arranged north-south and internally lined with alternating stones of low flat-topped slabs and higher lean pillars like the parapet of a battlement. There is a possible entrance at the

south-west corner. The quadrilateral and the cardinal orientation are critical.

Its surveyor, A.L. Lewis, was reminded of apparently
related structures in Brittany, also with gaps at their corners
and associated with rites of human cremation. Perhaps the
closest comparisons to Stonehenge's Stations are to be
found there, a thought all the more interesting because of
other evidence of Breton influence in the later phases of
Stonehenge.[17]

There are also two distant megalithic rectangles at Fortingall
by Loch Tay in Perthshire, standing 82ft (25m) apart. The
north-east site is arranged NE-SW, the south-west SSE-NNW.
There, in central Scotland, small megalithic rings known as
Four-Posters are common, being rings of four stones that
appear to form an oblong. It is an illusion. A true Four-Poster
is not a rectangle. Its stones stand on the circumference of a
circle.

The Fortingall sites were different. When Fred Coles saw
them in 1907 each had only three stones, but that was because
the pagan settings had been 'christianized' in the nineteenth
century by toppling and burying five of the original eight of
each site. This was proved in 1970 when a Leicester University
excavation led by Derek Simpson uncovered the lost stones in
their metre-deep pits.

The Fortingall oblongs possessed the singular trait of being
composed of eight stones, four tall at the corners, four lower in
each side, reminiscent of the 'high-and-low' stones of King
Arthur's Hall. The sites were rectangular and outsize, the
north-east 20ft 8in by 16ft 5in (6.3m x 5m), its partner
25ft 3in by 19ft 4in (7.7m x 5.9m) – more than double the
area of an average Four-Poster.

They had possible alignments, the sides of the north-east site
perhaps directed towards the minor summer moonset, a diag-

onal arranged east-west. The north-west's sides were orientated on the minor summer moonrise, a diagonal on the major summer moonset. It is astronomical conjecture. Even with the plans of the Thoms, made before the 1970 investigation, the deductions are possible rather than probable.[18]

Such angular settings were uncommon in Britain and Ireland. In Brittany they jostle. Infrequent in Morbihan, where horseshoes dominate, elsewhere they exist in Ile-et-Vilaine and the Côte-de-Nord. In Finistère, the *département* closest to Britain, there were almost a dozen, the now-lost granite quadrilaterals of Parc ar Varret and Lanvéoc on the Crozon peninsula, uprooted in the nineteenth century but planned and sketched before their destruction.

A square enclosure once stood at Lanvéoc, and at Morgat nearby there was a double line of large and small stones reminiscent of those at King Arthur's Hall, paired together around a rectangular core. Another rectangle with a row of menhirs down its centre was known on the Ile d'Ouessant, an island almost within sight of Britain. 'From Ushant to Scilly is thirty-five leagues.'

There were other oblongs at Ty-ar-c'Huré, Leuré and Landaoudec (even a polygon at Kermorvan near the fishing-port of Conquet), and the rectangle on Ushant in the Atlantic. All of them contained astronomical alignments, as recorded in French research of the 1920s: '*Tous obéissant, sans aucune exception, à la loi mégalithique d'orientation*'.[19]

Other than the Four Stations there is no comparable rectangle in Britain or Ireland with such definite astronomical sides and diagonals, but there is a remarkable correlation with similar alignments in the Crucuno quadrilateral three miles west of Carnac in the Morbihan. Its long sides lie neatly east-west towards the equinoctial sunsets, and the NE-SW diagonal is in line with the midwinter sunset. The rectangle was as out-

of-place in southern Brittany as the Four Stations oblong on
Salisbury Plain.

Crucuno is a magnificent rectangle, until recently protected
by gorse and bramble impenetrably bristling in and around it.
When the present writer with two colleagues visited it in 1980,
the gorse was head-high. Seeing scratched faces in the spiky
wilderness a black-bereted old farmer chortled, in Breton
dialect, '*a benn ar brochenn*' ('in the needles'), and wandered
back to his cows chuckling at the idiosyncrasies of megalithic
masochists.

Today the stones have been cleared of their undergrowth,
and from Crucuno hamlet – with its ruined *dolmen à couloir*
passage-tomb in which a witless youth lived for ten years, at
the end of the eighteenth century – a lengthy plod down a
rutted track, often squelching in mud, to the end of a hedged
field leads one to a corner where a gap gives entry to a gorse-
free, spectacular monument.

Crucuno was ruinous in the nineteenth century but was
restored in 1882–83. So meticulously were the long sides
arranged east-west that the validity of the reconstruction by
its restorer, a conscientious local hotelier, F. Gaillard, was
questioned, but an earlier plan of 1867 by Dryden and Lukis
vindicated the accuracy of his work. The rectangle was elegantly proportioned, its sides of spaced stones measuring 108ft
7in by 81ft 7ins (33.2 x 24.9m), which the Thoms pointed out
was equivalents to a ratio of 40:30 Megalithic Yards of 2.72ft.

Looking westwards from the eastern corner stones, the long
sides indicated the equinoctial sunsets in March and September, and the same would have been true, although less neatly,
of the sunrises in the opposite direction. G. Charrière calculated that the Crucuno diagonals were designed to point to the
risings and settings of the sun both at midsummer and midwinter, and this was corroborated, with reservations, by the

Thoms' survey. They added that it was also possible 'that the moon in its eight "standstill" positions was indicated', although Crucuno, 'unless it had foresights some distance away, could never have been more than a symbolic observatory'. If the lines, as at the Four Stations, were less for men to look along than for the sun or moon to travel into the rectangle, there would have been no need for longer alignments.[20]

Miniature rectangles and triangles

The Four Stations at Stonehenge (like the Aubrey Holes, ignored by visitors and disregarded as an unimportant remnant by some prehistorians) in reality merit discussion. Unlike counterparts such as Fortingall 350 miles to the north or Crucuno in Brittany 250 miles to the south, the Four Stations had no intervening stones along their sides. They seem to be an economy version, adequate as an unadorned template.

In its austerity the rectangle was similar to the simple 'boxes' on Exmoor, not many miles to the west. These almost neglected sites were not many sea-miles north of Finistère, where the majority of the straight-sided sites of Brittany had been erected. Like the contents of an untidy fairy's playpen, Exmoor is littered with miniature rectangles. Their distribution is significant. They are near the coast and close to river tributaries. It is as though voyagers, perhaps emigrants from Finistère in search of unclaimed land, had beached by Lynmouth's red-streaked cliffs and gone inland to the sheltered valleys between the hills.

Exmoor had been an uninviting region for Neolithic settlers. It had no flint or good stone in its upland of grim weather and poor soil. Just one megalithic tomb is known, Battle Gore

(Williton I, Somerset), whose denuded stones by the coast are miles from the unusual Bronze Age sites. Although only 30 miles north of Dartmoor, the upland of the river Exe has, until recently, been almost a prehistoric *terra incognita,* split between Devon and Somerset, a land that archaeology had forgotten. Distant from cities, its remoteness discouraged fieldwork. And the monuments have contributed to their own neglect. Whereas many Dartmoor rows are romantically megalithic, those on Exmoor are minilithic, dwarfed in grassy tussocks and weeds – tiny and fragile shafts of stone that can be overlooked from even a few steps away, sunken in peat and unalluring.

There are rectangles, 'quincunxes' and triangles, like exercises in Euclidean geometry. Because granite boulders were almost non-existent, the stones of slate, grit and shale were tiny and could easily be sledged by two or three men. Research in 1970 concluded that 'The unspectacular nature of many of the megalithic sites on Exmoor is doubtless due to the size and quantity of the local stones ready to hand without too much trouble'.[21] Unprotected and vulnerable, even during the twentieth century one in ten of the recorded sites has vanished, and of the remainder a quarter have lost stones.

In 1879 R.N. Worth commented, 'The antiquities of this district have never received the attention they deserve, and the Forest may therefore be commended to the attention of zealous and discreet archaeologists'. Apart from the studious attentions of his son and the Rev. J.F. Chanter in 1905 and 1906, who limited their fieldwork to the Devon side of Exmoor, and a few recent exceptions such as Leslie Grinsell's book of 1970, the neglect continued until the admirable survey and inventory published by the Royal Commission in 1992.[22]

There are stone circles at Porlock and Withypool, but it was the straight line that was obsessive on the moor. Finistère, over

200 miles from Barnstaple Bay, might seem an improbable birthplace for the Exmoor settings. Dartmoor was much closer. Less than 30 miles separated it from Exmoor's southern slopes. But the minuscule sites on Exmoor lie to the north, with the dreadful barrier of the Chains between them, a long, bleak ridge surrounded by mires and marshes. It was not impassable, but the passes between its hills were treacherous.

The double 'rows' (like Hoar Oak and Cheriton Ridge) of these hypothetical intrusions from overseas were unlike the long lines on Dartmoor. The 'rows' are small, short and wide, in formations easily construed as oblongs and rectangles. The ratio between length and width is so similar that such settings are more aptly called 'boxes'. It is an architectural ambiguity compounded by the question of the sites' antecedents. A major trait amongst them is that their builders aligned them towards cardinal points, often north-south, sometimes east-west – directions presumably obtained by bisecting the risings and settings of the sun. Astronomical analysis is needed.

Often of no more than four stones, these unobtrusive quadrilaterals are termed 'quincunxes' when there is a fifth stone at their centre. Such settings are not uncommon on Exmoor, occurring at Brendon Two Gates, Chapman Barrows, Trout Hill and elsewhere. In design they form an 'X' fitted inside an oblong, a saltire like St Andrew's Cross, its diagonals creating four triangles. It may be that from these already unusual settings that the even more strange shapes of triangles developed.

At Woodburrow Hangings, a site high up on the Chains, quincunx and triangle actually combined. A rather imprecise rectangle with a 2ft (60cm) high central stone had a triangle attached to its southern side. Complete when planned in 1891, a century later one side of the triangle was 'only 0.1m high and may be stumps of broken stones'.[23]

The ancestry of these little-mentioned, minilithic delicacies might seem inexplicable. But they are not exclusive to Exmoor. There are some on the Yorkshire Moors, others on the island of Anglesey. Such settings so many miles from south-west England make a Dartmoor origin for the triangles on Exmoor unconvincing. Proven three-stone settings in coastal positions in both Yorkshire and Anglesey make Brittany more plausible as the source of the Exmoor rectangles and triangles. In 1930 Frank Elgee mentioned several on the moors of Yorkshire, stating emphatically that 'Some triangles are certainly not the remains of circles', and listed them – Commondale Moor, Black Howes and Easington High Moor. Near Ramsdale, two miles from Robin Hood's Bay, three tall stones stood in an irregular triangle whose sides measured about 26 by 43 by 49ft (8 x 13 x 15m).[24] Almost 200 miles WSW on sea-bound Anglesey, there is a megalithic triangle of three gigantically heavy pillars at Llanfechell near Cemaes Bay on the north coast. Two miles away, at Llanfairynghornwy, another site 'possibly had three stones originally'. It is noticeable that every one of these triangles is coastal, close to bays convenient for landings.[25]

On Exmoor itself there are several, spread in 40 square miles from Furzehill Common in the west to Codsend. They lurk shyly at Clannon Ball, Challacombe, on Long Chains Coombe, Trout Hill, Lancombe and others, their midget stones camouflaged like winter-white stoats peeping from long grass. A sceptic might question a Breton ancestry for such eccentricities, claiming that whereas rectangles such as Crucuno are known in Brittany, no triangles have been recorded there. Scepticism is unjustified.

In Spring 1926, William Sitwell visited the elegant Crucuno quadrilateral. Near its centre there were 'three remarkable stones forming an equilateral triangle, six yards [5.5m] to each face. They are very much worn from exposure.' Like so many other stones in Brittany they disappeared, but not before they were planned. Sitwell added that at Crucuno 'there are so many remarkable combinations between the sides and the triangle within, that possibly the whole was prepared by ancient craftsmen as a tracing-board'.[26] He could have been describing the Four Stations at Stonehenge.

There were rectangles, even triangles in Brittany. Their abundance there and their scarcity in Britain and Ireland, their coastal distribution and the artefactual Breton/British links all support the argument for continental influence. Such a connection seemed to have been forgotten until the last few years, when the associations were suspected by the present writer. But there is a surprise. The Exmoor triangles were known 400 years ago.

Those tiny three-sided shapes have been known since the late sixteenth century. In his Latin *Britannia* of 1586, William Camden recorded them: 'this river [Exe] hath his head and springeth first in a weely barren ground named *Fxmore* . . . wherein, there are seen certaine monuments of anticke work, to wit, stones pitched in order, some triangle wise, others in a round circle'.[27] In Gibson's 1697 edition of *Britannia*, John Aubrey repeated Camden's words. Gough paraphrased the note in his own edition of 1806, but added nothing archae-ologically to it. Nobody else bothered.

Camden's reference to the Exmoor 'triangles' had a tortuous history. The quotation is from his *Britannia* of 1586, but the settings had already been referred to by William Caxton in his *The Discrypcion of Britayne* of 1480 – which itself was a distillation of John Trevisa's 1387 English translation of a compilation entitled *Polychronicon* (1327), by Ranulf Higden, a Benedictine monk of St Werberg's, Chester. The work was described by Caxton as 'a well-woven tissue of materials from many sources', namely reminiscences and guesswork by monks and clerics such as Gildas, Nennius, Geoffrey of Monmouth, Gerald of Wales and William of Malmesbury.[28]

It is likely that the triangles on Exmoor were first observed by some curious churchman, riding across the moor from a visit to a monastery in southern Ireland, perhaps musing about Merlin, magic and mobile megaliths, and from his horse spotting the Trinity-like settings lurking in the grass. That was no later than the end of the thirteenth century. Research into prehistoric innovations does not gallop in this country! Yet if there is a link between the Four Stations at Stonehenge, the angular settings in Finistère and the half-forgotten miniature peculiarities on Exmoor, research has at last advanced after a hiatus of six empty centuries.

A Breton origin for the Four Stations remains controversial. At this period, direct connections with Brittany are unproven. There are few identifiable artefacts in Britain, only architectural styles in chambered tombs and megalithic settings that are unlike anything indigenous. Nor were the Four Stations and other counterparts in Britain identical. They differed in size, angle and number of stones. What they did possess in common were celestial alignments, clear-cut directions that were not obvious in a circle. More than 30 years ago this was explained by the present writer:

It must be added, however, that had prehistoric man's prime intention been to design an astronomical monument it is unlikely that he would have constructed a circle. A line of stones for an alignment or a horseshoe of pillars for a calendrical calculation would have been more appropriate. A circle is an enclosure, it would have been an effective fence either for containing or excluding something spiritual but it would not have been the most efficient of observatories. Whatever astronomical function it had was probably only a part of its overall purpose.[29]

Squares and oblongs with their straight sides and their diagonals have the potential to contain a dozen sightlines – to the Meridian and Quarter Days; to the sun and moon rising and setting at their summer and winter extremes; even to a hill or distant mountain that was venerated by its society.

It does not follow that such constructions were for an astronomical exploration of the skies. Most sightlines are too short for precision, and most foresights of clumsy stones too inexact. It was not science but symbolism that was the cause of the quadrilaterals. King Arthur's Hall, the Fortingalls, Crucuno and the Four Stations all had sightlines, but their comparative crudity imply that it was a poetic rather than analytical vision of the cosmos that induced man to lay out the alignments. As the Thoms and Merritts observed, 'It should be understood that Crucuno, unless it had foresights some distance away, could never have been more than a symbolic observatory'.[30]

True of Crucuno and of the Four Stations, the conclusion would be just as relevant to the sarsen circle of Stonehenge that was to follow. As Richard Atkinson's sardonically commented, 'shots in the dark may miss their mark but may serve to awaken sleepers from their slumbers'.

CHAPTER 9:

THE GREAT CIRCLE, c.2450 BC

I should think one need no scruple to affirm that it is a British monument, since it does not appear that any other nation had so much footing in this kingdom, as to be Authors of such a rude and yet magnificent pile.

William Camden, *Britannia* (1695), p. 109.

Timber techniques in stone

Four and a half thousand years ago men began constructing one of the wonders of the ancient world. It was an astonishing and an optimistic enterprise, and it was built in a limbo of time, neither the end of the Neolithic nor the beginning of the Bronze Age, but during a blurred period of transition.

It was an age of innovation and disruption. The first metals were appearing in Britain – tiny objects of copper, trinkets of gold. Men searched for ores, prospectors crossed the seas and explored the coastlands of the Irish Sea. With the incomers came a conflict of creeds, of light or darkness, of the sun or the moon, of man or of woman as mother, of burial or cremation. It was an age of confusion.

In the middle of the third millennium BC a deep ditch and a mile-long outer bank was constructed at Durrington Walls, two miles from Stonehenge. The irregular enclosure had several entrances, one towards the river Avon. Inside the earthwork enclosure – to which the term 'henge' is often misapplied because this was a permanent settlement rather than a site only for seasonal gatherings – there were buildings. Outside, small earth-floored houses, 13ft (4m) square, perhaps thatched and wattle-and-daubed, surrounded the earthwork.

Despite its daunting size and the damage caused by centuries of farming, the site has been described, planned, even excavated on several occasions, first in 1951 and 1952 when lines of postholes were uncovered. The work was too limited to explain their significance.[1] A formidably ambitious exploration was undertaken in 1966–68, before the construction of a road through the centre of the site. With the help of earth-moving equipment the entire road area was stripped and the postholes of circular buildings of stout oak – one at least of 39m across (some 130ft) – were found in the interior. There were perhaps 20 or more structures, varying in size and as randomly scattered as an African kraal.[2]

A geophysical survey in 2003 located two concealed entrances, one at the north, a second at the south that had been blocked. Both were perhaps intended to mark cardinal points just as the nearby henge of Woodhenge did. More revelations came in 2005. Common rubbish can inform. Pits of broken pottery, burnt flints and discarded animal bones indicated the remains of long-forgotten ceremonies, in which hundreds of people had gathered for gluttonous meals and ceremonies of death. These had been midwinter assemblies.

The feasting had been prolonged and epicurean. The most tender cuts of pork from the meat of young pigs (that may have been fed on honey to make the flesh even more succulent) were half-roasted, then stirred in pots to make a thick, winter-warming stew. There may have been alcohol in the form of mead, also made from honey. These were gourmet banquets of early prehistory.[3]

Most of the pots were Grooved Ware and, once broken, were deposited in pits with flints, inedible pigs' jaws, a fragile bone pin, a flint arrowhead. In 2003 one pit was found to contain four phallic-shaped flints and two spherical flint nodules. There was also another 'phallic' flint with 'a naturally vulva-shaped hole through the middle deliberately put in a natural teardrop-shaped hollow'. 'The sexual symbolism of the phalli and balls were [sic] not lost on the excavators'.[4] Many more were found in the extensive excavations of 2005 – chalk phalli; testicles; 'cups' as representations of vulvae; incised plaques as female figurines. With cattle, crops and children, the people of Durrington Walls had need of as much fertility magic as they could conjure. As the director of the excavation, Mike Parker Pearson, observed, sex is often associated both with life and with death.

A probable reason for the gatherings and the festive indulgence was discovered in 2005 when a wide road of laid chalk, perhaps lined with an avenue of tall posts, was uncovered, leading from the east entrance towards the river Avon. It was thought that at sunrise families had carried the ashes of the recent dead to the river and cast them into the water that would take them into the world of the ancestors. It was a transition from life into eternity.

Indications that these had been formalized ceremonies appeared in 1967–68, when postholes of two successive timber circles were uncovered. The first was of lightweight, unroofed timbers, 76ft (23m) across with a south-east facing entrance. Quite soon after, it was replaced by a heavier setting of six concentric rings, the outermost 128ft (38.9m) in diameter. It also faced south-east. It may have been a secret place. With wickerwork between the uprights masking the interior of each ring, and with doorways at different positions, no profane person could see the rituals at the small heart of the structure.

Such multiple rings of posts are not unknown. There was one at Balfarg in Fife, another at the Sanctuary near Avebury. Even closer to Durrington Walls was Woodhenge. But none was as impressive as the nine circles, 312ft (95m) across, at Stanton Drew in Somerset that preceded the stone circles there.[5]

There was an astronomical subtlety at Durrington Walls. From the middle of its circles to the 13ft (4m) wide entrance was a distance of about 128ft (39m), apparently allowing an observer at the centre a broad 'window' almost 10° across, far too coarse for accuracy. There was no such latitude. The edges of the intervening posts of the inner rings overlapped, reducing the gap to less than a degree near 131°, aligned on the midwinter sunrise. It was a precision easier to achieve in wood than in rough stone. Uncertainty remains. It could be wondered whether the communal activities at Durrington Walls were for commoners, with the elite of society having the privilege of the stone circle at Stonehenge a mile or so away.

Stonehenge was an anomaly. On Salisbury Plain wood was found everywhere. It was treated by craftsmen and was frequently decorated. It was a time of change. Already in the wooded areas of southern Britain there were timber circles, ring-beamed to give stability to the uprights. In the

Netherlands, evidence preserved in a bog at Drenthe showed that some rings had carved ornamentation with 'pagoda-like protruding lintels', and many British sites may also have had attractive motifs carved and painted on their posts.[6] But, as wood does, they rotted. When it was decided to transform Stonehenge plainness and permanence were preferred to decoration and decay. Men built in stone.

Who the anonymous genius it was who envisaged the marvel will never be known. A committee seems unlikely. Generations of ever-more powerful leaders had steadily developed into dynasties, strong inter-marrying families whose members were aware of customs and ritual places overseas, in Holland, northern France and Brittany. They had considerable cross-Channel contacts.[7] They exchanged gifts (maybe including women), they knew the Dutch circles of wood and the Breton cromlechs and *fers-à-cheval*, colossal megalithic half-moons around Carnac. Such cosmopolitan chieftains had prestige and they accumulated wealth.

They were buried in novel, round barrows that over the centuries accumulated into cemeteries around Stonehenge, and became a sprawling necropolis that respected the ancestral ring of emptiness isolating the ring from the mundane world. There were many cemeteries, often raised against an ancestral long barrow – such as the Cursus group; the New and Old King barrows; Stonehenge Down, Winterbourne Stoke; Lake and Lake Down; and Wilsford, that included the rich barrows on Normanton Down. It may have been a member of that burial-ground who organized the beginning of the most ambitious project ever known in Britain. What is noticeable as the circle of Stonehenge rose, is how few, how modest and how remote the low mounds of early Beaker burials were, never encroaching on the native barrows, keeping well away from the developing circle (fig. 23).[8]

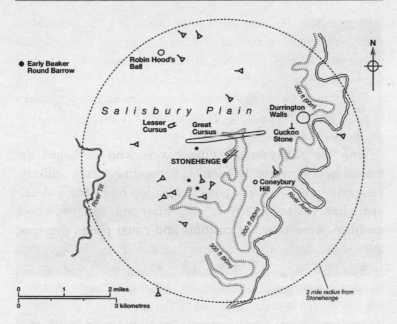

Fig. 23: The Stonehenge region in c.2450 BC,
showing the presence of early Beaker barrows.

There, the Welsh stones were lifted from their sockets and
the cavities were carefully backfilled. Excavation of the Q and
R Holes in 1954 showed that earth and dirty chalk had
tumbled back into the pits as the stones were dragged out.
This rubble had been rammed down before clean white chalk
was packed firmly on top of the holes and in the middle section
of the 'dumb-bells'. Then new holes to receive the sarsens were
dug. The fact that one of these, for Circle-Stone 3, cut into the
edge of Q4's pit proved that the bluestone rings had preceded
the huge circle.

Thirty sarsens were erected in a perfect circle. Thirty lintel-
stones were placed along their tops to form a structure three
times taller than a man. Inside it were five settings of two
uprights, with a lintel across them like constricted archways.

Fig. 24: The curving stones of the north-east lintels 130, 101 and 102.

Termed *trilithons* ('three-stones') by William Stukeley, they were arranged in a horseshoe-shaped setting that rose in height towards the south-west. Of the bluestones only the sandstone Altar Stone was left, upright near the centre of the new ring, close to the tallest trilithon. Outside the circle the Four Stations remained, their untooled roughness in contrast to the smoothed and ground faces of the sarsen ring. Beyond the entrance of the ageing earthwork was Stone 97 and, alongside it, the Heel Stone, 'corroded like worm-eaten wood', as Stukeley remarked of the outlying pillar at the Rollright Stones in Oxfordshire, 'by the harsh jaws of time'.[9]

Four assays, all from antlers (one from Stone 1 of the circle and three from the trilithons), provide a very wide converted range of dates from about 2620 to 2100 BC. A time around 2450 BC for the construction of the sarsen monument is feasible.[10]

Described so casually, one might think that there was nothing exceptional about Stonehenge, but reconsideration demonstrates how remarkable an achievement this monument was. The transportation of the stones over almost 20 miles of uneven countryside, the provisioning and shelter of the workers miles out on the exposed Plain, the shaping of the stones, the pre-planning of the design so that only stones of the right length, width and shape were selected, the manufacture of ropes and sledges, the lifting upwards of lintels six or more tons in weight – all these and many more problems leave one in astonishment and admiration that people with only primitive equipment could have completed their task.

The crux of their difficulty and their triumph was the height of the circle-stones. Despite the skewed site on which the ring was to stand, it was intended that the tops of its lintels were to be exactly level. Because of the 6in (15cm) fall of the land from south to north, and 1ft 3in (37cm) from west to east, some sarsen uprights had to be over 1ft (30cm) longer than stones on the other side of the circle. And the 30 stones were to be of similar width. All this had to be calculated and checked before the pillars could be chosen. The solutions lay in the working practices of earlier generations.

It was a society of skilled carpenters. One imagines a timber mock-up on the site. Two adjacent posts, where stones would stand, may have been erected with a wooden ring-beam across them. Observation over the centuries of how liquid dribbled over the rim of a filled tub, if the vessel were not level, would have shown how a trough of water could be used as a levelling-device. With a vessel placed on top of a ring-beam that tilted, water would spill. To overcome this, one of the supporting posts would be raised or lowered until the beam was horizontal and the water was still.

Then a third post would be set up near the second and the process repeated around the entire circumference, meticulously establishing the required heights of the posts. These were to be the templates for the stones as they arrived on site. A similar technique levelled the tops of long recumbent stones in megalithic rings 400 miles away in north-east Scotland.[11]

Getting the stones to the site

The source of the sarsens has seldom been disputed. Since the seventeenth century it has been accepted that they came from the Marlborough Downs, 17 direct miles north of Stonehenge. Some sarsens must have lain on Salisbury Plain itself, and this is probably where the Heel Stone and the Four Stations were found, but one simple fact shows that such erratics were uncommon. There is not one megalithic tomb near Stonehenge. The closest is at Tidcombe & Fosbury, 14 miles north-east and only a few miles from the sarsens of the Downs. The absence of any stone-built chamber in any other earthen long barrow on Salisbury Plain reveals how scarce large boulders and slabs had been. Although the small bluestones had lain conveniently nearby, when taller pillars were wanted for the sarsen ring men had to go a long way for them.

Enormous blocks of sarsen covered the upper slopes of the Marlborough Downs. People at the nearby Avebury used hundreds for the erection of great circles and avenues, and for Neolithic chambered tombs such as West Kennet and the Devil's Den.

Formed by the natural cementing of a bed of quartzite, itself created in a prehistoric sea from deposits of clays, sands and loams 26 million years or more ago, this thick layer of sacharoidal sandstone settled and concreted on the chalk of the sea-bed. When the sea retreated, coniferous forests grew on the exposed surface, the tree-roots penetrating the still-soft sand. Their holes can still be seen in some of the stones of

Avebury and Stonehenge. Eventually the freezing millennia of Ice Ages broke and cracked the bed of sarsen into gargantuan slabs, ideal for the building of a stone circle.

Sometimes called druid-stones, bridestones, or grey-wethers (from their similarity at a distance to grazing flocks, *wether* being an Old English word for sheep), the stones are better known as sarsens, perhaps because they are 'saracens' or 'foreigners' in their chalk landscape. There are other explanations.

The huge stone slabs in some prehistoric burial-grounds on the Chotanagpur plateau in northern India are known as 'sasans' and it may be that the 'sazzans', as they were once known in Wiltshire, and the 'sasans' of India have a common derivation from a long-forgotten word in the Indo-European language. There is also a local explanation. John Aubrey, writing about northern Wiltshire, noted, 'They are also (far from the rode) commonly called Sarsdens, or Sarsdon stones'. In Anglo-Saxon the word was the hybrid *sar-stan* or 'troublesome stone'. *Sar* had the meaning of 'grievous', as in several Saxon elegiac poems:

	. . . heart's
Sare aefter swaesne:	grief in those gone;
sorg bid geniwad	sorrow is renewed.
	'The Wanderer', line 50.

The phrase 'grievous stones' is apt for the reactions of those early farmers as they struggled to extract and drag unwieldy, half-buried sarsens from the fields. *Sar-stan* is just as alliterative and far more expressive than today's 'bloody boulder!'[12]

The stones were excellent for a megalithic ring. 'Those that lie in the weather are so hard that no toole can touch them', wrote Aubrey. 'They take a good polish'.[13] Lying embedded in turf and earth, they were dug out with wedges driven into natural fissures, levered free and manhandled onto hardwood sledges.

To lift one end of a 26-ton stone demanded the strength of 20 men heaving down on long timber levers, straining as they steadily shifted the slab until it could be lashed down and the long, slow, dragging journey to Stonehenge begun. Oxen may have been used for pulling the load, but the advantage of their strength is discounted by their slow brains and slow reactions in a crisis. Good traction animals when ploughing a level field, they are liabilities on slopes and twisting trails. Rollers are equally unhelpful. Except on prepared tracks or on flat, firm ground, they present problems on the hillsides and on wet patches, where they sink almost inextricably to the dismay and anger of their tired handlers.

Sledges would have been more likely, dragged by men along temporary rails, hauled on thick ropes of plaited thongs, guided round outcrops, tugged along the contours of the downs, slithering over the winter grass when the soil was hardest, moving day by grudging day towards Stonehenge. Such oak-built sleds, capable of supporting a huge sarsen, would have been very heavy, and for an average expedition a total payload of 30 or more tons can be assumed. Over 600 labourers were needed, travelling no more than half a mile a day, a tedious safari of more than a month before they reached Stonehenge.[14]

The route would not have been direct. Immediately to the south of the Marlborough Downs were marshes in the Vale of Pewsey, a lowland of ill-drained greensands with miles of swamp and wasteland, thick with reeds at its edges, willows and birches and alders growing on its islands. It was a wilderness, and only spoonbills and tiny reed-warblers were at home there. Today it is rich farmland. In prehistory it was wild and forbidding. To the east was Savernake, a primordial forest gloomy with oaks, ashes and thorns, which even now after centuries of clearance is a 'marvellously lovely woodland', but was then as much a barrier as a mountain range.

The sarsens had to be taken westwards. First a stone would have been moved cautiously down the slope of Overton Hill, then on, slowly upwards, towards present-day Bishops Cannings, Caneganmaerse ('Cana's marsh'), passing between the ridges and the wetlands, on to Coate, dragged around Etchilhampton Hill, along the line of the future Roman Lydeway, and on to Foxley Corner and the foot of Salisbury Plain. Fourteen miles had been covered. Weeks had gone by. Daily, helpers fetched local provisions, and had dragged the poles and skins of shelters for the cold nights of the long trek. But now, if Atkinson's proposed route is the correct one, and it is more plausible than many suggestions, the stone lay below the appalling slope of Redhorn Hill.

Here the escarpment climbed steeply, 250ft (76m) in half a mile, a slope of 1:11. Tiring for an unencumbered person, it would have been almost impossible for hundreds of men straining and slipping around the dog-leg of the easiest passage, heaving at taut, near-breaking ropes, jamming levers behind the sledge (the burden threatening to slither sideways on the bends), crawling and inching upwards until, days and nights later, the crest was reached. Then, on gentler downslopes, the group would have dragged past the conspicuous mound of the Ell long barrow, Wilsford N 3, where Thurnam was to find prehistoric and Saxon skeletons, across the Plain where the Bustard Inn now stands, and finally to Stonehenge, the weary weeks over, the trial of fatigue and accident (even death) concluded.

The exact route may never be known. Perhaps the hardships of Redhorn Hill were shunned and a less arduous but miles-longer way was preferred, moving from Etchilhampton south-westwards towards Lavington, then turning sharply eastwards up a long, steady valley towards Tilshead and Rollestone and Stonehenge. Whatever the chosen path, it was an undertaking to be remembered and told and retold – an exploit worthy of Merlin to be triumphantly vaunted by Geoffrey of Monmouth. That chronicler of legends recorded not a word about it.

Working the stone

It may have been decades after the first that the last, huge, exhausting sarsen was sledged past the Cursus to Stonehenge. During those years each earlier stone had been fashioned as though it was a block of wood, battered into a symmetrical shape to suit the design of the carpenters who had planned the new ring. The result was a masterpiece of woodworking, timber transformed into stone, decaying oak changed into enduring sarsen, a wooden house of the dead turned by the skills of men into an everlasting temple of the gods.

The tools used for this architectural metamorphosis were recognized in 1901 by Gowland during his excavations around the dangerously leaning Stone 56, the survivor of the tallest trilithon. He recovered over a hundred rounded mauls of sarsen, some no bigger than a tennis-ball but others as large as a pumpkin and weighing up to 64lb (29kg), more than most men could lift easily. It was with this repertoire of rough stones that people had shaped the pillars and lintels of Stonehenge. Jagged projections had probably been heated and then suddenly chilled with cold water before the largest mauls, encased in slings of leather with long handles 'in order that they might be used by two or more men', were whirled in high loops faster and faster then smashed down onto the sarsen, gradually pulverizing uneven lumps, slowly smoothing the surface. 'A more economical or efficient tool can hardly be imagined.'

Once the worst had been removed, gangs of workers lined up, four or five on either side of the stone, and with smaller mauls rubbed backwards and forwards on it as though it were a prehistoric washboard, sandy dust trickling away, scraping and scouring the surface into fluted ridges that would later be polished flat by a similar process. The effect of this broad tooling can be seen on the fallen trilithon 59, whose ripples were left unfinished by some exhausted group.

It must have been tiring and boring, and it must have seemed everlasting. Calculations suggest that in an hour of continuous rubbing no more than $6in^3$ ($98cm^3$) of dust would be removed.[15] If some 2in (5cm) of stone had to be levelled from the face of an average upright – wide, thick and more than twice the height of a tall man – the task would have taken almost 400 man-hours. Assuming eight people worked ten hours daily on the stone, they would have to spend four or five tediously long days before the sarsen could be turned over for its side to be dressed, then over again and its outer face smoothed, then over again for its second side to be polished, in all a fortnight or more of aching, day-long toil. Dishearteningly, there were 40 long sarsens to be dressed. With bad weather, harvests and illness, it was three or more years of literal and metaphorical hard labour.

In the turmoil of those years Stonehenge must have been a bustling, dirty, rowdy place, with the crashes of the hammer-stones, the rhythmical scrape and screech of the grinding mauls, the chatter, the bellowing of orders over the noise as the stones were levered upright, cries of warning, the distant shouting of a team dragging yet another sarsen across the last mile of the Plain. It will never be known how many people were involved, but it has been estimated that one-and-three-quarter million working hours were needed to build this sarsen phase of Stonehenge.

With an improbable thousand labourers (perhaps 1 in 20 of the inhabitants of Salisbury Plain), working long hours every day, hauling, shaping and erecting the stones, theoretically the project could have been completed in six months. The assessment is unrealistic. It is unlikely that any prehistoric community would have persisted so unceasingly, and the work of preparing the stones alone is quite likely to have taken far longer than a few months. Years, and quite probably generations, are more convincing. No sarsen could have been battered and ground and smoothed in just a few weeks. When one realizes that there were to be 30 pillars, 30 lintels and 15 massive uprights and lintels for the trilithons, the mere slog and drive required for the smoothing of the stones amazes the modern reader. This, however, was no more than the beginning.

Woodworking techniques demanded more than planed surfaces. The stones had to be connected together, as though dowelled by a carpenter. The top of each upright had to be bashed, chipped and scraped into two tenons, like bulbous pegs, to hold the lintels securely. The circle's lintels were delicately curved to follow the long line of the circle. They were chamfered, with bevelled edges, to fit firmly on their uprights. They had to have two deep mortise-holes pounded and pestled out of their undersides, the spacing neatly measured so that they could receive the tenons of the two pillars across which they would lie. The ends of these incredible lintels were also beaten into toggle-joints, with the V-shaped 'beak' of one end to be inserted into the V-shaped groove of the adjoining lintel. Like pieces of a geometrical jigsaw, they were to be socketed together, stone by stone, in a huge, immovable

Fig. 25: Lintel 156 lies on the ground, with its mortise-holes clearly visible.

ring high above the ground. In a timber building the result would have been an achievement for any prehistoric architect. In sarsen, it was a masterpiece.

The workers had to be fed, and they had to be sheltered if they came from far away. There may have been a temporary camp of expert masons dwelling on site during the warmer months of the year. It could have been such men who supervised the methods and decided on the order by which the uprights and the lintels were set in place. That such skilled artisans came from northern Brittany is little more than provocation. As the sarsens had come from the Marlborough Downs it is probable that men from there, accustomed to dealing with stones, were the masons.

A heritage of centuries of moving huge stones for megalithic tombs and circles made the task of coping with the sarsens of Stonehenge a familiar one. There was a straightforward technique for raising the uprights. Using rollers on the even ground, a stone was pushed forward until it was balanced at the edge of its ramp. A box-like pit had one sloping side, down which the lower end of the stone was slid until its base butted up against four or five thick poles standing protectively against the back of the stonehole. Stripped of their bark, these posts were sticky with sap, which lubricated the movement of the stone's heel as the sarsen was levered and pulled up. Ropes fixed around its top were attached to great sheer-legs of seasoned timber, that afforded extra leverage to the rope-handlers. Behind the stone other men jammed posts against it, preventing it from toppling backwards.[16]

The method was simple, but demanding of man-power. Oxen could not be used, and a stone three-quarters of the way to the vertical required a pull of a fifth of its dead weight to haul it the last few stages upwards. A hundred men, each exercising a strenuous and short-lasting pull of 100lb, would have been needed to move a 26-ton pillar of the outer circle. Stone 56 of the Great Trilithon – 50 tons of awkward sarsen – would have required twice that number, straining at a spread fan of ropes as the stone crunched and quivered slowly, apprehensively, into its deep hole.

Then, having checked with a plumb-line that the pillar was perfectly erect, chalk blocks, stones, bits of sarsen and blue-stone were crammed into the sides of the hole, wedging the rubble around the stone, holding it secure. Here there is a minor mystery. In the packing were pieces of fine rock from Chilmark, 11 miles away. They may have been imported because there was insufficient local stone. But their presence may have been the result of some magical belief, irrecoverable today.

Getting the lintels into position would have been the re-sponsibility of carpenters knowledgeable in the problems of lifting heavy ring-beams and fitting them onto the heads of wall-posts. Stone-masons lacked this experience. Other than Stonehenge there is no stone circle in Britain, Ireland or Brittany with lintels, and the capstones of the passages and chambers of the preceding megalithic tombs had almost certainly been dragged up the sides of the barrow mound. No remains of such ramps have been detected at Stonehenge, and other means must have been employed for positioning its lintels.

There are theories. The most plausible is that of building a rising platform or crib of squared logs under the stone, layer by layer, levering one end of the lintel up, inserting a beam under it, levering the other end, putting more logs beneath it for a floor, then commencing the stage above with the timbers at right-angles to those below. Although a mile of heavy timbers would have been needed at Stonehenge, the method had the advantage that the crib could quickly be dismantled and its joists re-used time after time.[17] Archaeologically, it is undetectable.

As long as the spacing of the tenons and mortises agreed with each other, and as long as the heights of the sarsens were level, the lintels could be moved forward onto their uprights. Any error, however, would have been disastrous, and today one can still see how the ends of some pillars and lintels were shaped into shoulders and steps to overcome the setback of a sarsen that was too short or a lintel that was too thick. Megalithic nuances such as these increase one's respect for the engineers of Stonehenge.

Examining the layout

Commonsense suggests that it was the trilithons that were set up first. Gaps in the outer circle were too narrow for any large stone to pass between them, although it is just possible that the erection of the circle and its internal archways went on together, with the uprights of the five trilithons rising above the stones of the ring.

The inner faces of the sarsen ring follow the line of an almost perfect circle. It is difficult to understand how this could have been achieved if the trilithons had stood in the way of a marker-rope swung from a focal point. It is feasible that the ring was laid out and built with one gap left by the truncated Stone 11 at the south and another at the north-west, where Stone 21 stands slightly outside the circumference. The huge pillars of the trilithons could have been dragged through these, erected and, once they were perpendicular, the gaps closed.

This might explain why the ramp for Stone 56 came in unexpectedly from the side where Hawley found the axe of chalk. It would also explain why Stone 21, unlike the other stones in the ring, had its ramp inside the circle because it could not have been pulled up from inside once the stones of trilithon 57–58 were erect.

In 1924 Hawley discovered the ramp of Stone 56. 'We came upon the incline in chalk rock for introducing the big stone to its place'. In 1979 Richard Atkinson embellished the statement. 'We found an impressive sloping ramp, cut in the chalk and filled with tightly-packed chalk rubble, running inwards and downwards directly towards the base of stone 56'. In *Stonehenge In Its Landscape* there was cautious agreement, 'perhaps but not certain'. By miscalculation it appeared that the ramp had been given a step which been backfilled 'to make the drop less steep'.[18]

Such an unusual approach could have been caused by the continuing presence of the Altar Stone as the long-established, indispensable backsight for the midsummer sunrise between the outlying Heel Stone and partner. If so, the pillar quickly became superfluous and was removed.

The five trilithons rise in height towards the greatest at the south-west. Trilithons 51–52 and 59–60, opposite each other and nearest the entrance, are 20ft (6.1m) high. The intermediate pairs, 53–54 and 57–58, are slightly angled inwards and stand about 21ft 4in (6.5m) tall. The 24ft (7.3m) ruined Great Trilithon, 55–56, at the apex of the horseshoe, once rose above them, standing a full 8ft (2.4m) above the lintels of the surrounding circle.[19] The grading of heights was deliberate. The effect drew the eye towards the massive Great Trilithon and the south-west, on the old axis but away from the summer solstice. Only the very top of 55–56 could be seen from outside the ring, its bulk concealed from all those forbidden to enter the circle.

For a megalithic ring that was constructed 4,500 years ago with the simplest of tools, the layout is amazingly symmetrical. Thirty heavy stones – long, ponderous blocks – were surmounted by 30 lintels whose tops were never more than 4in (10cm) from the horizontal, despite the skewed nature of the site, sloping both to north and east. Petrie, in his fastidious survey, calculated that the average error from the level was only 4in (10.2cm), a hand's width. The astonishing accuracy, attained by such pre-planning, was such that Stone 30 at the entrance was almost 1ft (30cm) shorter than Stone 10 at the south where the land was lower.

The regularity of the spacing also is noteworthy. The builders made the gaps half as wide as the sarsens surrounding them. How well the planners succeeded can be demonstrated by simple arithmetic. One stone with its gap measured 10ft 3in (3.1m). Thirty such combinations would produce a circumference of 315ft (94m). The actual perimeter is 306ft 4in

(93.4m), a deviation of no more than $3\frac{1}{2}$ in (9cm) for each stone and the gap by it.

There were two exceptions. Stone 11 at the south was shorter and more slender than the others, perhaps a late addition to fill the gap through which stones for the southern half of the ring had been dragged. And the gap at the north-east between Stones 30 and 1, facing the causeway to the henge, was wider than the rest, whereas the adjacent gaps between Stones 29–30 and 1–2 were narrower, producing an optical illusion of a broad, impressive entrance. Even the lintel above it, Stone 101, was heavier. Stukeley saw this: 'That impost which lies over the grand entrance, we said, was deeper and longer than the rest'.[20] He also noticed the better-finished interior of the ring:

> They set the best face of the stones inward – the stones of inside both of the outward circle and of the cell [the horseshoe of trilithons] are the smoothest, best wrought, and have the handsomest appearance . . . I find they took care to set those stones that had the best outward face, toward the front or entrance.[21]

The trilithons caused historical mistakes. Inigo Jones thought that there must have been six arches arranged in a hexagonal figure, one missing at the north-east having gone, 'not only exposed to the fury of all devouring Age, but to the rage of men likewise'. Stukeley was dismissive about the sixth. 'But this trilithon in dispute', he wrote sarcastically, 'must needs have been spirited away by nothing less than Merlin's magic'.[22]

The five trilithons formed an imposing, inner sanctum. Their inner faces were carefully smoothed, and although the arches were spaced well apart, the gaps between their uprights were

narrow like arrowslits in a tall, dark wall. There were occasional botches. Lintel-stone 156, lying across the prostrate
Altar Stone, has two deep mortise-holes on its underside and
also two shallower depressions on what had been its upper
surface. People had pounded holes on the wrong side.

There was an insistence on visual effect. Indeed, more
concern was shown over the heights of the stones than over
their safety, and on several occasions the experiments, sacrifi-
cing stability for spectacle, failed. When Stone 60 of the
northernmost trilithon was being dragged upright a huge
fragment broke from its base, leaving the pillar too short by
2ft 6in (76cm). Unwilling to lower the trilithon by so much –
because its counterpart, 51–52, at the east was already standing – the workers rolled boulders into the stonehole and
balanced the truncated sarsen precariously upon them. Its
partner, Stone 59, fell and shattered before AD 1575. By
1959 Stone 60 was leaning and shifting so badly that it was
straightened and set in concrete.[23]

To the south-west the pillars of trilithon 57–58 were erected
in extremely shallow holes, to ensure that the stones would be
of the same height as trilithon 53–54 opposite. Both fell
outwards on 3 January 1797 'with a considerable concussion',
58 lying flat but 57 tilted at a convenient angle for Victorian
boys later to slide down its inner face in hobnailed boots. The
stones were re-erected by a 60–ton crane in 1958.

The erection of the Great Trilithon was a similar compromise between dramatic effect and architectural prudence.
When two stones of exactly the right length could not be
found, the workers dug an 8ft 3in (2.5m) deep hole for Stone
56, reducing its height above ground to about 22ft (6.7m). As
its partner, Stone 55, was much shorter, but probably the
longest sarsen available, and its pit was much shallower. To
avert its collapse the masons battered the base of the stone into

a broad and ugly club-foot to stabilize it. They were not successful. Centuries before 1575 and the first good drawing of Stonehenge that showed its collapse, the stone fell, bringing its lintel, 156, down with it. Stone 55 broke. Today its clumsy foot pokes out anatomically close to the Friars Heel of the fallen Circle-Stone 14.

Despite the compromises, when the five trilithons and the circle were standing they would have awed prehistoric visitors. Nowhere else was there anything so overbearing. In the colossal ring the past dominated the present. It was a place where imagery, the transformation of tradition into new but recognizable forms, was more important than technical considerations of safety. The sarsen circle of Stonehenge preserved antiquity but absorbed it into a new form, a temple for the elite of a society whose customs and beliefs were as old as the ancestors, ghosts and gods of the past.

An observant eye will notice that the inner and outer sides of the uprights narrow towards the top, deliberately shaped to taper inwards. The effect has been likened to the Greek technique known as entasis.[24] This is defined as 'A slight convex curve in a column shaft to correct the visual illusion that straight lines give of curving inwards' (*Oxford English Dictionary*).

It was not illusion but delusion. At Stonehenge the effect was too crude. More probably the intention was merely to lessen the weight of the pillars. At their tops the inner sides of the trilithons were shortened into inverted triangles. Technically it was clumsy, but it did save muscles.

Whoever the genius was who planned Stonehenge – and there have been suggestions of an architect from Mycenae, Egyptian astronomer-priests, even a Beaker man from Mars, and, more probably, a native southerner[25] – the planner probably wanted a continuous run of lintels around the trilithon horseshoe. The graded heights defeated him. Planning the slopes, shaping the angled heads of uprights and calculating the positions of the tenon pegs and socketed mortises was too difficult for prehistoric technology in Britain. The compromise was five independent trilithons.

At some time the bluestones that had been returned to be set up inside the sarsen ring, only to be removed again, were brought back for a second time. Most of them were to form a rough circle; 19 others were for a more shapely horseshoe. There could not have been a more distinct difference in the way the two settings were treated. The stones of the horseshoe were elegantly composed, meticulously shaped and polished, and neatly arranged. The circle bluestones, like leftovers, were hastily and carelessly set up as though they had been no more than a method of using up the remaining stones.

Nineteen bluestones, all dolerites, were chosen for the graceful horseshoe that stood inside the five trilithons. Its open end was in line with trilithons 51–52 and 59–60 at the north-east, and its apex was within two paces of the Great Trilithon. All the pillars had been skilfully dressed, and they were graded in height, with the lowest at the open mouth a full 3ft (1m) shorter than bluestone 67 at the apex, its top 9ft 3in (2.8m) high.

Two of the stones had already been used. Stone 98 near the Great Trilithon had a long, deep groove down its side. Stone 66, broken and under the split Stone 55, has a projecting tongue. Atkinson persuasively suggested that the pair had once been fitted together so that their combined width would match that of a broad bluestone on the other side of the axis.[26]

Stonehenge was dark, claustrophobic, godlike. Stukeley was aware of the enclosing atmosphere:

Fig. 26: Trilithons 51–52 and 53–54 tower over bluestones 32 and 33, part of the bluestone horseshoe.

The stones that compose it, are really stupendous, their height, breadths and thickness are enormous, and to see so many of them plac'd together, in a nice and critical figure, with exactness; to consider, as it were, not a pillar of one stone, but a whole wall, a side, an end of a temple of one stone, to view them curiously, creates such a motion in the mind, which words can't express.[27]

He was so impressed by the trilithons that he climbed onto the top of 53–54: 'My Lord Winchelsea and myself took a considerable walk on the top of it, but it was a frightful situation'. In 1900 two Canadian cyclists climbed the same trilithon by rope-ladder – with their bicycles, by moonlight![28]

With his limited fieldwork elsewhere, Stukeley was unaware that the horseshoes were not native. They were Breton. There are at least 16 *fers-à-cheval* in Brittany, the farthest south being the dilapidated Kergonan on Ile-aux-Moines in the Gulf of Morbihan, 80 miles from Tossen-Keler on the north coast. There are others in Morbihan, including the pair on the former hill, now island, of Er-Lannic. As well as their shape they have stones graded in height and an astronomical axis, often towards a cardinal point or to a solar alignment.[29]

Equally unaware of those informative sites, no antiquarian after Stukeley wondered why Stonehenge contained such alien shapes. In his early manuscript about Stonehenge, Stukeley deduced that the trilithons formed a horseshoe because 'one end this Ellipsis being cut off for the Entrance it falls in very handsomely . . . the long extent of its winding arms & the most spatious opening at the entrance render it the proudest singularity in the world'.[30] He was perceptive.

But for almost four more centuries commentators were bleakly unimaginative about the settings, reporting, never enquiring: John Wood, 'Curved Lines of Pillars' (1747, p. 34); John Smith, 'originally an Ellipsis, or oval' (1771, p. 56); Sir Richard Colt Hoare, 'a large oval' (1812, p. 147); William Long, 'in horse-shoe form' (1876, p. 59); Herbert Stone, 'in horseshoe style' (1924, p. 9); Robert Cunnington, 'the form of a horseshoe' (1935, p. 13); Richard Atkinson, 'set in a horseshoe' (1956, p. 27; 1979, p. 40). No one asked why. Even the encyclopaedic *Stonehenge In Its Landscape* shrugged 'a horseshoe' (1995, p. 29).

There is an almost perverse archaeological ambivalence between what is agreed about foreign artefacts and what is ignored about foreign architecture. For years it has been accepted that there were cultural contacts between Bronze Age Wessex and Brittany. Research in 1979 confirmed that 'Links are demonstrable between southern Britain, Brittany and central Europe in the early bronze age'. The axes, daggers and ornaments of gold, amber, jet and faience in

round barrows near Stonehenge are like those of the war-
rior graves in northern Brittany. 'In the Early Bronze Age
southern Britain and Brittany presented a single cultural
province'.[31]

Megalithic horseshoes are plentiful in Brittany, particularly
in the Morbihan, 'land of the sea', whose inhabitants were
experienced seamen. In Britain and Ireland horseshoe shapes
are unusual. As well as his *allée-couverte,* John Aubrey may
have recorded one at Avebury, a Breton *fer-à-cheval,*
although its surviving sarsens are traditionally identified as
the remains of a 'North Circle'. Of the two reliable observers
before its disruption, Stukeley thought it had been a concentric ring. A geophysical survey in 1989 discovered no
traces of it, but did detect depressions and anomalies, which
along with the two surviving standing stones and one fallen
stone indicated a horseshoe setting. Aubrey had planned it as
such. The resistivity survey concluded that 'it is therefore at
least possible that Aubrey's Plan A version of this area may
yet turn out to be the most accurate of all'. There is
independent support. The axis from the centre of the mouth
to the apex of the setting is due north, an orientation often
found in Brittany.[32] It can be no more than conjecture. Short
of finding a Breton vase-support or shards of Neolithic
Chasséen or Conguel ware, the interpretation is just a tempting possibility.

Cromlechs, huge ovals like Ménec West, contained solar
alignments along their axis. By 'cutting' such enclosures in half
a horseshoe would be formed, with a mouth facing the foresight of a tall pillar at the curved apex. Similarly immense ovals
also exist along the west coast of Britain – the Twelve Apostles
near Dumfriess; Loch a Phobuill and Pobull Fhinn on the
island of North Uist; and in Caithness at Achnagoul. They are
all near the sea (see Appendix 2).

There was nothing extraordinary about these megalithic mavericks from overseas. They did not have to be of large stones. Nor did they have to come from Brittany. Near Penrith in the Lake District, the henge of Mayburgh was 30 direct land-miles from the coast, even farther from the Solway Firth and along the river Avon. It faced the typically British henge of King Arthur's Round Table, but it was not British. With its absence of a ditch, its cobble-piled bank and its subtly domed interior, it was Irish – and as out of place at Penrith as the Sphinx would be outside Stratford-upon-Avon.

Like the great ovals, it is significant that the horseshoes in Britain and Ireland are also near a bay or river-mouth, as though set up by seafarers. There is a fine example in Caithness at Achavanich, 'field of the holy man', by Loch Stemster five miles from Lybster Bay and only six north of the immense 'Breton' oval of Achnagoul. The setting has a characteristic Breton 'high-and-low' trait, with taller stones on its eastern side.[33] Astronomically it is aligned NNW towards the most northerly setting of the winter moon. Like other horseshoes, it was composed of local material.

Another horseshoe, this time inside a stone circle, exists at Croft Moraig, one of the farthest from the sea of these foreign sites. Significantly it is only two miles from the Fortingall rectangles on the other side of Loch Tay. The ruinous Hethpool, 12 miles from Budle Bay in Northumberland, might be another horseshoe. Its size matches large Morbihan *fers-à-cheval* such as Kergonan and the Champ de la Croix.[34]

Of Stonehenge's three horseshoe settings, the first, a semi-circle of bluestones, is feasible. Two others are certain, one of bluestones, one of trilithons. That horseshoe is graded in height up to the Great Trilithon and the mid-winter sunset.

The few horseshoes and rectangles in Britain and Ireland (but more than 1,300 stone circles) demonstrate how atypical the unusual settings inside Stonehenge were if created by natives. Conversely, there are numerous ovals, horseshoes and rectangles in Brittany, a *département* only a twelfth of the size of Britain and Ireland. The horseshoes erected inside Stonehenge were as alien to British architectural styles as the tinkling bells of a Buddhist shrine in Salisbury Cathedral.

The comparative densities make it plausible that the plan of Stonehenge was influenced by the Breton geometry and astronomy of the rectangle, and the monumentality of the horseshoe. Archaeologically, such associations are well attested.

What remains unclear is the reason for these Breton intrusions. Were there, as Childe speculated, 'megalithic saints', who 'sailed to the coasts of Scotland, Ireland and the remoter isles'.[35] Invasions, immigrations or missionaries are not essential. Brittany and southern England were so close that cults could be transmitted by a few individuals carrying gifts to cousins across the water. Rather than aggression, ideas are likely. With the possibility that the regions shared something of a common language, such cross-Channel links and beliefs are not unlikely.

Stonehenge had been a place of light. The sun had shone there at midsummer, its rays shining between the stones into the heart of the ring. It had been a place of warmth and growth when the year was bright. But later men had turned towards darkness and the midwinter sunset, and the despair of the year when leaves had fallen and there were long, chilled hours of darkness. It was a change from celebration to supplication that life would return.

Tis the yeares midnight, and it is the dayes,
Lucies, who scarce seaven houres herself unmaskes,
The Sunne is spent, and now his flasks
Send forth light squibs, no constant rayes;
The worlds whole sap is shrunke,
The generall balme th'hydroptique earth hath drunk,
Whiether, as to the beds-feet, life is shrunke,
Dead and enterr'd.[36]

> John Donne, 'A Nocturnall upon S. Lucies Day,
> Being the shortest day', Poems, By J.D. with
> Elegies on the Authors Death (1633), pp 187–88.

CHAPTER 10:

THE AVENUE, PORTALS, CARVINGS AND DEATH, c.2400 BC

This figure has a special importance because it can be related to similar figures on standing stones and tombs of the same general period in Brittany. There they seem to represent, in highly simplified form, the mother goddess.
Sir Mortimer Wheeler, *The Times*, 26 February 1958, p. 9.

Positioning the Slaughter Stone

When the final sarsens and bluestones were erect, with the Altar Stone removed from its outdated horseshoe and placed near the centre of the circle, Stonehenge was complete. It was stark in its simplicity. Like a newly built house empty of people, furniture and decorations, it was little more than naked evidence of an astounding architectural achievement.

Enhancement followed. Portal stones were set up at a widened entrance. An earth-banked avenue extended from the circle towards the Cursus. Carvings were ground into some of the sarsens. The Altar Stone became the centrepiece of ritual. From its austere beginnings, Stonehenge was transformed into a ceremonial meeting place for the elite of society.

Today, to the south-west of the Heel Stone, the wrinkled, pock-marked slab of the Slaughter Stone (Stone 95) lies by the entrance, half-buried alongside the end of the bank. Large, long and heavy, comprising 28 tons of elephantine sarsen, its name is pseudo-romantic. So are its legends. Its prostrate condition is confusing.

The stone was not regarded as a sacrificial slab until the late eighteenth century. It might be wondered why it was Stone 95, rather than the Altar Stone (Stone 80) at the heart of Stone-henge, that was selected as the stone of sacrifice. The Altar Stone was unsuitable. Being a dressed, polished block of pale-green sandstone, long and smooth-sided, it was quite unlike the Slaughter Stone, whose rough pits, hollows and crevices offered the impressionable mind gruesomely evocative recep-tacles for gouts of blood before disembowelled corpses were borne to the altar for the final rites.

Towards the end of the eighteenth century, Stukeley's gentle proto-Christian druids of the Age of Reason lost favour.[1] The Age of Romantic Credulity preferred fantasies to philosophy, the macabre to meditation and torture to contemplation. Writers exploited the whimsies. Matthew Lewis – of the much-quoted line, 'The worms crawl in and the worms crawl out' – to the shuddering delight of his readers wrote *The Monk* in 1796, a morbid mixture of murder, outrage, satanism and indecency that became a discreet bestseller. Mary Shelley's *Frankenstein* (1818), with its man-made monster, and Charles Maturin's demonic *Melmoth the Wanderer* (1820) added to the 'gothick' horror stories that landowners read in newly planted 'druidical groves' around genuine prehistoric barrows. Stone circles became centres of sacrifice, thronged with sanguinary priests examining human entrails for auguries of the future.

In *Macbeth* Shakespeare wrote, 'Blood will have blood'.[2] Two centuries later Hanoverian devotees of the macabre were insisting that the druidical past had been dripping with real gore, and that the Slaughter Stone provided it. The sarsen was ideally situated, lying like a butcher's slab at the very entrance to the circle. In 1776 the author of *A Description of Stonehenge* enthused about 'a large stone lying within the entrance of the area, which in all likelihood served by way of a table, upon which the victims were dissected and prepared'. In 1799 Edward King called it 'the slaughtering-stone', a slab 'on which the victims were immolated'. There was worse. 'It is not without reason suspected that they proceeded to even more criminal lengths, and finished their horrid sacrifice with a still more horrid banquet'.[3]

Long before that age of escapist delusion, neither William Camden nor Inigo Jones had given the sarsen a name, the latter merely referring to 'the [four] great stones which made the entrances', locating two of them outside the causeway. His dimensions of 'seven foot broad, three foot thick and twenty foot high' (2.1 x 0.9 x 6.1m) correspond so closely to those of the Slaughter Stone that he must have measured it when it was standing. If it had lain in the ground he would not have known, without digging, that it was 'three foot thick'. He also wrote that the stone was 'twenty foot high', rather than 'long', an obvious indication that it stood. As well as the Slaughter Stone, two adjacent stones, D and E, may have survived for some decades after Jones' observations.[4]

John Aubrey identified the Heel Stone as 'one whereof

(sc. 'w') lieth a good way off, north-eastward from the circu-larish bank'. On his plan he showed the Slaughter Stone but only as a mark, not indicating if it was upright, but 60 years later it certainly was down. 'One at the entrance', wrote Stukeley, is 'a very large stone, at present flat on the ground', perhaps collapsed because of the digging of treasure-hunters or by the 'unfortunate colony of rabbits lately transplanted thither'.[5]

None of this explained why the stone should have been levelled, but it is possible that it stood inconveniently in the way of carters and waggoners coming to plunder Stonehenge of its smaller stones, a practice that dated from medieval times. Hawley discovered that just to the north-west of the Slaughter Stone the causeway had been churned up to a depth of 8in (20cm) by Tudor and Stuart treasure-seekers, perhaps even by Inigo Jones and his companions who dug there, leaving broken glazed platters and glass bottles behind them. John Aubrey noted 'severall pathes worne by Carts' across the bank and ditch.[6]

The Slaughter Stone may have been thrown over to be broken up, surviving only because of its bulk and weight. A line of drill-holes across one corner shows an attempt to break it up, but by 1750 it was safe. Stone-robbing ceased around the mid-eighteenth century, perhaps from a Romantic dread of spectral reprisals.

Excavations by Cunnington and Hawley did not confirm that the Slaughter Stone had stood. They were suggestive, but not conclusive. History helped. Literature and art combined to show that Stone 95 had once been upright. Some 50 years before Jones, around 1568–69, topographical artist Joris Hoefnagel sketched Stonehenge. As mentioned in an earlier chapter, four contemporary half-aerial illustrations of Stone-henge have survived – not Hoefnagel's but that of a friend; a derivative watercolour by William Smith; an engraving dated 1575 by 'R.F.'; and 'an incompetent re-engraving for the 1600 edition of Camden's *Britannia*.'[7]

Of these, two show only the sarsen circle, but both 'R.F.' and the Camden include the Slaughter Stone and its companion. In the 'R.F.' engraving the two sarsens are erect boulders, and in the Camden, 20 years before Inigo Jones, they are drawn as upstanding pillars. Jones' nephew, John Webb, corroborated this. 'He hath described in his Draught two Stones . . . these were the two parallel stones that *stood* [my italics] upon the inside of the Trench, at the Entrance from the North-East'.[8] Close to the circle, and inside the ditch and bank, they were the Slaughter Stone and an adjacent pillar, the now missing Stone E.

It was supposed that the Slaughter Stone had been part of the first phase of Stonehenge, but two C-14 assays from antlers found by Hawley in the hole of Stone E – 1935 ± 40 bc (OxA-4838) and 2045 ± 60 bc (OxA-4837), around 2400 BC – resolved the uncertainty.[9] The Slaughter Stone was a contemporary of the sarsen circle. There is architectural confirmation. As a sarsen whose sides had been dressed with stone mauls, a fact noted by William Cunnington in 1802, it is probable that it belonged to the time of the lintelled ring.

Although a few sarsens had been incorporated in earlier phases of the henge, they had not been shaped. The Heel Stone of Phase I was untouched. So were the Four Stations stones. What patches of tooling they possess, 'could have been done after their original erection; and apart from this tooling they are much more like the Heel Stone, in that they are substantially natural boulders'.[10] The Slaughter Stone was different. The part that had been below ground was rough. Above ground it had been smoothed in the same manner as the other sarsens.

Just to the west of the Slaughter Stone, Hawley came across a very large and deep hole. In it were two antlers. 'No doubt that a large stone once stood in the hole'. The pit is known as 'E', some 3m from Stone 95. Equidistant to the west was a third hole, for a vanished stone named 'D'. Hawley thought the hole had been where the Slaughter Stone had stood.[11] The perceptive Stukeley anticipated Hawley's discovery of Stone E by 200 years. 'There can be no room to doubt but that there was another fellow to it [the Slaughter Stone] . . . and these two made a grand portal'. He could not have known that they were accompanied by Stone D. He also deduced that they had straddled the axis of Stonehenge 'from the altar down thro' the middle of the Avenue', something confirmed by modern excavations and surveys.[12]

There is a puzzle. The three stones were not symmetrically placed to the entrance. D was just over 3m from the west end, but the Slaughter Stone was almost 6m from the east. An absent fourth stone may have balanced the setting. Unfortunately, Hawley did not excavate the area.[13]

There is further speculation. Some 10ft (3m) apart, the Slaughter Stone, D, E and the hypothetical fourth would have been an imposing entrance for processions approaching Stonehenge. Many henges and stone circles had impressive portals – such as Long Meg & Her Daughters, Swinside and Mayburgh in Cumbria; perhaps Arbor Low in the Peak District; and, nearer to Stonehenge, Maumbury Rings in Dorset and Gorsey Bigbury and Priddy South in the Mendips. Four tall pillars at Stonehenge would proclaim the strength of the great circle to every person approaching the monument.

At present, lying where it does against the 'bank', the Slaughter Stone seems to be a fallen portal stone at the edge of the entrance. It is an illusion. The sarsen was never so close. It had been set up at a time when the entrance had been

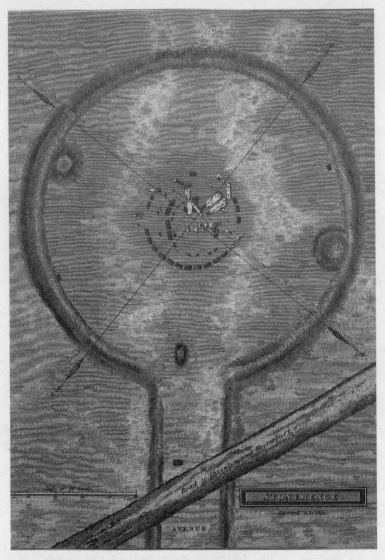

Fig. 27: Philip Crocker's 1810 plan of Stonehenge shows the prostrate Slaughter Stone lying well clear of the bank and ditch at the north-east entrance of Stonehenge. Today it is against them, because the eastern end of the ditch has been backfilled.

widened, part of the easternmost bank having been levelled and thrown into the ditch. When Hawley finished excavating the infilled ditch he left its rubble piled up like a bank that extended to the Slaughter Stone. Possibly he wanted to reproduce the original appearance of the earthwork. But visitors to the ring should visualize Stone 95 as it once was, standing free of the entrance.

Originally the western edge of the causeway had been aligned upon the northernmost rising of the winter moon. Beyond it, the Heel Stone had marked the midpoint of the lunar swing from minor to major rising. Now, with an extended entrance, the axis changed. Men of a new cult tipped basketloads of chalk into the ditch and broadened the entrance to realign the circle. Once about 35ft (11m) wide, the space was about 62ft (19m) across.

The result was drastic. Whereas the axis of the original entrance had a compass-bearing of 46.55°, the new bearing shifted some 4° to 49.90°, almost in line with the Heel Stone and very close to an alignment on the midsummer sunrise. The alignment is long enough to be measured, and its accuracy is good enough to think that it was intended. With stones missing, however, belief is not certainty and reservations remain.[14]

The orientation was not perfect, being only 'where the sun rises, or nearly so, at the summer solstice'.[15] Stukeley was right. The direction was not exact but it sufficed. It converted Stonehenge into a solar monument in which the former sight-line to the moon was reduced to insignificance. There is documentary proof. In 1810, when the enlarged entrance remained intact, a plan was made of Stonehenge 'by the assistance of an able surveyor' and with 'a strict attention to accuracy'. The draught made by Philip Crocker, a former Ordnance surveyor, for Sir Richard Colt Hoare (fig. 27) shows the 59ft (18m) broad space between the banks with the Slaughter Stone lying over 16ft (5m), five long strides, from the south-eastern terminal – far from where it has been supposed to stand.[16]

Avenues at stone circles

The visual effect of the quartet of pillars was made even more dramatic by the construction of a long approach leading uphill towards them. Just outside the entrance, two ditches of an avenue were dug, their chalk used to heap up a pair of inner banks a dozen or so strides apart. Trampled down, rutted by wagons and weathered, their faint lines can still be made out. The Avenue was the first of a series of spectacular settings to awe visitors as they neared the ring.

From Stonehenge the way went straight downhill for a third of a mile. Many years later an extension was added, swinging to the east and then curving southwards towards the river Avon, widening slightly. It was never finished. An excavation in 1973 found proof only of its eastern ditch.

It is quite possible that the first straight stretch of the Avenue was purposely directed towards a stream, ending downslope just above Stonehenge Bottom, some 65ft (20m) below the circle. The association between ritual monuments and water has already been noted. There may have been a winterbourne running in the deep, wide gully. Such intermittent streams, common in chalk landscapes, rise only in winter months. (Similar 'magic' brooks existed nearby, as the villages of Winterbourne Dauntsey, Earls, Gunner, Monkton and Stoke attest.) Even recently people recall water flowing here. The avenues of other stone circles in the region had connections with streams – both the Beckhampton and Kennet at Avebury, and Stanton Drew in Somerset. It may have been only when the Stonehenge Bottom winterbourne became infrequent that men decided to extend the Avenue to the deep, reliable river of the Avon.[17]

A walk today up the slope between the eroded banks towards the Heel Stone and the framework of stones and trilithons gives a thin impression of what the effect must have been more than 4,000 years ago. As with other architectural changes at Stonehenge, the layout of the Avenue from the river was a stage set, designed to bring the past into the present. From the Avon a visitor would see a sequence of ancestral survivals, first only ancient long barrows before the newer round barrows came into sight. As the walk to Stonehenge is described in *Stonehenge Landscapes*:

> Then, quite suddenly, and increasingly quickly, as the last slope is tackled, all is forgotten as the skylined profile of the great monument of Stonehenge fills the view ahead. All that has been seen on the way, all that it symbolized, is now overtaken and replaced by the overwhelming and central experience of the stones themselves.[18]

Unexpectedly, the banks stopped three strides short of the henge's entrance, just where the northernmost row of causeway postholes were. It was as though it were a sacrosanct space.

Like the Slaughter Stone and its partners, the Avenue was a late addition to the sarsen circle. Three radiocarbon assays from the north-west ditch and one from the south-east indicated a period for its construction between 2580 to 1890 BC, perhaps around 2400 to 2300 BC, a time during which many other avenues were being added to stone circles and henges elsewhere in Britain.[19]

In 1719, at the very onset of his fieldwork at Stonehenge, Stukeley was the first antiquarian to recognize the Avenue. Pleased with his discovery, he was surprised that it 'was never observ'd by any who have wrote of it, tho' a very elegant part of it, and very apparent'. 'The two ditches that form'd the outside of it are very visible the whole length'.[20]

He added a further sentence in his manuscript that, strangely, has hardly been discussed in Stonehenge literature. 'There is not one stone left therof, yet a curious eye without difficulty will discern a mark of the holes whence they were taken tho' the ground is so much trod upon'. At a later date and with a thicker quill a heavy line was drawn through the words. Then, after writing 'This magnificent Walk or Entry is made up of two', the words 'rows of stones containing fifty on a side' were deleted.[21]

Stukeley did not always help himself. When his book was published in 1740 he omitted any reference to stones in the Avenue. In a letter of 28 May 1740, his friend Roger Gale rebuked him:

> I think you have omitted a remarkable particular, which is that the avenue up to the chief entrance was formerly planted with great stones, opposite to each other, on the side banks of it, for I well remember we observed the holes where they had been fixt, when you and I surveyed the place.[22]

At least five years before that letter, Stukeley clearly believed that the circle and its unquestionably stone-lined Avenue had been erected long before the Christian era. He and Gale had found the holes. In an independent manuscript, 'The history of the temples of the antient Celts', there was an illuminating, undeleted passage written before 1724. It provides firm evidence of his clear-headed archaeological thinking about those stones. The druids, he said, built Stonehenge. And they had built it before the birth of Christ:

> It may be reckond bold to assert an Avenue at Stonehenge when there is not one Stone left. But I did not invent it, having been able to measure the very intervals of almost every Stone. From the manifest hollows left in their stations and probably they were taken away when Christianity first prevaild here. Millions of Persons have traversed the ground over many times without ever discerning it . . . I am thro'ly convincd of my self: I dont wonder so much at the 99 which are gone as at the poor one remaining.[23]

This is doubly interesting. It reveals Stukeley's pre-Christian thinking about Stonehenge and the druids. It also demonstrates his keen archaeological eye. No previous fieldworker mentioned an avenue of stones. Inigo Jones never drew it. Nor did John Aubrey. Both men had been concerned with visible features inside the earthwork. Both mentioned the very obvious outlying Heel Stone, their silence on any other stone implying that there was nothing else. Vandals had already removed such vulnerable sarsens as those exposed outside the circle.

That the banks had once supported stones is not unlikely. There were counterparts within 40 miles to north, west and south – the Kennet and Beckhampton avenues at Avebury; the two avenues at Stanton Drew; perhaps others at the Dorset rings of Hampton Down, Little Mayne and Rempstone. That one at Stonehenge has been disbelieved may be no more than prejudice.[24]

Prejudice had already questioned the existence of the Beckhampton avenue at Avebury. For part of the nineteenth century and, with few dissenters, throughout the twentieth

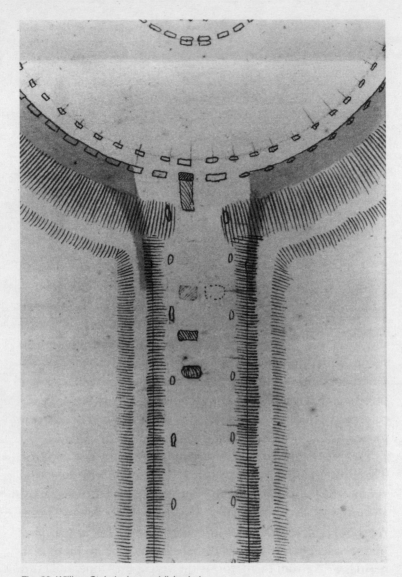

Fig. 28: William Stukeley's unpublished plan
of the Avenue stoneholes, as observed by
Stukeley and Gale in 1719.

century, a majority of scholars such as Rev. W.C. Lukis took it for granted that Stukeley's obsession with having a tail for a landscaped Holy Serpent led him to invent a non-existent Beckhampton avenue. Only a tri-university excavation in 1999 vindicated him, finding stoneholes where he predicted they would be.[25]

At Stonehenge the vandalism of the Middle Ages had not stopped. It continued in Tudor times. Jones recorded only four stones at the earthwork's north-eastern entrance – the Slaughter Stone and its partner, E, just inside the entrance, and the two portals opposite them outside the bank, that 'lie so broken, and ruind by time, that their proportion in height cannot be distinguisht, much lesse exactly measured'. One of them had gone by Aubrey's time.[26]

Aware of the former existence of those portals, it would not have been difficult for Stukeley and Gale to find where they had been. From the disturbed holes that no stone-robber had thought of tidying, Stukeley would know what to look for in the supposed avenue, namely similar faint traces of weathered, overgrown pits from which sarsens had been dragged. Some distance beyond the ring, inside the banks, Gale and he had detected two regularly spaced lines of grass-covered, shallow indentations that led to the entrance.

If, as in other avenues in Britain and Brittany, the stones rose in height towards the entrance, then those farthest down the hill had been not only the smallest but also the most exposed and accessible. Stukeley believed that robbery persisted during the centuries – as the nearby village of Amesbury grew, there was a systematic reduction of the Avenue. 'The Church is mostly raised from them, for tis the very same stone, the Lord of the Mannors house & outhouses in all likelihood partook of the plunder, perhaps the parsonage house & large barns'.[27] Stone after stone was taken, a depredation that stopped only at the very largest of the pillars, the Slaughter Stone. It defied destruction, but even that great sarsen was thrown down and attacked with chisels. It was the only survivor of the ghost-avenue.

Concern that such stones could have been idolatrous may have caused Stukeley's change of mind. He thought that the outlying Heel Stone had been a sacred pillar at which religious visitors bowed before entering the circle, because 'a part of the religious worship in patriarchal times consisted in a solemn adoration, or those silent bowings: the first bowing might be perform'd at this stone'. To have stones lining the holy Avenue might have appeared too similar to the idols set up along the approaches to pagan temples. He eliminated them.

Fig. 29: Bluestones 49 and 31 stand in front of the north-east entrance, through which the Heel Stone can be seen.

In August 1721 he drew a plan of a stone-lined avenue with the prostrate Slaughter Stone, two fallen sarsens, the erect Heel Stone and the outlines of many other stones in two long lines inside the earthen bank. Three years later he rejected them. By

6 June 1724, in another plan, except for the Heel Stone all the sarsens had disappeared.[28]

It is a pleasure to record that after years of dismissal, even derision, Stukeley has been proved correct about the former existence of the Beckhampton at Avebury, and now, arguably, one at Stonehenge. '*Iustitia omnibus*', he might have rejoiced, 'justice for all'.

When the sarsen circle was finished, the high banks and stones of the Avenue barred all but the privileged from the circle. People could look, but they could not see the interior. Stonehenge had become a secret place. Walking towards it along the Avenue, the faded lines of the Cursus behind them, processions moved towards the Heel Stone, crossed the causeway with its looming pillars, and entered the circle. Whether they came for festivals, inaugurations, alliances or funerals, whatever the occasion these would not have been quiet gatherings. There would have been shouting, wails and screams, the blowing of horns, an excitement of noise very different from the seemliness of an audience today.

Inside Stonehenge it was oppressive, almost spartan, but every stone, every height had meaning. Through the wide space between the sarsens, people came to the outer circle of bluestones. It was planned. The two stones at the north-east, 49 and 31 (fig. 29), had been set wider apart than the others and they differed from each other. The peaked Stone 49 on the right was taller and leaner than the broader stone to its left. Like many other paired stones in western Europe the differences had been chosen for effect, perhaps 'male' to the right, 'female' to the left, like the arrangement of men's and women's beds at the Orkney village of Skara Brae.

It may be fanciful to see that contrast repeated in the treatment of the Four Stations stones. From the centre of Stonehenge, looking westwards to Stones 93 and 94, it is

94 on the right that had been encircled by a ditch. Turning to the east and Stones 91 and 92, it is 92 on the right that once stood in the middle of the trench around it. Phallic symbolism or meaningless coincidence? The question is unanswerable. But there was nothing meaningless about the art that had been added to the ring over the years.

The art of Stonehenge

In the Early Bronze Age, groups moving towards the circle would have been aware of carvings on the circle-stones to their left. Over slow centuries as the barrow cemeteries became bigger – but no closer – symbolic messages had been added to the sarsens. Yet despite the attentions of Inigo Jones, John Aubrey, even William Stukeley, it is hardly 50 years since the art was first recognized.

It was about five o'clock in the evening of 10 July 1953, the light being favourable, that Richard Atkinson decided to photograph the most elegant of all Stonehenge's graffiti, the chiselled name on the inner face of trilithon 53 of IOH;LUD;- DEFERRE, an unknown but uneradicated seventeenth-century visitor to the ring. Atkinson recalled later, 'I had the good fortune to notice the prehistoric carvings immediately beneath it'.[29]

'This was no psychic phenomenon but tangible fact', enthused Mortimer Wheeler in The Times.[30] Since 1953 many more carvings have been discovered, the majority depicting axes – 3 being on the outer face of Stone 3, not far from the entrance to the sarsen ring, and 26 on the lower half of Stone 4. Low down on 3 was a very faint trellis or lattice pattern.

Today all these carvings are weathered and barely distinguishable, except in very favourable light, but they are important. They are the only carvings on the outside of the circle and, intentionally, the two stones, 3 and 4, frame the exact east, that part of the horizon where the sun rose twice yearly at the vernal and autumnal equinoxes. Like a Christian cross outside a cathedral, the carvings carried meanings to everyone privileged to see them, like a circle of death standing in the square of the living world.

Without exception the carvings at Stonehenge are on stones in cardinal positions – 3 and 4 at the east, Stone 53 due south, and Stone 57 at the west. Stone 53, the one photographed by Atkinson, had at least 14 axes and what seemed to be a dagger. Doubts were expressed that in reality the 'dagger' might be two superimposed axes, but digitally enhanced images later proved the original interpretation to be correct. What could be another dagger 'or possibly a human figure' was recorded at the far right of the sarsen.[31] The axes and the dagger(s) were British weapons of the Early Bronze Age. The shape of the flanged axes was that of implements of the Arreton Down style; the dagger was a form known at Camerton-Snowshill.[32]

To the west of Stone 53 was trilithon pillar 57. Its art was quite different from the others. High on its inner face, well out of reach from ground-level, was a rectangular carving over 3ft (1m) square. At its top was the outline of a semi-circle. Almost erased by children sliding down the stone before its re-erection in 1958, the carving was akin to the anthropomorphic 'figurines' known in the chambered tombs of Brittany. An even smaller and even more worn version can be seen below it. In 1958 another was found on the fallen lintel 121, just behind 57. Originally it would have been on the underside of the lintel, in between the two uprights, and would have been difficult to make out against the shining of the sky above it.[33]

To be seen properly, all the Stonehenge carvings require favourable light. Crawford recorded how 'Stone 3 went dead soon after 11.10 and Stone 4 was at its best soon afterwards'. The ideal time would be early on a sunny morning. This was as true of the leaning granite pillar known as Le Tiemblage at St Samson-sur-Rance, in northern Brittany. On it is an art gallery of cupmarks, axes and rectangles, but they are invisible except between 11a.m. and midday on a sunlit morning.[34]

It has to be wondered why there are so many carvings. Very few are isolated and some are cramped together, suggesting that they are an accretion made over the years, possibly centuries. As will be seen, the motifs are intimately connected with the dead and it could be that they are records of individual events, of midwinter sunsets, of deaths of leaders, of the inauguration of new chieftains. Archaeology cannot recover the answer. Camden lamented four centuries ago that 'the authors of so noble a monument are thus buried in oblivion'.[35]

What the symbols signify can partly be explained from their origin. The weapons are British. The motifs are not (see Appendix 3). There are three distinct corpora of megalithic art in Britain, Ireland and Brittany. Between their imagery there is little overlap. The spirals of Ireland are uncommon elsewhere. Cup-and-ring marks, profuse in Britain, are rare overseas. The recognizable axes, yokes and daggers of Brittany are seldom found in either Britain or Ireland.[36]

On prehistoric stones and boulders in Britain there are almost 900 carvings, the majority of them being non-representational cup-and-ring markings. Of motifs similar to those at Stonehenge, however, there are only four sites, fewer than 0.5 per cent![37] There were concentric rectangles on a small slab in a cist at Ardross, five miles from Scotland's Cromarty Firth. 'Such a slab could only have been of use for the inmate of the grave'. Axe-carvings exist in two Scottish sites and one in Dorset.[38]

In the Kilmartin cemetery by Loch Fyne in south-west Scotland, two cairns contain such carvings. One, Ri Cruin, was opened in 1870. Of three cists, the central one contained stone. On it was a pattern like the teeth of a garden rake, similar to carvings of hafted axes in Breton tombs such as Gavr'inis and Mané Lud. The western slab of the cist had eight carvings of axes. No bones were found, but the clay lining the grave was dark and sticky, and emitted a 'very close unpleasant smell'. At the far end of the cemetery, the cairn of Nether Largie North also covered a cist in which a body had decomposed. All that was left was a human molar tooth, which 'fell to pieces when it was lifted'. There were two large axe-carvings on the end-slab, and the underside of the capstone was covered in cupmarks and impressions of flat, bronze axes.[39]

Further evidence of a funerary axe-cult came from a round barrow at Badbury in Dorset, 6 miles from Poole harbour and less than 30 from Stonehenge. Before it was ploughed in 1845, a hasty rescue excavation revealed its elaborate construction. Under a chalk capping, a massive sandstone wall surrounded a wide ring of sharp, dark flints. It covered a central cairn of sandstone. (This prehistoric preference for combining different colours and textures was repeated at Stonehenge around the Altar Stone.) Inside the Badbury cairn was a heavy slab. On it were carvings of cupmarks, two bronze daggers with oval pommels and two flat, triangular axes of early Breton type. Research in 1939 concluded that 'The Badbury stone therefore represents an art-style, presumably of magico-religious significance, which has undoubted connexions with, and probably originated in, megalithic carvings such as those of the Breton passage-graves'.[40]

Of all the hundreds of megalithic rings in western Europe there is only one, other than Stonehenge, that has a possible axe-carving. This is the Irish multiple-stone circle of Drombeg in Co. Cork, a ring with a central cremation. The recumbent stone, lying in line with the midwinter sunset, has a debatable outline of a stone axe around a deep cupmark on its upper surface. The circle is not far from the coast.[41]

A comparable ritual site is the spacious *fer-à-cheval* of Er-Lannic North, in southern Brittany. It is partly submerged in the Gulf of Morbihan, and it stands alongside another enormous horseshoe of stones now hidden beneath the sea. Four of Er-Lannic's stones have carvings. Three are of axes – two of stone, one with a full blade. The fourth is like an inverted yoke with a straight line on either side of it.[42] One 'axe' stone stands at the north, the others frame an alignment towards the midsummer sunset.

It can hardly be coincidence that these carvings occur in important cardinal and solar positions. As Drombeg lies in the same area as many Irish wedge-tombs, believed to be derived from the *allées-couvertes* of Brittany, its inclusion does nothing to diminish the idea that the axe-cult at Stonehenge, associated with the sun and with death, was also associated with funerary traditions from Brittany. Drombeg, Er-Lannic and Stonehenge were exceptions. By far the majority of axes were carved on the slabs and capstones of chambered tombs in Brittany, whether Neolithic *dolmens à couloir* or the later *allées-couvertes*. The motifs could be realistic axes with an obvious blade. Others are abbreviations – some in the etiolated shape of an 'f', some even more economically with the crossbar of the blade missing so that they resemble a shepherd's crook. There are also controversial 'weapons' that look like daggers, but this interpretation has been questioned.[43]

Quite frequently in the Breton tombs, the carvings are in

proximity to a domed or rectangular motif. A remarkable example occurs at the Table des Marchands near Locmariaquer. The end-slab bears a large, liberally carved 'buckler' or 'shield', supporting a roof-stone on whose underside a gigantic handled axe has been engraved. The so-called bucklers 'seem to represent an anthropomorphic figure similar to the anthropomorphic *stelae* found free-standing in some of the early passage-graves', such as Gavr'inis, Table des Marchands, and especially Les Pierres-Plates. Some have a pair, even pairs of breasts. There are also necklaces, arms and, at the top, a small 'n' representing the head. Other figures are austere, no more than an outline as severe as a rectangle like those on Stone 57.[44] They can be seen in *dolmens à couloir* and in *allées-couvertes*. In one of the latter, Prajou-Menhir near Lannion, three are associated with axes and apparent daggers.

Whatever the version, its presence in a tomb reaffirms the connection with death of the carvings in Brittany. The most evocative representations exist in the angled passage-tomb or *allée-coudée* of Les Pierres-Plates, by the south coast of the Morbihan. No fewer than eight of the stones in its passage carry sub-rectangular frames, sometimes double or treble, with a central vertical groove forming two panels in which there are breasts. One just beyond the bend in the passage is a big figurine with three concentric outlines, a central dividing line and four breasts in pairs with concentric arcs between them.[45]

It would demand special pleading to deny that the rectangular figurine carved on Stone 57 of Stonehenge was not related to these Breton motifs. This special pleading would become intentional bias if it refused to recognize the additional proof that exists on the sarsen. Just above the left-hand top corner of the rectangle is another carving of a Breton axe, the economy version like Charlie Chaplin's walking-stick – a protective weapon against desecrators.

With its enormous, art-decorated sarsens Stonehenge looked as unmoving as a mountain, an incomparable work of architectural timber, carpenters laughing at masons. There was nothing like it in Brittany. There were bigger menhirs, huge megalithic pillars like Kerloas in Finistère and the jagged monsters at Kerzerho near Carnac. There were the unbelievable 300 or more tons of the colossal Grand Menhir Brisé at Locmariaquer, but there was no monument like Stonehenge.[46]

Its complexity has invited speculation. The 30 uprights of the circle included the diminutive Stone 11 at the precise south. It has been proposed that this architectural anomaly represented the 29½ days of the lunar month, and that the 19 bluestones of the inner horseshoe stood for the years of the moon's cycle from major to minor and return. It is speculation.

Arithmetically it could be argued that the 97ft 6in (29.7m) diameter of the sarsen ring was achieved by the use of a 3ft 3in (0.99m) yardstick, which was converted by a multiple of three into a convenient measuring rod of 9ft 9in (2.97m). From the middle of the circle five rods would have determined the radius of 48ft 9in (14.9m).[47] This is feasible, the system containing as it does persuasive multiples of 3 and 5 (numbers reflected in the 30 sarsens and the 5 trilithons with their 15 stones). It is mathematically interesting, but it is not conclusive. Statistics like these demand confirmation from at least 5, more certainly 10, almost identical sites, as was demonstrated for the moon-orientated recumbent stone circles of Scotland.[48] There are no rings similar to Stonehenge. It is unique.

In its design the circle was impressive, but the architecture was more than prosaically functional, more than a simple huge sarsen edifice. It was a centre of ritual, and the ritual was expressed by the fastidious choice of shapes, textures and colours. Many early societies chose a selection of materials for their ceremonial monuments and burial-places, often in a form that was linked to the sun or moon. Stonehenge was not an exception.

As privileged groups moved towards the innermost, most secret part of the ring, their eyes would have been sensitive to the subtleties of form, materials and shades around them. The combinations were a microcosm of their world. It was not a phenomenon confined to Stonehenge or to Salisbury Plain. Nor was it limited to stone circles. Burial-places contained similar mixtures of local materials, frequently obtained only by effort.

A barrow at Charlton Marshall in Dorset was built of alternating layers of flint and chalk. The empty grave of Huish Champflower in Somerset was covered in thick bands of turf and brushwood. On the Yorkshire Moors a barrow at Saintoft was composed of a variety of sand. Another mound consisted of clean, water-worn pebbles and nodules of half a dozen different varieties of stone from two-and-a-half miles away. A barrow on Wapley Moor contained a thick layer of white sand, thought to have been brought from a distance of seven miles.

In Aberdeenshire, the recumbent stone circle of Easter Aquorthies was polychromatic. All its stones were local granite but those to the east were light pink, to the west dark grey, the flankers light grey, and the recumbent reddish granite attractively streaked and flecked with white quartz. One of the most ruinous of those rings, Balquhain, two miles to the north, had an even wider mixture. Its stones were a medley of colour and shape. The tall outlier of the circle is a distinctive pillar of blotched white quartz with roseate seams. A stone on the east is red granite; the east flanker is a dark, almost black basalt; the 'foreign' recumbent is an attractive white-grained granite while the west flanker is a reddish quartzite.

The custom was widespread in western Europe. The façade of the splendid passage-tomb of Newgrange in Ireland was a startling mixture of black stones and white quartz. Similar contrasts occurred in Brittany. The side-slabs of the burial mound Jardin-aux-Moines, in the mythical forest of Brocéliande, were alternating red schist and white quartz. The Alignements du Moulin near St Just had a tall row of tall, thin grey pillars, opposite one of low, shiningly white quartz boulders.

When Stukeley returned to Stonehenge in July 1723 he discovered, in the Cursus barrow cemetery, comparable contrasts in a round barrow. This was the twin bell Amesbury 44E, that he trenched into more than half-a-mile north-west of the ring. It was not a simple mound. Under the turf was a capping of chalk, then a layer of fine earth, then a band of flints and then more soil, before the burial with its articles of bronze, amber, faience and gold.[49]

The heart of Stonehenge itself consisted of a similar, evocative combination of shapes, colours and carvings. There were tall, thick stones rising high above more slender ones. Colours of grey looked down on blue near green. There were textures of obdurate sarsen, smooth dolerite and delicately grained sandstone. It all had meaning.

The very presence of alien carvings on chosen stones provides two insights. The lesser, because it is obvious, is that the images are evidence of contacts and of a cult from Brittany, already evident in the existence of the bluestone and trilithon horseshoes. More important, these depictions of axes, figurines and an axe-less haft (handle) are indications of a belief in a protectress of the dead. With that comes the likelihood that some ceremonies at Stonehenge were also connected with death. Funerary rites are probable, conducted within the deep heart of the circle.

It is a strange coincidence that the Saxons called the ring 'the hanging stones', as though they were gibbets. It may not have been a coincidence that in much later history a man hanged and 'hung in chains' should be buried at the centre of the ring.[50] In one of his drawings Stukeley showed a gallows with its victim standing conspicuously on the bank of the Wansdyke, not far from Avebury.[51] Such sights were commonplace in his time. At least three names of 'Gallows Hill' survive in Wiltshire to this day. It is possible that some corpse had been cut down and buried inside Stonehenge for superstitious reasons. Folk memories can be long.

Stonehenge was unique, and its stones guarded their secrets. Occasionally there are whispers, murmurs of fact for those who listen. Stone 53 stood to the east of the Altar Stone, Stone 57 to the west. That silent trinity provides an insight into the rites at Stonehenge.

CHAPTER 11:

THE ALTAR STONE, c.2400 BC
ONWARDS

Webster *was much possessed by death And saw the skull
beneath the skin* . . .

T.S. Eliot, 'Whispers of Immortality',
Poems (1920), lines 1–2.

Idiosyncrasy and conjecture

Until 1901, the south-west arc of Stonehenge was chaotic. A
long stone lay in two pieces, half-embedded there near the
middle of the ring. Crushing it was the bulk of a broken top of
a huge trilithon pillar. Against it, also over the long stone, was
another whose far corner covered the side of a fourth tumbled
pillar, the end of which was hidden by the bottom half of the
broken slab.

Adding to the chaos was the partner to the broken sarsen (once the tallest sarsen in Stonehenge), tilted sharply forward and propped heavily on a low standing stone. It was as though giants had been playing pitch-and-toss with sarsens, dolerites and sandstones. The first stone of this disarray, part-buried under the two stones and pressed into the ground, was the Altar Stone (Stone 80). Stukeley wrote: 'Other buildings fall by piece meal, but here a single stone is a ruin, and lies like the haughty carcase of Goliath'.[1]

The Altar Stone was not an altar. Nor was it used for human offerings to the gods. Its disposition is a series of contradictions. Near but not at the middle of Stonehenge, the prostrate stone has everything odd about it. Although it lies across the north-east/south-west axis of the circle, it is nearly 10ft (3m) south of the ring's centre. Nor is it at right-angles to the axis, but skewed $6\frac{1}{2}°$ away from 90°. It is not equidistantly placed across the axis – 8 ft 6in of its length lies to the west, but only 7ft 11in to the east (2.6m, 2.4m). Neither is it level. In his punctilious survey of 1877, Petrie noted that it was tilted, higher to the east by more than 7in (18cm).[2] It is a study in idiosyncrasy.

Everything is arguable about it. How and why was it brought to Stonehenge? Did it once stand? Is it in its original position? Why is it not central to the circle? What was its function? Could it have been one of a pair? Only its fictitious name has remained constant.

An ambiguous sentence in John Aubrey's *Monumenta Britannica* seemed to claim that there had been a partner to the Altar Stone. Aubrey was told by Randal Chaldicot, rector of Bishopstone, a village just east of Aubrey's home at Broad Chalke, that 'Philip, Earle of Pembroke (L[d] Chamberlayne to King Charles I) did say that an Altar-stone was found in the middle of the Area here; and that it was carried away to St. James (Westminster)'.[3]

Thinking that this might have been St James's Palace near London, in 1868 William Cunnington, grandson of Hoare's colleague, wrote to the Clerk of the Works asking if he knew the whereabouts of the exciting stone. 'No such stone now exists there', was the courteous but disappointing reply.[4] Many decades later, G.M. Engleheart thought that 'St James' might be a place much closer than London. He believed that the village of Berwick St James, less than four miles south-west of Stonehenge, could be a likely candidate, a stone being taken there to be laid across a brook. It was common practice. Earlier, John Aubrey had been informed by Mrs Mary Trotman, another inhabitant of Bishopstone, that 'one large stone was taken away to make a Bridge'. This observation was repeated by Stukeley.[5]

In 1933 Engleheart wrote that two sarsens, once forming a footbridge, had been re-erected at the corners of the street through the village. The present writer, having seen the stones, wondered whether they were bluestones rather than sarsens. They were neither. They were Jurassic limestone, not local to Salisbury Plain but unlikely to have been associated with Stonehenge.[6] Their presence, so close to but not associated with Stonehenge, may be further and independent evidence of glaciation.

Re-reading Aubrey's comment about the Earl of Pembroke, where he said that the stone was 'carried away to St. James', it occurred to the writer that the Earl may not have been referring to St James's Palace or to Berwick St James, but to a stone taken for an altar in a Wiltshire church dedicated to St James. There are some 15 of these, alphabetically from Ansty to Tytherington, but the nearest to Stonehenge is at the Domesday village of Berwick St James itself. The old church there, with its Norman tower and doorway (and its early silver chalice now in the British Museum), has a Jacobean communion-rail which could have had a slab, probably one from the horseshoe of bluestones, brought to it during early seventeenth-century renovations. It is possibility, not proof. Whatever the truth, it shows that Aubrey's information did not mean that the Altar Stone had a counterpart.[7]

It was first called the Altar Stone in 1620 by Inigo Jones. He stated that, inside the ring,

> there is a stone appearing not much above the surface of the earth (and lying towards the East) four foot broad, and sixteen foot in length. Which, whether it might be an *Altar* or no, I leave to the judgement of others, because so overwhelmed with the ruines of the Work, that I could make no search after it, but even with much difficulty, took the aforesaid proportion thereof.[8]

It rests on rising land, 5ft (1.5m) above the bench-mark of the Heel Stone that was further down the slope to the north-east. Stukeley described it thus:

> Our altar here is laid toward the upper end of the *adytum* [the inner sanctum of a temple], at present flat upon the ground . . . 'Tis a kind of blue coarse marble, such as comes from Derbyshire, and laid upon tombs in our churches and churchyards . . . This altar is plac'd a little above the focus of the upper end of the ellipsis.[9]

A pale greenish-grey sandstone, the stone is flecked with fragments of mica and garnet grains. It is the largest of the 'foreign' stones, measuring some 16ft long, 3ft 6in wide and about 1ft 9in thick (5m, 1.1m, 0.53m), and weighing over 6 tons. The two fallen sarsens lie on it 'and their weight has probably pressed it down to its present position'.[10] It had been carefully dressed to shape. As usual, the curious Stukeley was perceptive about the sandstone: 'Tis 20 inches thick, a just cubit, and has been squar'd. It lies between the centers, that of the compasses and that of the string: leaving a convenient space quite round it, no doubt, as much as was necessary for their ministration'.[11]

William Cunnington, in a letter to John Britton, remarked that the sides of the stone 'still retain marks of the tools with which it was originally wrought', writing in a second letter, 'Now to return to Stonehenge, I will pledge myself to prove that the altar stone was worked with tools of some kind, also that Mr. King's "Slaughtering Stone" stood erect'.[12]

Investigating the Altar Stone's disposition

In 1958, when trilithon 57–58 was being restored, a small excavation was made around the Altar Stone to determine whether it had ever been intended to stand upright. The north-western end had been battered by treasure-seekers, but originally had been squared off. The other end was more informative. It had been dressed to an 'oblique, bevelled outline, [pointed] very much like the bases of some of the sarsens' to facilitate the erection of the stone.[13]

It is known, of course, that the Altar Stone had once been erect. It had acted as the backsight towards the Heel Stone and the midsummer sunrise, standing at the open mouth of the bluestone semi-circle. When, later, the stones were dismantled the Altar Stone, with its distinctive appearance, was probably re-used to be placed in a special position. It was situated in front of the tallest of the pairs of lintelled sarsens, the Great

Trilithon, 55–56. Whether it stood or lay flat is its most debatable question.

Stukeley believed that it was always flat. 'The trilithon of the upper end of the *adytum* was an extraordinary beauty. But alas through the indiscretion probably, of some body digging there, between them and the altar, the noble impost is dislodge'd from its airy seat, and fallen upon the altar, where its huge bulk lies unfractur'd'.[14] Others disagreed. It is believed that an erect Altar Stone had been pushed to the ground by the fall of trilithon 55 and its lintel, 156, tumbling it askew of the axis.

Trilithon 55, now broken in two halfway along its length, had always been unstable. Faulty construction caused the collapse. As explained in earlier chapters, it was paired with Stone 56 – 50 tons of sarsen, at almost 30ft long (9m) with over 8ft (2.5m) of its length in its stonehole. The 10 tons lighter Stone 55, at only 24ft long (7.3m), only had a mere 4ft (1.2m) in the ground. To counteract the instability its base had been shaped into a club-foot, 'a large projecting foot left in working, to go under ground'.[15] When 55 inevitably fell, its partner, 56, was pulled out of true, and leaned more and more precariously until straightened by Gowland in 1901. The collapse of the trilithon is unquestioned. Whether it knocked over an upright Altar Stone or simply collapsed onto a supine stone has been debated ever since.

The disaster occurred centuries, perhaps millennia ago. A sketch of AD 1575 showed Stone 55 lying on the ground. The trilithon could have collapsed in prehistoric times. Roman coins, including *sestertii* of Antonia (36 BC–AD 37) and Emperor Commodus (AD 161–192), were found in Gowland's 1901 excavation 'only in the superficial layers' near the trilithon, not under the fallen, broken sarsen.[16]

Many Stonehenge students favoured a standing Altar Stone – Charleton (1663), pp 32, 52, and, much later, Hawkins (1966), p. 56; Atkinson (1979), p. 57; Richards (1991), p. 61; Castleden (1993), p. 135; Cleal et al. (1995), p. 268; North (1996), pp 460–61; Souden (1997), p. 39; Ruggles (1997), p. 218; Burl (1999), pp 195–97; and Chippindale (2004), p. 271. Charleton was convinced that Stonehenge was a Danish monument, and argued that the Altar Stone, although 'now lying along and broken', was 'at first set upright', and was a *Kongstolen* or throne 'for the king to stand upon, and shew himself to the people, at the time of his Inauguration'. He was wrong. The others cited form an honourable list. So do their opponents. It is interesting to see how widespread the belief in a supine Altar Stone was amongst early antiquaries – Jones (1655), p. 57; Stukeley (1740), p. 28; Wood (1747), p. 54; and Smith (1771), End, plate 3. In the nineteenth century, authors include Long (1876), p. 54; Fergusson (1872), p. 93; Petrie (1880), p. 18; Stevens (1882), p. 95; Barclay (1895), p. 4, plate II. Later still to be added are Stone (1924), p. 19; Cunnington (1935), pp 16–18; Stevens (1936), p. 14; Niel (1975), p. 50; and Freeman (1998), p. 7.

Recent opinion has favoured an erect stone. Popularity, however, may not equate with reality.[17] Stone circles with internal standing stones are rare in the south of England. There are a couple in Cornwall, and two dubious ones at the destroyed Wiltshire rings of Tisbury and Winterbourne Bassett. It is an insignificant minority, at the most 4 of almost 150 rings in the counties of Cornwall, Devon, Dorset, Somerset and Wiltshire. Stonehenge is unlikely to be added to the brief list.[18]

Writing in 1924, E.H. Stone was sure that the stone had never stood:

Some persons have supposed that this stone once stood upright. There is, however, nothing to support such a theory, and all the evidence which can be gained from an examination of the stone itself and from a consideration of its position indicates that it was placed where it now lies as forming part of the original design of the structure [and] would have an obvious use as a dais or platform.[19] It should be added that, from the centre of Stonehenge, an upright Altar Stone 12ft (3.7m) high would have hidden the 8ft (2.3m) tall bluestone 67 behind it, utterly spoiling the visual effect of the carefully graded heights of the bluestone horseshoe of which 67 was the apex.

There have also been practical experiments to test whether the Altar was ever upright. Fernand Niel believed the block had always lain flat:

Wishing to determine this more precisely, I reproduced the fall of the Great Trilithon by means of a scale model. The Altar Stone in the model was displaced in the way described above [slightly shifted from the horizontal by Stone 55's collapse]. It is therefore quite likely that it originally had a symmetrical position in relation to the axis. It would be rather surprising if it had not.

In 1998, Freeman agreed.[20] Elsewhere in Wiltshire, archaeological features lying across the axis of a monument are not unknown. R.H. Cunnington, the great-great-grandson of William Cunnington (who excavated at the Altar Stone in 1802), remarked that at Woodhenge the shallow grave of a child had been dug 'in precisely the same relative position as the Altar Stone at Stonehenge. It lies across the axis and at right-angles to it and halfway between the centre and the circumference of the inner ring'.[21]

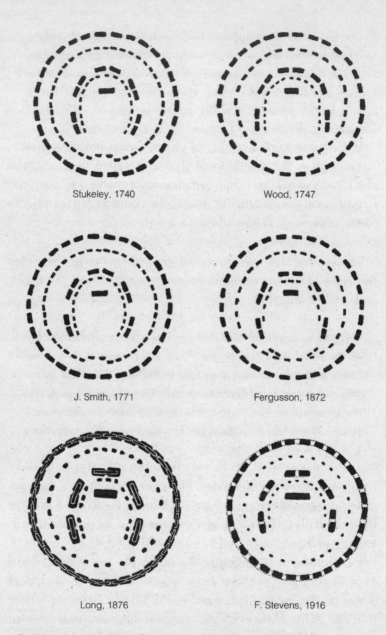

Stukeley, 1740

Wood, 1747

J. Smith, 1771

Fergusson, 1872

Long, 1876

F. Stevens, 1916

Fig. 30: Antiquarian plans of Stonehenge, showing a prone Altar Stone.

For the truth about the Altar Stone, the choices are simple. Originally it had either been upright or it had been supine. For the first alternative there are three possibilities – that it had fallen of its own accord, that it had been pushed over in Roman times or in the Middle Ages before 1575, or that it was flung down by Stone 55.

If the Altar Stone had simply fallen, then it probably would have been in the direction of its ramp where the disturbed chalk was weakest. This remains unprovable because the hypothetical ramp and pit would be concealed beneath the stone itself, with the bulk of Stone 55b on top of it. If it *had* fallen, however, then of its original 16ft (4.9m) length, about 4ft (1.2m) would have been in its hole, meaning that the pillar would have had to 'kick' back a further 4ft (1.2m) to account for 8ft (2.4m) of the stone to be east of the axis. It is possible but unlikely, because no force except gravity had been applied. The likelihood is that the pillar would have tumbled with its base over or just a little to the east of its damaged pit. It should also be recalled that, although far from conclusive, Stukeley had burrowed under the Altar Stone in search of its hole but found only 'perfect solid chalk, that had never been stir'd'.[22]

There is a second objection. The chances of the stone being so neatly disposed at nearly 90° from the axis are statistically highly improbable, the odds being in the region of 165:1 against, when allowing for its slight $6\frac{1}{2}°$ diversion from the right-angle. If its position had not mattered it could have lain anywhere between 1° to 181° and 179° to 359°.

For Roman or medieval interference, the same objection is as cogent. Had Romans intended to destroy a centre of druidical resistance, they would have smashed the sandstone into fragments. If medieval thieves had uprooted it, then once the stone was out of its hole there was nothing to prevent them dragging it away, as had happened to so many bluestones and lintels before 1575.

For the third theory, that an upright Altar Stone had been slammed down by Stone 55, then Niel and Freeman are probably correct that the stone could never have been thrust into its present position by the fall of the trilithon. Mechanically it would have been almost impossible for that to have occurred. Three stones – 55b, lintel 156 and bluestone 67 – are the keys. A likely sequence would begin with Stone 55, standing precariously in its insecure pit on the south-western weather side of Stonehenge, exposed to heavy gusts and gales beating in across the unprotected Plain. The stone would begin to shift. At a critical angle of tilt its lintel would slip out of 55's peg. Then, still held temporarily by the peg of 56, it would swing anti-clockwise downwards, tugging 56 out of the vertical, smashing into bluestone 67 which would be hurled to the west (explaining why it now lies at an angle). Finally, the free-falling lintel would drop onto the end of 67 and across the western edge of the Altar Stone.

The tons of 55 had already fallen almost directly forward, breaking in two and hitting the Altar Stone which, if standing, would have been forced forward towards the centre of the circle. It could never have been edged so far to its left that it fell so nearly at right-angles across the axis, as it does today. Nor could it have been shifted after the catastrophe. Logic demands that it was prone, lying flat perhaps as a symbolic 'doorway' or 'entrance', with bluestone 67 rising in front of it, its top forming the bottom of a 'window' through the gap between the trilithon where the midwinter setting sun would shine across the circle between the sarsens at the entrance and up to the Heel Stone and its companion.

Speculation becomes near-reality by the knowledge that there were supine stones in similar cross-axial situations in two other ritual monuments in Wessex – the Sanctuary near Avebury and Woodhenge near Stonehenge. By coincidence, both were excavated by Maud Cunnington.

At the Sanctuary a 6ft (1.8m) long but only 2ft (60cm) deep near-central stonehole was found at the SSW between the two outer rings of postholes.[23] It is an insight made even more relevant to the Altar Stone by the existence of a comparable stonehole at Woodhenge, less than two miles from Stonehenge. Like its counterpart at the Sanctuary, it lay between the two outer rings of postholes. The shallow 6ft 6in (2m) long hollow lay east-west. The sarsen that had been there was later broken up.[24]

The probable explanation for the eccentric position of the Altar Stone was that, by design, it separated a third of the circle from the rest of Stonehenge. To reach that sanctum was akin to passing through a cathedral to reach the Lady Chapel and its mysteries. The Altar Stone formed a 'cell' that was made special by the grandeur of its high bluestones and towering trilithons, by its chosen association with the midwinter sunset, and by the presence of the only art inside Stonehenge.[25]

The six concentric rings of posts at Durrington Walls would have been difficult to reproduce at Stonehenge. Timber was plentiful on Salisbury Plain. Stone was scarce. Yet the stone circle contained artistic and ritualistic triumph of a different kind. Stonehenge did not possess six rings but it did have four; the sarsen circle, the bluestone circle, the sarsen horseshoe and the bluestone horseshoe. It also had a discrimination not available in wood – the selection and arrangement of three types of stone (sarsen, bluestone and sandstone), distinctive in their colours and textures. It was not megalithic wallpaper. The stones, the colours and the arrangement formed the essence of Stonehenge itself.

Even in ruin and with stones removed, it is possible to see
how carefully the area had been designed (fig. 31). Directly in
front of the Altar stood the tallest bluestone, 67, and behind it
was the Great Trilithon. These were gigantic but plain stones.
To their left and right were subtleties.

To the left (south) of the Altar Stone was trilithon 53–54.
There were carvings on Stone 53 but a bluestone, now missing,
would have hidden any decoration on the left-hand side of the
sarsen's inner face. There was none. The famous dagger and a
dozen or more axes were ground and pecked out on the far side
of Stone 53, to the right of the obscuring bluestone, leaving them
in full view of anyone standing at the Altar Stone. To the right
(west) of the Altar Stone there were carvings of a figurine and the

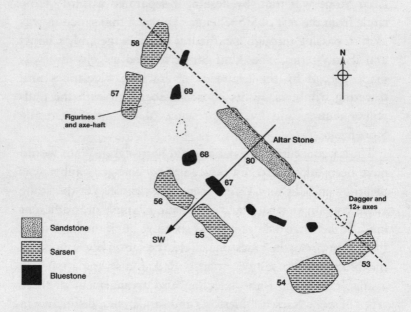

Fig. 31: The Altar Stone area, showing stone
types and positions of carvings c.2400 BC.

haft of an axe on Stone 57, the left-hand sarsen of trilithon 57–58. Bluestone 69 and a lost one between it and 68 concealed the right-hand side of 57. The carvings, however, could be seen head-high to the left above the bluestones, placed, like Stone 53, where they would be visible from the Altar Stone.

Today the carvings are without life, dull and flat, just weatherworn representations, little more than moribund graffiti to the modern mind. Not then. Their people did not see them like that. And it is still just possible to see what they saw (fig. 32).

Years ago I visited the decorated palaeolithic cave of Les Combarelles near Les Eyzies in the Dordogne. In those un-commercial times it had no electricity. One was led through the blackness by a guide with an acetylene lamp. The cave had few paintings but a multitude of carvings, deeply cut figures of reindeer, mammoths and bison, and the effect was like an animated magic lantern show. In the semi-gloom the lamplight flickered over the engraved outlines of creatures that appeared, moved, vanished. '*Ici le dos*', '*ici le nez*', '*les yeux*' – the animals were for a moment reborn, features and images appearing briefly. This is how palaeolithic people saw them. In the midwinter sunset at Stonehenge, the carvings of axes and the figurines would have emerged in the wavering flames of torches, coming briefly into life before the night reclaimed them.[26]

'Bare ruined choirs' wrote Shakespeare in 'Sonnet 73', and it is true of Stonehenge, its meaning as nearly erased as church medieval wall-paintings, where the bright colours and sermons of the sickle-bearing skeleton of Death have been obliterated by puritanical iconoclasts and nineteenth-century plaster. At Stonehenge, human vandals were unnecessary. Time and weather were the destroyers.

Fig. 32: Trilithon 57, in a supine position,
with its carved figurine and 'axe'.

But fragments of glory remain. The Altar Stone is still there,
lying close to where it was placed before the collapse of Stone
55 disturbed it. Bluestone 67 can be seen under the lintel that
once rested high on the top of the Great Trilithon. Trilithon 56
was straightened and set in concrete in 1901. Its companion, as
fragments 55a and 55b, is down, broken.

It demands vision to recreate the scene, re-erecting the
trilithon and the bluestone, and having the Altar Stone lying
across the axis of Stonehenge in front of them. The wreckage
has been so harsh that imagination is demanded. Imagination

can be persuasive even when proof is absent. There must have been ceremonies, processions along the stone-lined avenue, inaugurations, the exchange of gifts, weapons and gold, of daughters in marriage from leaders overseas. There must have been seasonal festivals to mark the important times of the year, such as early February when ewes came into milk; the beginning of May and the first grazing of pasture by cattle; August and the harvest. Worst were the nights at the end of October, when it was the turning point of the year and the barrier between the world of the living and the limbo of the dead vanished, and vicious, vengeful spirits moved through the darkness of night.

There were midsummer dawns when the sun rose by the edge of the Heel Stone. At midwinter there would have been the burning, shivering flames of torches when the dying sun and year sank and disappeared behind the Great Trilithon. It was the dramatic climax of the year.

The effect was calculated by the position of the adjacent stones. Behind the Altar Stone the tallest of the bluestones, 67, stood 8ft (2.4m) high, blocking the lower part of the narrow gap between sarsens 55 and 56 of the Great Trilithon. A 3ft (1m) wide 'window', like an inverted triangle, had been fashioned there above the top of the bluestone. It was behind that aperture that the setting midwinter sun would pass. Momentarily. At the latitude of Stonehenge the late December sun would move across five miles of the skyline during the eight short hours of the day. As it sank towards its setting it would pass across the 'window'. From its first glimpse at the left to its final glinting at the right, it would have been seen for no more than four or five but intense seconds, the ending and death of the year.[27]

Imagination can bring dead bodies to be laid on the Altar Stone, mourners huddled in the cramped secrecies there, the corpse carried southwards to the small entrance and to the barrow that had been prepared for it. Imagination can persuade. Proof is absent. But, as so often, William Stukeley half-antici-pated this by several centuries. His drawing of 6 June 1724, *A peep into the Sanctum Sanctorum*, shown as the frontispiece of this book, depicts that powerful scene perfectly.[28]

CHAPTER 12:

THE ARCHER AND BEYOND, c.2300 BC

Beaker burials at Stonehenge and Boscombe Down

For several centuries, groups of people making Beaker pottery had been drifting into Britain from the continental mainland. There is no evidence that they were welcomed. Beaker graves with early forms of the ware such as the 'European' style were never buried in the native cemeteries around Stonehenge.

To the contrary, the incomers kept away from those. There is a remote barrow near the east end of the Cursus, and two near, but not in, the Lake group. Even a century or two later, with arguably the finest of beakers – those known as Wessex-Middle Rhine – there was little change. Amongst the almost 400 barrows (bowls, bells and discs) in the four great parishes within a mile-and-a-half of Stonehenge (Amesbury, Durrington, Wilsford and Winterbourne Stoke), only four barrows

contained those pots, even though the style endured several
centuries from 2450 to 2000 BC. What integration there was
came slowly, if at all.[1]

There is, however, evidence of hostility. In 1978, while re-
cutting a trench west of Stonehenge's north-east entrance,
archaeologists unearthed the skeleton of a young man. His
'grave' was a crudely dug pit, and in it his corpse had been
laid on its back with the right arm across the chest. He had
been healthy, about 25 to 30 years of age, although a slight
deformation of the spine had given him a rather twisted
posture. He had been somewhat bow-legged, and the wear-
ing-down of some of his ankle-bones showed that, like
many of his contemporaries, he had been accustomed to
squatting rather than sitting when eating or talking with
friends.

There was a dark slate wristguard on his arm (to protect the
arm from the lash of a bowstring). Three broken flint arrowheads lay by his skeleton. When the bones were cleaned, the
tips of the arrows were seen embedded in the man's ribs. They
had been fired at short range, one from the right into the chest,
another into the side and a third from behind to the left,
penetrating the heart and killing the man instantly.[2] He may
have been a stranger who had offended by breaking some
taboo. Antagonism between newcomers and natives may have
been the cause of his death; local people angry at a desecration
of their sanctuary. Two of the killing arrows were not a Beaker
form (the Green Low type, with a tang longer than its barbs)
but the native Conygar style of barb and tangs, equal in length,
and it is possible to imagine an unexpected encounter, a
panicking flight, the death and the burial in the earthwork
ditch as an offering to the circle.

It is known that he had been killed in the Early Bronze Age.
Five radiocarbon assays from his bones provided an upper and

lower range of calibrated dates for his death.[3] The median of those dates indicated that he died around 2300 BC.

It was a time when the sarsen circle of Stonehenge had been standing for a century or more. Perhaps not by coincidence, 2300 BC is also very close to the 'date' for the Beaker skeleton of a man in a timber-lined grave on Boscombe Down, east of Amesbury. The Stonehenge Archer, as he has mistakenly been called (as well as, fancifully, the 'King of Stonehenge'), was not the most prepossessing of human beings.

Young middle-aged, 30 to 35 years of age, stocky, about 5ft 8in (1.7m) tall, he was partly crippled, ungainly in his walk. In spite of the riches left with his body, the body itself had been repellent. He had suffered from a severe and very painful dental abscess. His breath would have stunk. For some horrifying reason, when he was a full-grown adult his left kneecap had been agonizingly cut off. The leg became infected, the bones of his lower leg eroded, the wound suppurated and reeked. 'People would have been able to pick him up downwind', observed a pathologist. The leg never recovered. It would not flex, leaving him with an awkward gait.

What distinguished his burial, under its small round barrow, was not his physique but the objects left with him. By his head were the cremated remains of three young children. There were also the intrusive bones of two more children, a youth and two grown men. With the burial there were weapons and two sandstone wristguards, one dark, one red. There were fifteeen barbed-and-tanged flint arrowheads and three tanged copper knives, all different, all continental (one of Spanish metal).

The number five (or a multiple of it for Beaker arrows) was known elsewhere. Five, ten, even fifteen frequently lay with burials in Germany. John Mortimer found five at the Callis Wold 100 barrow near Pocklington in Yorkshire. With them were traces of a possible bow. Five seems to have been chosen as a convenient amount for quivers, and is an indication of elementary numeracy among these societies. Despite Callis Wold, however, five arrowheads with a burial are unknown elsewhere in Britain where one, three and even seven are common. The fifteen with the Archer may be an indication of his foreign origins.[4]

There were also ornaments – a shale bead from Kimmeridge in Dorset; a bone pin, probably for a cloak; and two delicate gold 'basket ear-rings' that are now thought to be tresses for the hair. They are rare in Britain. There were five beakers. One was an All-Over-Corded vessel, almost useless for dating as the style endured unchanging for 500 years. Two other beakers had been impressed with plaited cord, also uncommon in Britain but well-known on the continent.

And there were tools, including a collection of flints, some broken, some in mint condition; a spatula of red deer bone; a black 'cushion' stone used for metalworking; and four boars' tusks, which in Europe were frequently found with a smith's equipment. The lavish collection of archery, ornaments, tools and pots made the burial look like the funeral of a king of the gypsies, a rich collection of offerings to the dead man by his followers.

Close to his grave was another, containing the skeleton of a 25- to 30- year-old man. He also had a pair of golden hair tresses, a boar's tusk and a cord-plaited beaker. During his lifetime his left thighbone had been broken. Physical abnormalities indicated that he had been related to the Archer. Both men had unusually articulated skulls, and both had bones fused together at the back of the heel, the *calcaneum* and the *navicular* – morphologically an exceptional trait and, presumably, a family trait. What the men's relationship was is unclear. Father and son is unlikely, but brothers, cousins? From the evidence of their teeth the older man had once lived close to the Alps, whereas his relative came from southern England.

Radiocarbon assays revealed that they had lived at some period between 2400 and 2200 BC.[5]

There is a whimsical classical coincidence. Their injured legs may have caused them to limp, the Archer certainly, the other man perhaps. The indications of a connection with metalworking creates an unlikely relationship with the Olympian deity, Hephaestos of Greek mythology (called Vulcan by the Romans), who was god of the forge and smiths. Legend has it that he limped.

Less speculatively, a third Beaker grave was found on Boscombe Down half a mile from the others. It contained the remains of four adults and two children.[6] They were not local. Analysis of the men's teeth revealed a very high proportion of the Strontium isotope, indicating a source with a strong radioactive environment. In the British Isles, this occurs in Cornwall, the Isle of Man, north-west England, the Scottish Highlands and Wales. The oxygen isotopes caused by people drinking water eliminates three (Cornwall and the Isle of Man as too warm, Scotland too cold). The only acceptable parts of Britain are the Lake District, and north and south-west Wales.

Before over-enthusiasm persuades believers that this proves that such men brought the bluestones from the Preselis, there must be a realistic reminder that the stones, whether arriving by glaciation or human transportation, were on Salisbury Plain some four centuries earlier than the burials in the mass grave. Worse, the Welsh origin for the burials is probably mistaken. The writer has been reliably informed by two independent authorities that the isotopes indicate that the people more probably came from Brittany.[7]

Returning to the Archer, his nickname of the 'King of Stonehenge' is misapplied. The three burials were all found on Boscombe Down, far outside the exclusion zone of the native cemeteries and three long miles from Stonehenge. This was an age when the only transport was by foot, and it would have been an hour's walk with the additional barrier of the river Avon separating the incomers from the ring. Beaker communities and the sarsen circle were separate entities.

The cult of the sun continued. In barrow after barrow the body lay with its head to the north, a direction only obtained by finding the midpoint between the sun's north-east rising and north-west setting at midsummer (table 6).

Period	North	NE	East	SE	South	SW	West	NW
Early–mid Beaker	5	0	2	1	2	0	0	0
Late Beaker	5	1	0	1	0	0	0	0
Early Bronze Age (Wessex I)	3	2	0	1	0	0	0	0
Early Bronze Age (Wessex II)	3	1	3	1	1	0	2	0
TOTAL	16	4	5	4	3	0	2	0

Table 6: Orientations of skulls in the round barrows near Stonehenge.

The passing of a millennium

For a long, drawn-out thousand years, Stonehenge decayed in neglect. Perhaps during that period the Great Trilithon collapsed. A thousand years is easily mentioned but it would take the present far back into the past – back through two World Wars, a deadly outbreak of influenza, the Boer War, an epidemic of cholera, the investigations of Cunnington and Hoare, the Napoleonic Wars, the Jacobite Risings, William Stukeley, the Great Plague, John Aubrey, the Civil War, the Wars of the Roses, the Hundred Years War, the Black Death, Geoffrey of Monmouth and Henry of Huntingdon, the Norman Conquest, as far back in time to the century when Ethelred, King of England, was paying unsuccessful bribes of Danegeld into the ever-deeper purses of Danish raiders. A thousand years is a very long time.

Over the millennium of Stonehenge's negelect, taboos waned. The centuries-old half-mile void around Stonehenge was infringed. Amesbury 11 – a fine bell barrow with a cremation, a Bronze Age urn and bone tweezers ('well made and perfect') – was built within 120yd (110m) of Stonehenge (fig. 33). Only the tweezers survive.[8]

There was a half-hearted attempt to enhance a tumbledown ring. In 1923 Hawley and Newall located two very irregular rings of pits that had been dug outside the circle. Known as the Y and Z Holes, the innermost group, Z, was about 12ft (3.7m) outside the sarsens and the Y Holes a further 24ft (7.3m) away, but the so-called 'circles' could deviate by as much as 4ft (1.2m) and 8ft (2.4m) respectively. Temporarily 'distinguishing these holes by lettering', Hawley and Newall's identification has been retained for more than 80 years.

Fig. 33: View of bell barrow Amesbury 11, a late round barrow, with Stonehenge to the left.

Numbered clockwise from the north-east entrance, the intention may have been to have 30 pits in each ring to correspond with the number of sarsens in the outer circle, but the project was never completed. For some reason the work began at the SSE outside Stone 9 with the digging of Z9 and Y9. With no possibility of a helpful marking-out rope, because of the obstructive sarsens, the rings of pits became ever more erratic and the workers gave up. The last hole of the outer ring, Y7, was only half-dug. Z8 was not even begun, perhaps because Stone 8 and its lintel had already fallen over the intended spot.

There was a motley of finds in the holes that had never been created to hold stones. There was some poorly fired Deverel-Rimbury ware of the Middle Bronze Age, pieces of bluestone and rhyolite, a human tooth, as well as Romano-British pottery and other later material. Yet there were still murmurs of old beliefs. The holes near the north-eastern entrance received traditional deposits. Y30 had two antler-picks and three complete antlers at its bottom. Z29 contained another antler. Four radiocarbon dates (three from Y30, one from Z1) were converted into their probable true upper and lower ranges, averaging around 1725 BC.[9]

There followed a long period of social stagnation. It has been suggested that there may have been an outbreak of plague, possibly widespread across Europe where there are other signs of collapse and disturbance as far away as Greece and the Aegean. Perhaps not by coincidence the population of Britain, having been increasing steadily up to 1300 BC, diminished sharply the next century or two, and by the end of the millennium had been halved. Recovery was slow.[10]

Who the architect of Stonehenge was will remain unknown forever – man or woman, many people, a succession of planners, British or Breton. There is no identity, just anonymity.

What can be stated unequivocally was that the long-forgotten genius was not the Stonehenge Archer nor the well-built man in Bush Barrow, with his daggers, bronze axe and luxurious gold possessions. Both were too late.

In his *Hydriotaphia, or Urne Buriall* of 1658, philosophizing over burnt bones from the pagan Anglo-Saxon cemetery at Walsingham in Norfolk, Sir Thomas Browne wrote:

> What song the *Syrens* sang, or what name *Achilles* assumed when he hid himself among women, though puzzling Questions, are not beyond all conjecture . . . But who were the proprietaries of these bones, or what bodies these ashes made up, were a question beyond Antiquairism, not to be resolved by man.[11]

It is to be wondered what obsessive urge compelled Stonehenge's designer and the labourers who struggled with something at the very horizons of their abilities to create such a monster. It may have been no more than a determination to erect a megalithic impossibility that would astonish from that time to ours.

It could have been arrogance, a compulsion to outdo the gigantic menhirs the person had seen in Brittany. Near Carnac there were the astounding rows of Kerzerho. A line detached from the others had some jaggedly rough pillars wrenched from the living rock. They tower above humans, vast, crude blocks high as a house. Nearer to Britain was the stupendous stone at Kerloas near Brest, a hundred tons of granite dragged from its source a mile-and-a-half away and hauled up a slope to stand 33ft (10m) high at the crest of the hillside.

These were colossi, but even they were dwarfed by the prostrate Grand Menhir Brisé at Locmariaquer. Weighing at least 300 granite tons it probably collapsed and broke during the futile endeavour to erect it, and today it lies in four shattered fragments, testimony to people's ambition exceeding their ability. Resolved to set up a stone beyond all others he had the mountainous slab dragged from Kerdaniel over two miles away.[12]

Men did succeed in the erection of Stonehenge, and inside its British circle they included two horseshoes in respectful imitation of the *fers-à-cheval* in Brittany. For a time, the long stone-lined avenue, the portals, the solar tunnel from the Heel Stone, the great sarsen circle, the 'male' and 'female' stones, the carvings, the sanctum of the Altar Stone concealed between the sarsen and bluestone horseshoes, and the Great Trilithon and its window to the midwinter sunset stood as a triumphant declaration of man's genius and piety.

It did not endure.

Through the indifference of men, Stonehenge mouldered year by year, becoming frailer in the snows and rains. Freezing earth loosened the holes in which the sarsens stood. Winds blowing in from the south-west imperceptibly but steadily shifted some uprights from the perpendicular. Even a steady breeze exerted a quivering push on an exposed surface, and a sudden winter blast, howling across the Plain at a hundred destructive miles an hour, would smash against a pillar of the Great Trilithon as heavily as a 3-ton hammer-blow. It was man's neglect and God's effect that toppled many of the sarsens.

Today, all that is left is the wreckage, changing with every colour of the day, shadows of clouds drifting darkly across the stones like the wraiths of people who once walked there. In summer wild flowers grow inside the ring, and the sarsens glitter and glow goldenly as though eternity had its home there, caught in an everlasting circle of sunlight. Then death returns. In 1900 Florence Antrobus wrote:

To my mind the magic of Stonehenge is never more powerfully felt than during the wild tempestuous autumnal gales that usually sweep across the Plain in October . . . Thoughts rise suddenly of the many tragedies, feasts, sacrifices, mysterious rites that must have been enacted here in far-off, bygone days.[13]

Those days are finished. The people have gone. The ring is a broken cage around which sightseers wander as though in an empty zoo. It stands outlined against the sunset like the bared ribs of a galleon shipwrecked on the shores of Time.

When Stonehenge entered history is not entirely conjectural. It was not in the late fourth century BC, when the explorer Pytheas circumnavigated Britain. His allusion to a 'spherical temple' where the moon appeared to move along the rim of the skyline could not have referred to Stonehenge as it was too far south in Britain for that lunar phenomenon. Nor did the Romans record its existence. The ring does not appear in the writings of Caesar or Tacitus, and the Romano-British people who visited the curiosity lost articles and enjoyed picnics there, but wrote no existing letter about it.

Stonehenge became history when settled Saxons were farming on Salisbury Plain, especially around Amesbury (Ambres-byrig, 'Ambre's *burh*'). The name of that town is first recorded around AD 880. It began before then, probably around AD 700. Saxon burials were inserted into at least three prehistoric barrows in the neighbourhood.[14] It may have been at that time that the hybrid word *stan-hencgen* developed, describing the lintelled sarsens that looked like 'hanging-frames of stone'. By then what the circle had been called by its builders had been forgotten for almost 2,000 years.

There is a final irony. In cars, caravans and coaches people drive into the parking-area at Stonehenge. They alight, pass through the turnstile, go to the stones. Preoccupied with the desolation of the monstrous sarsens, few notice the unobtrusive, neglected slabs that commemorate the Aubrey Holes. Even fewer wonder at the stump and the fallen pillar that are the remains of the once impressive Four Stations. Finally, visitors return to their vehicles, put away cameras and souvenirs and drive onto the busy A360.

The irony is that, whether pedestrian, motorist or one of a coach party, most have been completely unaware of the one reason why Stonehenge stands where it does, even though the evidence lies conspicuously close to where coaches are parked. On the ground is a line of four large, white-painted rings, indicating the position of a tree and three high posts of pine that were erected in the Middle Stone Age, 10,000 years ago. Probably carved, perhaps painted, the posts were aligned on a tree that may have been a sacred totem. The four were in a neat east-west row 120ft (37m) long, some 820ft (250m) northwest of where Stonehenge would stand.

That row, so remote in time, so overlooked, established the sanctity of an area that has endured for almost 500 generations.

APPENDIX I:

ANCIENT WORDS ALONG THE ATLANTIC FRINGE

With very few exceptions, Breton, Cornish and Welsh words appear not to be derived from French, German or Latin. However, it is clear that they share the same origin, as can be seen in the charts below.[1]

English	German	French	Latin	Breton	Cornish	Welsh
ice	eis	glace	glacies	rew	skorn	rhew
rain	regen	pluviale	pluvial	glao	glaw	glaw
river	fluß	rivière	flumen	aven	avon	afon
sleep	schlaf	sommeil	somnus	kousked	cusca	cysgu
small	klein	petit	parvus	bihan	byghan	bychan
stone	stein	pierre	lapis	men	maen	maen
sun	sonne	soleil	sol	heol	hewl	haul
wind	wind	vent	ventus	gwent	gwynys	gwynt

A: Everyday world

English	German	French	Latin	Breton	Cornish	Welsh
black	schwarz	noir	niger	du	du	du
blue	blau	bleu	caerulus	glaz	glas	glas
brown	braun	brun	fulvus	gell	gell	llwyd
green	grün	vert	viridir	gwer	gwer	gwyrdd
red	rot	rouge	ruber	ruz	ruth	rhudd
white	weiß	blanc	albus	gwenn	gwyn	gwyn

B: Colours

English	German	French	Latin	Breton	Cornish	Welsh
arm	arm	bras	brachium	breh	bregh	braich
ear	öhr	oreille	auris	scouarn	scovarn	tywysn
eye	auge	oeil	oculus	lagad	lagas	llygad
finger	finger	doigt	digitus	bis	bys	bys
foot	fuß	pied	pes	troad	tros	troed
hand	arbeiter	main	manus	dorn	dorn	llaw
head	kopf	tête	caput	penn	pen	pen
mouth	mund	bouche	oris	genou	ganow	genau
shoulder	schulter	scapulaire	humerus	skoaz	scoth	ysgwydd

C: Human body

English	German	French	Latin	Breton	Cornish	Welsh
cattle	vieh	bovine	pecus	chatal	gwarthez	gwartheg
cow	kuh	vache	vacca	buoh	bugh	bigylu
goat	ziege	chèvre	caper	gavr	gavar	gair
snake	schlange	serpent	serpens	near	gorthfyl	neiddr

D: Animals

English	German	French	Latin	Breton	Cornish	Welsh
one	eins	une	unus	gwm	un	un
two	zwei	deux	duo	daou	deu	dau
three	drei	trois	tres	teir	try	tri
four	vier	quatre	quattuor	peder	peder	pedwar
five	fünf	cinq	quinque	pemp	pymp	pump
six	sechs	six	sex	c'wheh	wheyg	chwech
seven	sieben	sept	septem	seiz	seyth	saith
eight	acht	huit	octo	eiz	eth	wyth
nine	neun	neuf	novem	nerven	naw	naw
ten	zehn	dix	decem	deg	dek	deg
eleven	elf	onze	undecim	unneg	unnek	un ar ddeg
twelve	zwölf	douze	duodecim	daouzeg	deudhek	deuddeg

E: Numbers

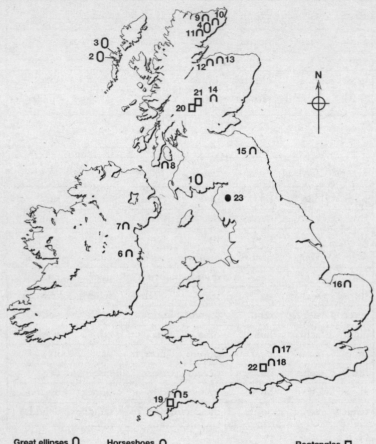

Great ellipses ◖

1. Twelve Apostles
2. Pobull Fhinn
3. Loch a Phobuill
4. Achnagoul

Horseshoes ∩

5. East Down
6. Lugg
7. Carn Beg
8. Machrie Moor 1
9. Latheronwheel
10. Broubster
11. Achavanich
12. Haerstanes
13. Cowiemuir
14. Croft Moraig
15. Hethpool
16. Arminghall
17. Avebury North
18. Stonehenge

Rectangles ▢

19. King Arthur's Hall
20. Fortingall SW
21. Fortingall NE
22. Stonehenge

'Irish' henge ●

23. Mayburgh

Fig. 34: Map of ellipses, horseshoes and rectangles in Britain and Ireland.

APPENDIX 2:

BRETON MEGALITHIC SETTINGS IN BRITAIN AND IRELAND[1]

site	locality	material	earthwork	miles from sea
Twelve Apostles	Dumfriesshire	stone	no	9
Loch a Phobuill	North Uist	stone	no	3
Pobull Fhinn	North Uist	stone	no	4
Achnagoul	Caithness	stone	yes	8

1: Great ellipses

site	locality	material	earthwork	miles from sea
Achavanich	Caithness	stone	yes	5
Arminghall	Norfolk	stone	yes	20
Avebury (N)	Wiltshire	stone	yes	48
Broubster	Caithness	stone	no	6
Carn Beg	Co. Louth	stone	yes	2
Cowiemuir	Moray Firth	earth	no	2
Croft Moraig	Perthshire	stone	yes	30
East Down	Cornwall	earth	no	12
Haerstanes	Moray Firth	stone	no	4
Hethpool	Northumberland	stone	no	16
Latheronwheel	Caithness	stone	no	1
Lugg	Co. Dublin	timber	yes	5
Machrie Moor I	Arran	stone	no	2
Stonehenge IIa	Wiltshire	bluestone	yes	31
Stonehenge IIb	Wiltshire	bluestone	yes	31
Stonehenge III	Wiltshire	bluestone	yes	31
Stonehenge III	Wiltshire	sarsen	yes	31

2: Horseshoes

site	locality	material	earthwork	miles from sea
King Arthur's Hall	Bodmin Moor	stone	yes	7
Fortingall NE, SW	Perthshire	stone	no	45
Stonehenge, Four Stations	Wiltshire	sarsen	no	31

3: Rectangles

site	locality	material	earthwork	miles from sea
Mayburgh	Westmorland	earth	yes	33

4: Irish 'henge'

APPENDIX 3:

ALIEN CARVED MOTIFS
IN BRITAIN AND IRELAND

Amongst the various motifs carved on prehistoric stones in Britain and Ireland, figurines and axes are almost unknown.

In a 1989 paper on British prehistoric rock art, R.W.B. Morris listed almost 900 sites from northern Scotland to southern England. The great majority of them had abstract cup-and-ring markings; representational art is almost non-existent.[1] There was one possible rectangle, a 'lattice' like a chess board, found engraved on a cist at Ardross near the coast of Ross and Cromarty. The stone is lost.[2]

Axes were almost as rare. Apart from Stonehenge, they have been recorded on only four other sites, all on stones of burial cists and intimately associated with death. Three of them were in the Kilmartin Valley by the sea-linked Loch Fyne on the Kintyre peninsula of south-western Scotland, at the cairns of Nether Largie Centre and North, and at the nearby cairn of Ri

Hafted stone axes from the realistic to the stylized

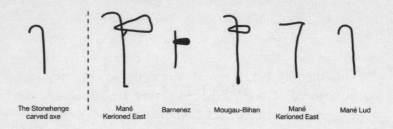

| The Stonehenge carved axe | Mané Kerioned East | Barnenez | Mougau-Bihan | Mané Kerioned East | Mané Lud |

Figurines (a) with breasts, and (b) with heads, into (c) figurative rectangles

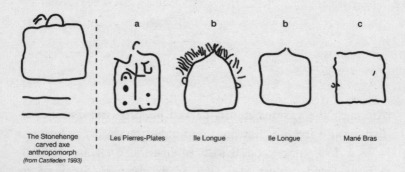

The Stonehenge carved axe anthropomorph *(from Castleden 1993)* — Les Pierres-Plates — Ile Longue — Ile Longue — Mané Bras

Fig. 35: Comparison of axe and figure carvings
at Stonehenge and in Breton chambered tombs.

Cruin.[3] The fourth, again on a cist, came from a bowl barrow at Badbury in Dorset, some eight miles north of Poole Harbour.[4]

In Ireland, what seems to be an axe was carved on the recumbent slab of Drombeg stone circle in Co. Cork, close to Rosscarbery Bay on the south coast. The ring contained a central burial.[5] The scarcity of such motifs in these islands, their proximity to the sea and their proliferation in Brittany suggests that the latter was their origin.

In Brittany, carvings of axes on standing stones, in the passages and chambers of megalithic tombs, even occasionally on cromlechs, are commonplace. The motifs can be realistic with a recognizable blade and haft. Others are symbolic carvings in the shape of the letter 'f', or even more economically with the crossbar of the blade missing so that they look like a shepherd's crook.[6] Frequently they are associated with an outlined domed or rectangular shape with carved, sometimes sculpted circles considered to be breasts, and have been considered to represent a weapon-bearing protectress of the dead. As S. Twohig observed, 'The most frequent and widespread naturalistic motif is the axe'.[7]

Among many examples, axe-carvings can be seen in the tombs of Gavr'inis; Grah-Niaul; Kercado; Mané Kerioned B; Mané Lud; Mané Ruthuel; Penhape; Petit-Mont; and the Table des Marchands, all in southern Brittany.[8]

In contrast to the single, rather dubious 'rectangle' of Ardross in Scotland, figurines in Brittany occur almost as frequently as axes. Twohig notes that these so-called 'bucklers' or shields 'seem to represent an anthropomorphic figure similar to the anthropomorphic *stelae* found free-standing in some of the early passage-graves'.[9] Some have multiple pairs of breasts which identify the sex, some with loops for arms, several with necklaces. Others are austere, no more than the outline of a plain rectangle.

The constant appearance of these shapes in tombs – whether early *dolmens à couloir* like Les Pierres-Plates or later *allées-couvertes* such as Crech-Quillé – reaffirms their intimate relationship with the dead. Often well-protected from weather in roofed tombs, there are good examples to be seen in Gavr'inis; Goërem, Gâvres; Ile Longue; Kercado; Luffang, now open to the sky and the stone removed; Les Pierres-Plates; Mané Bras; Mané Ruthuel; Penhape; Table des

Marchands. There are good casts of them in the Musée Miln-Le Rouzic at Carnac-Ville.[10]

Some are lavishly decorated. The big stone inside Table des Marchands may originally have been an open-air statue-menhir, re-used to stand awesomely at the back of the tomb because of its evocative imagery. Ten feet (3m) high and wide, with its ogival body filled with symbolic axes and with a large and realistic one carved in the roof-slab above it, the slab was almost identical to the free-standing statue-menhirs of southern France.[11] There, particularly in the Aveyron region where there is a fine exhibition in the Musée Fenaille at Rodez, the figurines, some 6ft (2m) or more high (like the 'Dame de Saint-Sernin'), are naked under a large cloak. They have eyes, arms, necklaces and breasts. Ancestral to the enclosed 'guardians' of the tombs in Brittany, those Breton motifs in turn were the inspiration of the less evocative figurines at Stonehenge.[12]

The existence of many axes, some questionable daggers and three figurines on the sarsens of Stonehenge is clear evidence of Breton imagery being adopted by the natives of Salisbury Plain, and an association with rituals connected with death is probable.

ABBREVIATIONS

Ant	Antiquity
Ant J	Antiquaries Journal
Arch	Archaeologia
Arch J	Archaeological Journal
Arch W	Archaeology in Wales
Archaeo	Archaeoastronomy
BAR	British Archaeological Reports
Brit Arch	British Archaeology
CA	Current Archaeology
JHA	Journal for the History of Astronomy
JRAI	Journal of the Royal Anthropological Institute
OJA	Oxford Journal Of Archeology
PBA	Proceedings of the British Academy
PPS	Proceedings of the Prehistoric Society
PSAL	Proceedings of the Society of Antiquaries of London

PSAS   *Proceedings of the Society of Antiquaries of Scotland*
WAM   *Wiltshire Archaeological Journal*

NOTES

Note: The author/date system is used here, for entries where full details are cited in the Bibliography. Where full details are not in the Bibliography, details are given here in full at their first appearance in each chapter, with the author/date system used thereafter.

For Stukeley's 1721–24 manuscript, the first page cited is that of Burl & Mortimer, *Stonehenge. An Unpublished Manuscript by William Stukeley, 1721–4* (Yale University Press, London, 2005). The original manuscript page is then cited in brackets.

Preface

1. Atkinson (1956), p. 166; Atkinson (1979), p. 169.
2. Christopher Marlowe, *Tamburlaine the Great*, Part 1, ActII, Scene 7, lines 23–24.

3. Aubrey, *c*.1665–93 (1980 ed.), p. 25.
4. Stukeley as a fool: Piggott (1985), p. 152. The manuscript: Burl & Mortimer (2005).
5. A traveller in the Preselis: Atkinson (1979), p. 176.
6. Samuel Pepys, *Diary*, 11 June 1668.

Introduction

1. Distribution of 17 long and over 200 round barrows around Stonehenge: Grinsell (1978), pp. 24–25; Exon et al. (2000), pp. 3, 76–107, 111–12.
2. The footpath and landscape: Richards (1985), p. 24, plan.
3. The Cursus 'long barrow': Stukeley (1724), p. 90 (p. 75); Stukeley (1740), p. 41; Hoare (1812), p. 128; Maud Cunnington, 'List of the long barrows of Wiltshire', *WAM 38* (1914), pp. 383–84; Grinsell (1957), p. 137. The excavation: Richards (1990), pp. 72–96.
4. Salisbury Plain: Stukeley (1740), p. 9.
5. Souvenirs: *The Diary of John Evelyn, I-III*, ed. A. Dobson (Macmillan, London, 1906), vol. II, p. 83.
6. Emerson (1914), pp. 2, 6–7; Browne (1867).
7. Detailed references to the additions, subtractions and changes to Stonehenge are given in the relevant chapters that follow.
8. Diameter of the ditch from middle to middle, and the banks: Walker & Gardiner, in Cleal et al. (1995), pp. 24–25.
9. Tacitus, 'Britain', vol. XI, p. 61, in *Tacitus on Britain and Germany*, trans. H. Mattingly (Penguin, Harmonsworth, 1948).
10. Counting systems: Burl (1976b). Units of measurement: Druid's Cubit, Stukeley (1740), pp. 6, 15; a and b units: M. Behrend, 'A forgotten researcher: Ludovic McClellan Mann' (Institute of Geomantic Research, Occasional Paper 7, Cambridge, 1977); Megalithic Yard and Rod: Thom (1967, and earlier papers); regional yards: Burl (2000), pp. 50–53, 106; Boyne Yard: A.H. Powell, *PPS 60* (1994), pp. 86–90. Sumeria and Assyria: A.E. Berryman, *Historical Metrology* (Dent, London, 1953), pp. 54–55. The dimensions quoted for Stonehenge are those provided by reliable surveyors such as Petrie, Hawley, Atkinson and Thom, using chains and tapes. Computer-generated dimensions have produced slightly different lengths: Walker & Gardiner, in Cleal et al. (1995), pp. 21, 24.
11. Bowing stone: Stukeley (1740), p. 33.
12. Edward King, *Munimenta Antiqua*, vol. I of IV (G. Nicol, London, 1799), p. 172; Anonymous (1776), p. 7.
13. Les Mousseaux: Burl (1985), pp. 100–101.
14. The Four Stations: Duke (1846), pp. 142–46; Hawkins (1966), p. 134; Hoyle (1977), p. 30 ff; Ruggles (1997), p. 219.
15. Sarsen circle: Atkinson (1979), p. 38; Walker & Gardiner, in Cleal et al. (1995), p. 26.
16. 'Trilithon': Stukeley (1724), p. 33 (p. 15); Stukeley (1740), p. 25.
17. Bluestone circle and horseshoe: Atkinson (1979), pp. 49, 53–56.
18. Name of the Altar Stone: Jones (1655), p. 57, p. 75.

19. Numbering of the stones: Wood (1747), p. 54; Smith (1771), pp. 54–57, end plan; Hoare (1812), p. 145; Petrie (1880), pp. 9–12.
20. Numbering of the Aubrey Holes: Hawley (1921), pp. 30–33.

Chapter 1

1. Henry of Huntingdon: Henry of Huntingdon (1991 ed.), p. 7.
2. *Stan-hengen:* Gover et al. (1970), pp. 360–61.
3. Stukeley (1724), p. 35 (pp. 12, 17).
4. Stonehenge as the Second Wonder of Britain: Henry of Huntingdon (1991), pp. 7–8. The First Wonder was the caves and winds in the Peak District; the Third was the Cheddar Caves; and the Fourth was rain from hills falling onto the Plain.
5. Robert de Torigny: Long (1876), pp. 7–8.
6. Diodorus Siculus 'of Sicily': *Library of History, Book II, 35*, trans. Oldfather (1929), pp. 37–41. Pytheas: B. Cunliffe, *The Extraordinary Voyage of Pytheas the Greek* (Allen Lane, London, 2001). Callanish: Burl (1999), pp. 59–65, 178–80.
7. Geoffrey of Monmouth and St Augustine: Geoffrey of Monmouth (1969 ed.), p. 240. Stonehenge and Merlin: Geoffrey of Monmouth (1969), pp. 172–74. Popular ignorance of history: *Daily Telegraph*, 4 April 2004, p. 5.
8. William of Newburgh (1996 ed.), pp. 398–99.
9. Iron Age burial: Walker & Montague, in Cleal et al. (1995), pp. 159–61. 'No clear picture': Walker, in Cleal et al. (1995), p. 337. Hoard by Stone 7: Hawley (1921), p. 29.
10. Roman period coins: Davies, in Cleal et al. (1995), pp. 431–32. Roman destruction: Atkinson (1979), pp. 85–86.
11. The tablet: Camden (1637), p. 254; Aubrey (1980 ed.), p. 92; Stukeley (1740), p. 31. John Lyly, c.1554–1606, author of *Euphues*, and Sir Thomas Elyot, c.1490–1546, scholar and diplomat: from their dates they must have inspected the tablet independently, perhaps many years apart, making its ultimate disappearance all the more regrettable. *Defixiones* and Roman chariot-races: Aubrey Burl, *Catullus: a Poet in the Rome of Julius Caesar* (Constable & Robinson, London, 2004), p. 89.
12. Place names – Amesbury: Gover et al. (1970), pp. 358–59; Durrington: Gover et al. (1970), pp. 364–65.
13. Lanfranc and Ireland: Burl (1984), pp. 181–82.
14. Gerald of Wales (1982 ed.), p. 84.
15. Harroway: Timperley & Brill (1983), pp. 46–50. Along with Ridgeway and Icknield Way, one of the oldest highways in Britain: Taylor (1979), pp. 185, 193.
16. 14th-century sketches of Stonehenge – Merlin: Chippindale (2004), p. 23; rectangular Stonehenge: J. Michell, *Megalithomania* (Thames & Hudson, London, 1982), p. 22.
17. The four sketches: Chippindale (2004), pp. 34–36, plate 1; Bakker (1979), pp. 107–111; Burl (1994), p.88.
18. Camden, *Britannia* (1637), pp. 251–54.

19. It has been wrongly claimed that Robert Gay's inane *A Fool's Bolt soon shott at Stonage* was earlier than Jones' book. Gay himself denied it. 'As for a description of the saide fabricke, I would referr you to Architector Inigo Jones in his book, entituled *Stonehenge restored*'. Legg (1986), p. 7.

20. Plan of Stonehenge: Jones (1655), pp. 1–2. Excavations: Webb (1725), pp. 11, 16. Plans of Stonehenge, nos. 6, 7: Jones (1655), pp. 63, 64; Leapman (2003), pp. 197–200.

21. One entrance: Aubrey (1980 ed.), p. 80, plate VII; Webb (1725), p. 16.

22. The portal-stones: Jones (1655), p. 57, F.

23. Roman monument: Jones (1655), p. 63, plan 7, p. 68. First edition of the trilogy: Piggott (1971). The edition remains a collector's item. A copy, with its Wenceslaus Hollar portrait of Jones, rebound and with a slight tear, was recently priced at almost £2,000.

24. Walpole: Leapman (2003), p. 199.

25. Charleton (1663).

26. Jones, Charleton and Webb: Piggott (1971) pp. i-ii.

27. Avebury exceeding Stonehenge: Aubrey (1980 ed.), pp. 21, 36.

28. *John Aubrey's 'Brief Lives'*, ed. Dick (1949).

29. Druids: Aubrey (1980 ed.), p. 25. Not Roman: Aubrey (1980 ed.), p. 83. Conjurer: *Wiltshire. The Topographical Collections of John Aubrey*, ed. J.E. Jackson (Devizes, 1862), p. 4.

30. Diameter of the circle: Aubrey (1980 ed.), p. 75; Thom, Thom & Burl (1980), pp. 122–23.

31. The north-east entrance: Aubrey (1980 ed.), p. 80, plate VII.

32. The imagined avenue: Aubrey (1980 ed.), p. 76, p. 80, plate VII.

33. Aubrey Holes: Aubrey (1980 ed.), p. 76; Hawley (1921), p. 30.

34. The stone and Merlin's heel: Aubrey (1980 ed.), p. 95; Burl (1991), p. 3. Broome stone circle: *WAM* 97, 2004, p. 278. Avebury and the Devil: Burl (2002), pp. 146–47. Smith and the wrong 'Heel Stone': Smith (1771), p. 51.

35. The barrows and burials: Camden (1637), pp. 253, 255; Aubrey (1980 ed.), pp. 83, 99–100.

36. Duke of Buckingham: Aubrey (1980 ed.), p. 93. Plate VII, fig. 2, shows the position of the pit.

37. Seven planets: Aubrey (1980 ed.), p. 82; Smith (1771), pp. 57–58, 65–66, plate I.

38. Starlings and Pliny: Aubrey (1980 ed.), p. 142.

39. The 1721–24 Cardiff manuscript, MS 4. 253: eds. Burl & Mortimer (2005); Hutton (2005).

40. Stukeley's model – Letter to Maurice Johnson, 6 June 1716: Piggott (1985), p. 40. Aubrey on Avebury and Stonehenge (1980), p. 21; Stukeley (1724), p. 21 (Preliminary, p. 1).

41. Stukeley and Wilton House: T. Lever, *The Herberts of Wilton* (John Murray, London, 1967), p. 149; Lukis (1885), pp. 251, 253.

42. Date of Stonehenge: Stukeley (1724), p. 31 (p. 13). Halley: Stukeley (1724), p. 31 (p 13).

43. Entasis: Stukeley (1724), p. 43 (p. 25); Atkinson (1956), p. 23.

44. Excavation at the Altar Stone: Stukeley (1724), p. 66 (p. 47).

45. The 'bowing' Heel Stone: Stukeley (1724), p. 108 (p. 97).

46. Stones in the avenue: Stukeley (1724), pp. 77–78 (p. 59). Not mentioned in the book: Stukeley (1740), p. 35, table 28, p. 54. Gale's letter of 20 May 1740: Lukis (1885), p. 268.

47. Stukeley's barrows are noted in chapter two. His theodolite: Atkinson (1985).
48. Summer solstice: Stukeley (1724), p. 93 (p. 76). 'Or nearly': Stukeley (1740), p. 56.
49. The patriarchal religion: Stukeley (1740), Preface, v.
50. The stones: Defoe, *A Tour Through the Whole Island of Great Britain* (Yale University Press, London, 1991), p. 81. No history: Defoe, *A Tour Through the Whole Island of Great Britain* (Penguin, Harmondsworth, 1971), p. 201.
51. John Wood and the Crescent at Bath: T. Mowl & B. Earnshaw, *John Wood. Architect of Obsession* (Millstream Press, Bath, 1988), pp. 191–93. The stones of Stonehenge: Wood (1747), p. 53; Petrie (1880), p. 16.
52. Highwaymen: James Waylen, *The Highwaymen of Wiltshire* (E. & W. Books, London, 1970), pp. 11–62; C. Millson, *Tales of Old Wiltshire* (Countryside Books, Newbury, 1982), p. 24; P. Pringle, *Stand and Deliver* (Museum Press, London, 1951), p. 115.
53. Stukeley writing about John Wood: *Diary*, 3 August 1763; Lukis (1885), p. 275.
54. The summer solstice at Stonehenge: Smith (1771), pp. 63–64.
55. Hoare (1812), pp. 126–59. William Cunnington at Stonehenge: R.H. Cunnington (1975), pp. 109–21.
56. Atkinson (1956), p. 166; Atkinson (1979), p. 168.

Chapter 2

1. Aubrey (1980 ed.), pp. 76, 93.
2. Mary Trotman: Aubrey (1980 ed.), pp. 87, 95, 100. Augering: Walker, in Cleal et al. (1995), pp. 9, 107. 'Coming up red': G.W. Meates, *Lullingstone Roman Villa* (1955), pp. 11, 15.
3. The 1574 sketch: Stone (1924), pp. 147–48.
4. Camden (1695), p. 96; Hawley (1924), p. 35.
5. Jones and sacrifices: Webb (1725), p. 66.
6. Hayward at Stonehenge: Stukeley (1740), p. 32. Rabbits near the entrance: Stukeley (1724), p. 94 (p. 79). At Winterbourne Stoke: Stukeley (1740), p. 13.
7. Abraham Sturges: Wood (1747), p. 60. The Altar Stone: Stukeley (1724), p. 67 (p. 46).
8. Collapse of trilithon 57–58 – Gypsies: Browne (1867), pp. 19–20; 'Letter of Dr. Maton, May 30, 1797', Easton (1815), pp. 64–66; W.J. Maton, 'Account of the Fall of some of the Stones of Stonehenge', *Arch 13*, 1800, pp. 103–106.
9. Boles Barrow is categorized as 'Heytesbury 1' after the parish in which it lies. The identification is necessary. As an example, the whimsically named but unlocated Fairy's Toot megalithic tomb in Somerset is officially classed as 'Butcombe 1'. Leslie Grinsell compiled detailed county gazetteers – Dorset, Gloucestershire, Somerset, North Devon – for barrows in their architectural types, namely long, plain round, bell, disc, pond and saucer. The barrows of Wiltshire are listed in Grinsell (1957).
10. Boles Barrow – Letter of William Cunnington, July, 1801: R.H. Cunnington (1975), p. 15. A three-volume collection of Cunnington's letters about his barrow excavations is in Devizes Museum: Vol. 1, 324/2594; II, 324/2595; III, 324/2596. His work at Boles Barrow is in III, Book 10, pp. 1–31.

11. The Altar Stone: R.H. Cunnington (1975), pp. 39, 164.
12. Station stones 92 and 94: Hoare (1812), pp. 144–45; Cleal & Walker, in Cleal et al. (1995), pp. 272–74.
13. Amesbury 4 bowl barrow: Stukeley (1724), p. 105 (p. 93); Stukeley (1740), p. 46; William Cunnington, in R.H. Cunnington (1975), p. 114; Hoare (1812), p. 127.
14. Slaughter Stone once erect: Stukeley (1724), p. 41 (p. 25); Stukeley (1740), p. 16; R.H. Cunnington (1975), p. 151.
15. Beamish: Long (1876), pp. 86–87.
16. The plans of Wood and Hoare: Petrie (1880), p. 3; Wood's stones: Petrie (1880), p. 16.
17. The precise planning: Petrie (1880), p. 13.
18. An unfinished Stonehenge: Petrie (1880), p. 16.
19. The Slaughter and Heel Stones as gateways: Petrie (1880), p. 17.
20. Astronomy and units of measurement: Petrie (1880), pp. 18–21.
21. Stone 56: Petrie (1880), p. 33.
22. The gypsy: George Borrow, *Lavengro: The Scholar, the Gypsy, the Priest*, chapter xxxii.
23. *The Times*: Balfour (1979), p. 175.
24. The erection of Stone 56: Gowland (1902), pp. 40–45; Gowland (1903), pp. 3–7.
25. Concrete at Stonehenge: Long (1876), pp. 117–18. In Roman times: L.S. de Camp, *The Ancient Engineers* (Ballantyne, New York, 1963), pp. 183–84.
26. Base of 55: Stone (1924), p. 91, plate 21.
27. Stonehole of 55: Gowland (1902), pp. 52–53; Gowland (1903), p. 39; Allen, in Cleal et al. (1995), pp. 198–99.
28. Use of sarsen mauls: Gowland (1902), pp. 67–72; Gowland (1903), pp. 26, 31–32.
29. J.W. Judd, 'Note on the nature and origin of the rock-fragments found in the excavations made at Stonehenge . . .', *Arch 58*, 1902, pp. 106–18; the bluestones: p. 56.
30. Shaping bluestones at their source: Judd, note 30, pp. 117–18.
31. Unshaped circle-stones: Burl (1993), p. 88. Hammer-dressing of The Hurlers, Bodmin Moor: R. Radford, *PPS I*, 1935, p. 134. Moses: *Exodus XX*, 25.
32. Dressing of the sarsens: Judd, p. 60.
33. 'A dangerous mess': Lawson, in Cleal et al. (1995), p. 345. Stones leaning or prostrate: Gardiner, in Cleal et al. (1995), p. 344, fig. 188.
34. Office of Works: Hawley (1921), p. 17.
35. Restoration of stones: Hawley (1921), pp. 18–30; Hawley (1922), pp. 36–51.
36. A polygon: Hawley (1928), p. 163. Segments of the ditch, Hawley (1922), pp. 36–51. East against west: Hawley (1928), p. 157. No theories: Hawley (1923), p. 20.
37. 'High-and-low': Burl (1993), p. 57 et al.. Brittany: Burl (1985), pp. 39–40, 91–92. Colours: Stukeley (1724), pp. 23–24 (p. 3). Arran: A. Jones, *Brit Arch 32*, 1997, p. 6.
38. Y & Z Holes: Hawley (1925), pp. 37–50. Tracking days: Hawkins & White (1966), p. 146.
39. The causeway postholes: Hawley (1924), p. 35; Hawley (1925), p. 22.
40. Passage and palisade: Hawley (1926), pp. 2–3.
41. The bottle of port: Hawley (1921), p. 34. The macehead: Hawley (1925), pp. 33–34.

42. The Aubrey Holes: Hawley (1921), pp. 30–33; Thom & Thom (1978), p. 146; Hawkins & White (1966), pp. 140–45. 'Holes in the Argument': Burl, *The Bulletin of the Center for Archaeoastronomy 4 (4)*, 1981, pp. 19–25.

43. H.H. Thomas and the Preselis: Hawley (1921), pp. 39–40.

44. Dr Samuel Johnson to Mrs Thrale, 9 October 1783: Long (1876), p. 45.

45. Aubrey Hole 32: 1848±275 bc (C-602). 'bc' indicates that the 'date' has not been calibrated and needs correction to the true date given by testing it against the annular growth of tree-rings. Such calibrated dates are followed by bc, hence 3020–1520 bc from the ± 275. All dates are quoted by their laboratory and sample number – C-602 means Chicago, sample number 602. Other laboratories for Stonehenge assays are: BM, British Museum; HAR, Harwell; OxA, Oxford Radiocarbon Accelerator; UB, University of Belfast. Bayliss, Housley & McCormac, in Cleal et al. (1995), pp. 516–26.

Chapter 3

1. 'Essentially it was an idea', Francis Pryor, *Britain* BC: Life in Britain and Ireland Before the Romans (HarperCollins, London, 2003): 'There must however have been a small element of migration', domestic animals 'had to be introduced from outside', pp. 121–22.

2. V.G. Childe, *Prehistoric Communities of the British Isles* (Chambers, London, 1940), p. 34.

3. *AA Book of the Seaside. A Guide Mile by Mile to Britain's Coastline* (Drive Publications Limited, Basingstoke, 1972), pp. 62–63.

4. Severn-Cotswold/Brittany tombs: F. Lynch, *Megalithic Tombs and Long Barrows in Britain* (Shire, Princes Risborough, 1997), pp. 45, 54. Sea-crossings: Cunliffe (2001), p. 154. Timbers at Balbridie: Ralston & N. Reynolds, *Balbridie. Excavations 1977–80* (HMSO, London, 1981); *CA 84* (1982), pp. 23–25. Somerset Levels: Coles & Orme: p. 59 ff. Masts and sails: Twohig (1981), pp. 63–64, 91, 114; P. Gelling & H.E. Davidson, *The Chariot of the Sun. And Other Rites and Symbols of the Northern Bronze Age* (Dent, London, 1969), pp. 43–67, 155–58; G. Burenhult, 'Rock carving chronology and rock carving ships with sails', *Mémoires du Musée de l'Université du Lund* (Lund University, 1972), pp. 151–62.

5. Fussell's Lodge: Ashbee (1966), pp. 36–37.

6. Burl (1976b).

7. Ashbee (1966), pp. 36–37.

8. Abelard and Breton: 'Historia Calamitatum' in, B. Radice, ed., *The Letters of Abelard and Heloise* (Penguin, London, 1974), pp. 94–95. Camden and Welsh: Dick (1949), p.51. Lhuyd and Cornish: P.A.S. Poole, *William Borlase* (Royal Institution of Cornwall, Truro, 1986), pp. 71–72.

9. South Newton 1: Hoare (1812), pp. 75–76. Upton Lovell 2a: Annable & Simpson (1964), pp. 49, 104.

10. Normanton Down: Castleden (1992), pp. 221–22.

11. Easton Down: Thurnam (1869), p. 184.

12. Stonehenge burial: Hawley (1928), p. 169.

13. Oxendean: Hoare (1812), p. 66; *WAM 32*, 1948, pp. 216–17.

14. Boles Barrow: Hoare (1812), pp. 87–88; J. Thurnam, *Memoirs of the Anthropological Society 1* (1865), p. 472; H. & W. Cunnington, *WAM 24*, pp. 107, 116. Tilshead 2: *WAM 13*, 1872, p. 341.

15. Old Ditch barrow (Tilshead 2): Hoare (1812), p. 87; Thurnam, *WAM 13*, 1872, p. 341. Skulls: *WAM 38*, 1913, p. 401. Meyrick, 'Thurnam, MS. Catalogue collection of skulls, Cambridge', *WAM 52*, 1948, pp. 216–17.

16. Schulting & Wysocki, 'In this chambered tumulus were found cleft skulls . . .', *PPS 71*, 2005, pp. 107–38, table 3, p. 123.

17. Old Ditch barrow, the largest long barrow in south Wiltshire – violently cleft, 'and doubtless during life': Cunnington letter to Coxe, 7 September 1802, R.H. Cunnington (1975), p. 164.

18. Arrowhead, 'Giant's Grave': Thurnam (1869), p. 194; *PSAL III* (1867), p. 170.

19. John Milton, 'On the Morning of Christ's Nativity', 'The Hymn', 1645, stanza 14, line 3. T. Hobbes, *Leviathan I* (1651), chapter III.

20. Pits near burials: Hoare (1812), p. 21.

21. Tilshead 2: Hoare (1812), p. 91; Grinsell (1957), p. 144.

22. Thurnam (1869), p. 171.

23. Knighton barrow: *WAM 38*, 1914, p. 390.

24. Tilshead 2: Grinsell (1957), p. 144.

25. Knook 2: Hoare (1812), p. 83.

26. Long barrows and the east: Hoare (1812), p. 21.

27. Ashbee (1984), pp. 80–81.

28. Winterbourne Stoke 1: Thurnam (1869), pp. 379, 420.

29. Modest barrows: Ashbee (1984), p. 21.

30. *Cordon sanitaire*: Exon et al. (2000), p. 107.

31. Allen, in Cleal et al. (1995), pp. 474–76.

32. Mesolithic postholes – astronomy: Newham (1972), pp. 23–28.

33. Excavation: Vatcher (1973), pp. 57–63. C-14 assays: Burl (1979), p. 65. Pine charcoal: Limbrey, *WAM 68*, 1973, pp. 62–63. C-14: Bayliss, Houseley & McCormac, in Cleal et al. (1995), pp. 470–73. Totem-poles: Allen, in Cleal et al. (1995), pp. 470–73.

34. 'Noble *Ippodrom*': Stukeley (1724), p. 90 (p. 75).

Chapter 4

1. Causewayed enclosures: Oswald, Dyer, & Barber (2001).

2. Robin Hood's Ball: Hoare (1812), p. 170. Excavation: N. Thomas, *WAM 59*, 1964, pp. 1–27.

3. Cursus 'alignments' – Pleiades: Lockyer (1909), pp. 154–55. Stars: North (2001), pp. 180–85. Equinox: Darvill (1997), note 184. Imprecision of the equinox: Thom (1967), pp. 23–24. 'Instruments': Thom (1967), p. 107.

4. 'Three parts': Darvill (1997), p. 184.

5. 'Cursus': Barclay & Harding (1999). Ireland: C. Newman, 'Notes on four cursus-like monuments in Co. Meath, Ireland', in Barclay & Harding (1999), pp. 141–47. France: I. Kinnes, 'Longtemps ignorées: Passy-Rots, linear monuments in northern France', in Barclay & Harding (1999), pp. 148–54.

6. Assay OxA-1403: Allen, in Cleal et al. (1995), pp. 477, 487. Cursus building: Barclay and Bayliss, in Barclay & Harding (1999), pp. 11–29; Russell (2002), pp. 115, 117, 119. Young men racing: D. McOmish, *Brit Arch 69*, 2003, pp. 8–13; Barclay & Harding (1999), p. 2. Dating. C-14: Allen, in Cleal et al. (1995), p. 477. Antler: Stone (1947); 1950 ± 105 bc = 2910–2460 BC: Barclay and Bayliss, 'Cursus monuments and the radiocarbon problem' in Barclay & Harding (1999), pp. 11–29. Excavations: J.F.S. Stone (1947); *Arch J 104*, 1947, pp. 7–19; P. Christie, *WAM 58*, 1963, pp. 370–82; Richards (1991), pp. 79–82. Lesser Cursus assays: 2690 ± 100 bc (OxA-1405), 2600 ± 120 bc (OxA-1404): Allen, in Cleal et al. (1995), p. 481.

7. Chariot-races: Stukeley (1724), pp. 90–91 (p. 75); Stukeley (1740), p. 41. Young male athletes: D. McOmish, *Brit Arch 69*, 2003, pp. 8–24.

8. Water: Francis Pryor, *Britain* BC: *Life in Britain and Ireland Before the Romans* (HarperCollins, London, 2003), p. 217; Barclay & Harding (1999), p. 2.

9. Western deep ditch: Christie, *WAM 58*, 1963, p. 374.

10. Dates of avenues to stone circles: Burl (1993), p. 23.

11. Access to an inner sacred area: Harding, in Barclay & Harding (1999), p. 34

12. Walk along the Stonehenge cursus: Exon et al. (2000), p. 52; H.P. Chapman, *PPS 71*, 2005, pp. 159–70.

13. Curious pebble: Hoare (1812), p. 165, Amesbury 56 bowl barrow at the west end of the Cursus.

14. L.P. Hartley, *The Go-Between* (1953), Prologue.

15. Sinodun: Loveday, in Barclay & Harding (1999), pp. 59–60.

16. Brittany: Burl (1985), 'Guardian, female, of the dead', p. 173; Twohig (1981), pp. 128–30.

17. 'Female hills': Tuck (2003), pp. 81–107.

18. Old Hags and stones: Grinsell (1976), pp. 43–44, 157.

19. Carved figurine: B. & J. Coles, *Sweet Track to Glastonbury. The Somerset Levels in Prehistory* (Thames & Hudson, London, 1986), p. 81, plate VII.

20. The Cuckoo Stone: Ruddle, *WAM 31*, 1901, p. 331; Stukeley (1724), p. 31 (p. 13), p. 80 (p. 62)

21. Barclay (1895), pp. 25, 26. There is a sketch of the Cuckoo Stone, p. 25.

22. Stones and the Devil: Grinsell (1975), p. 15; Grinsell (1976), p. 114. The Bulford river stone and its neighbours: Brentnall, *WAM 51*, 1946, p. 432.

23. Cuckhold Stone: Gover et al. (1970), p. 365. The Heel Stone: C.E. Ferry, 'The Stonehenge bird', *Ar Quatuor Coronatum 7*, 1894, p. 189.

24. The stone in the river: E.H. Stone (1924), pp. 143–44.

25. Heel Stone pre-dating Stonehenge: Douglas, in R.H. Cunnington (1975), pp. 149–50. James Douglas: B. Marsden, *The Early Barrow Diggers* (Tempus, Stroud, 1999), pp. 16–19.

26. Callanish: Burl (2000), p. 203; Long Meg: Burl (2000), pp. 119–20; Grand Menhir Brisé: Bailloud, Boujot, Cassen & Le Roux, *Carnac. Les Premières Architectures de Pierre* (Éditions du CNRS - CNmhs, Paris, 1995), p. 467.

27. Errors about the Heel Stone: Barclay (1895), p. 11.

28. Early mentions of the Heel Stone: Aubrey (1980), p. 95; Long (1876), pp. 7–31; Jones (1655), pp. 55, 57.

29. Stukeley and the Heel Stone – a portal: Stukeley (1724), p. 76 (p. 57); use unknown: Stukeley (1740), p. 33.

30. Heel Stone, Wood's Stone: Wood (1747), pp. 33, 44, 48, 52, 58, 81ff.

31. John Smith and the Heel Stone: Smith (1771), pp. 63–64. Maligned: Burl (1991), p. 2.

32. Mortuary centre: Stone, Piggott & Booth, *Ant J 34*, 1954, pp. 155–77; Wainwright & Longworth (1971), pp. 9–10, 192–93. C-14 assays: 2625±40 bc (Gro-901a); 2450±150 bc (NPL-191); 2635±70 bc (Gro-901). The third assay led to Piggott's famous dismissal of the findings as 'architecturally unacceptable . . . roughly a millennium too high!' (*Ant 33*, 1959, pp. 289–90), because of its mistaken association with much later beakers.

33. Climate and catastrophe: Burgess (2001), pp. 43–45; Darvill (1987), pp. 75–77; *Arch Ireland 2 (2)*, 1988, pp. 71–74; *Ant 71*, 1997, pp. 581–93; H. Dalfes, G. Kukla & H. Weiss, eds., *Third Millennium* BC Climate Change and Old World Collapse (Springer Verlag, Heidelberg/Berlin, 1997).

34. Circle-henges: Burl (1976a), pp. 27–28, 274–82.

Chapter 5

1. Atkinson's phases: Atkinson (1979), pp. 215–16.

2. Cleal's phases: Cleal, in Cleal et al. (1995), pp. 477–91.

3. Avenue alignments: Gardiner, in Cleal et al. (1995), p. 329.

4. Francis Pryor, *Britain* BC: Life in Britain and Ireland Before the Romans (HarperCollins, London, 2003), pp. 237–38.

5. Atkinson (1979), pp. 70–71; Cleal, in Cleal et al. (1995), p. 483.

6. 'Major to minor': Cole Porter, 'Every time we say goodbye', *Seven Lively Arts* (1944). Wandering moon: Milton, 'Il Penseroso', line 65. Inconstant moon: Shakespeare, *Romeo & Juliet*, Act II, Scene 2, line 109.

7. Hawley (1925), pp. 24–25.

8. J.E. Wood (1978), pp. 62–63.

9. Hawley in 1922: Hawley (1924), p. 35; in 1923: Hawley (1926), p. 3.

10. Newham (1972), p. 15.

11. Heggie (1981), p. 202; Cleal, in Cleal et al. (1995), p. 145. See also pp. 111, 164.

12. Contemporary postholes: Hawley (1925), p. 24.

13. Midwinter moonlight: Thom (1971), pp. 22–23.

14. Postholes in groups: Allen, in Cleal et al. (1995), pp. 140–42.

15. Central settings, causeway and 'A' Holes contemporary: Hawley (1926), p. 3.

16. B. & J. Coles, *Sweet Track to Glastonbury. The Somerset Levels in Prehistory* (London, Thames & Hudson, 1986), p. 110.

17. Trampled ground: Hawley (1926), p. 2.

18. Irregularity of the 'circles': Allen, in Cleal et al. (1995), p. 148. No structures recognized: Allen, in Cleal et al. (1995), p. 151, fig. 70; Hawley (1926), p. 16.

19. Tentative 30m circle: Cleal et al. (1995), fig. 69, p. 141. Half the area of the so-called ring has not been excavated. For anyone wishing to examine the 'evidence', the respective postholes are nos 2332, 2328 at the south; 3180, 2746 at the east; 2697 at the north; and 2421 at the south-west.

20. The Stonehenge timber circle unlikely to be early: Walker, in Cleal et al. (1995), p. 107. Possibly as early as 3000 BC: Allen, in Cleal et al. (1995), p. 479; Gibson (1998).

21. Screened passageway: Allen, in Cleal et al. (1995), p. 150.
22. Alignments on cardinal points: Thom (1975), pp. 19–21; Burl (1987), pp. 74–75; Stukeley (1724), p. 101 (p. 87), Stukeley, 'The history of the Temples of the Antient Celts', Par. I, Bodleian Library, Eng. misc. c. 343, p. 207.
23. Disrupted projects in prehistory: Burl (2000), pp. 40, 198, 207, 281, 365. An unfinished Stonehenge: Petrie (1880), p. 16.
24. A.W.R. Whittle, 'Traditions and structures of meaning', in Cunliffe & Renfrew (1997), p. 148.
25. C-14 assays: Bayliss, Housley & McCormac, in Cleal et al. (1995), p. 522.
26. Contents of the ditch terminals: T. Darvill, 'Sacred geographies', in Cunliffe & Renfrew, (1997), pp. 178–79.
27. 'Curated': Serjeantson, in Cleal et al. (1995), p. 449; 'curation': Ramsey & Allen, in Cleal et al. (1995), p. 529.
28. A. Lawson, 'Structural history', in Cunliffe & Renfrew (1997), p. 21.
29. Radiocarbon assays: Bayliss, Housley & McCormac, in Cleal et al. (1995), p. 522.
30. The 'craters' and their contents: Hawley (1924), pp. 31–33.
31. Palisade trench and posts: Walker & Montague, in Cleal et al. (1995), pp. 155–61.
32. Tacitus, *On Britain and Germany, XI*, p. 61. Dickens, *A Child's History of England* (1853), Chapter I.
33. Large posthole: Hawley (1926), p. 2. It is posthole 1c: Cleal et al. (1995), fig. 69, p. 149. The postholes to its north-west are 1b and 1a respectively. Major southern moonrise: allowing for lunar parallax, a declination of 30.12°, a latitude of 52.18° and a skyline height of 0.5°, the azimuth is 142.12°.
34. Lake long barrow: Hoare (1812), p.209. Landscape: Exon et al. (2000), pp. 108–109.
35. Heel Stone and the summer solstice: Smith (1771), p. 51.
36. Not quite the solstice: Stukeley (1724), p. 122 (p. 113). Faulty compass: Atkinson (1985), S62.
37. Shakespeare: *A Midsummer Night's Dream*, Act IV, Scene I, line 139.
38. H. Wansey, *Stonehenge* (1796), p. 61 in Legg (1986) pp. 107–111; Duke (1846), p. 133; A. Herbert, *Cyclops Christianus* (John Petheram, London, 1849), p. 98; Stevens (1896), p. 88.
39. Lockyer (1909), p. 68; Stone (1924), p. 130; Atkinson (1956), pp. 15, 52.
40. False photographs: Chippindale (2004), p. 137.
41. The Heel Stone and the summer solstice: Niel (1975), p. 53.
42. The three centres – Aubrey Holes, 3ft 6ft (1m) SSW of sarsen centre: Thom & Thom (1978), p. 149; The earthwork centre, WSW of the sarsen centre: Petrie (1880), plate II, p. 39.
43. The importance of hills: A.L. Lewis, 'On the relationship of stone circles to outlying stones or tumuli or neighbouring hills', *JRAI 11*, 1883, pp. 176–91; Cope (1998), pp. 97–104, 386; Ruggles (1999), pp. 98, 106–107, 140; Burl (2000).
44. The burial: Hawley (1928), pp. 170–72; Atkinson (1956), p. 51; Gibson (1998), p. 117.

Chapter 6

1. The Aubrey Holes: Aubrey (1980 ed.), pp. 76, 80.
2. J. Leasor, *The Plague and the Fire* (Allen & Unwin, London, 1962), p. 24.
3. Hawley (1921), p. 30.
4. Calibrated dates: Bayliss, Housley, & McCormac, in Cleal et al. (1995), pp. 522–24. Newall, *Ant 3*, 1929, p.82.
5. Hawkins, 'Stonehenge: a Neolithic computer', *Nature 202*, 1964, pp. 1258–61; Hoyle (1977), pp. 79–81.
6. Hawkins (1964), note 5, p. 1259.
7. Hawkins (1966), p. 140.
8. For details of the henges and sources of excavation reports, see the gazetteer in Harding & Lee (1987).
9. Thom, Thom & Thom (1974), p. 83.
10. Thom, Thom & Thom (1974), note 9, p. 83.
11. Aubrey Holes and posts: Cleal & Walker, in Cleal (1995), pp. 106, 107, 112. Boscombe Down: *CA 195*, 2004, pp. 106–107.
12. Hawley (1928), p. 172.
13. Atkinson, Piggott & Stone (1952), pp. 14–20.
14. Newall, *Ant 3*, 1929, p. 83; Newall, *Stonehenge* (HMSO, London, 1953), p. 9.
15. Hawley (1923), p. 14.
16. J. Evans, *Land Snails in Archaeology* (Academic Press, London, 1972), p. 103.
17. J. Evans et al., 'Stonehenge – the environment in the Late Neolithic and Early Bronze Age . . .', *WAM 78*, 1983, p. 13.
18. Coneybury Hill: Richards (1991), pp. 44, 74–75, 98–96. Radiocarbon assays: Cleal et al. (1995), p. 57; the pit: Cleal et al. (1995), p. 57, 3100 ± 100 bc (OxA-1402); the ditch: Cleal et al. (1995), pp. 163, 487.
19. Cleal & MacSween, eds., *Grooved Ware in Britain and Ireland, Neolithic Studies Group, Seminar Paper 3* (Oxbow, Oxford, 1999); A. Gibson, *Prehistoric Pottery in Britain and Ireland* (Tempus, Brimscombe Port, 2002), pp. 84–87.
20. J. Thomas, *Re-thinking the Neolithic* (Cambridge, Cambridge University Press, 1991), p. 59.
21. Grooved Ware and beakers: Grant & Yorston, *Ant J 18*, 1938, p. 402; V.G. Childe, *Prehistoric Communities of the British Isles* (Edinburgh, Chambers, 1940), pp. 45, 84, 87; S. Piggott, *Neolithic Cultures of the British Isles* (Cambridge, Cambridge University Press, 1963), pp. 322–27.
22. Four types of Rinyo-Clacton ware: Cleal & MacSween (1999), note 19; Gibson (2002), pp. 84–87; Garwood, in Cleal et al. (1995), pp. 145–76.
23. Rivers: Cleal, in Cleal and MacSween (1999), note 23, pp. 4, 5; Stukeley (1740), p. 14.
24. Discovery of pottery: Cleal, in Bradley & Gardiner, eds., *Neolithic Studies. A review of some current Research* (Oxford, Oxford University Press, 1984), p. 150.
25 Snail Down stakeholes: N. Thomas, *Snail Down, Wiltshire. A Bronze Age Cemetery* . . . (Wiltshire Archaeological and Natural History Society/English Heritage, 2005). Sites III, VI, VII, X-XIV, XVI, XVII, XIX.

26. Grooved sherds at Stonehenge: Piggott, *Ant 10*, 1936, p. 221.
27. D. Clarke; T. Cowie & A. Foxon, *Symbols of Power* (Edinburgh, National Museum of Antiquities, Scotland, 1989), pp. 54–55.
28. Solar spirals: M. Brennan, *The Stars and the Stones. Ancient Art and Astronomy in Ireland* (Thames & Hudson, London, 1983), pp. 189–90.
29. C. Richards & J. Thomas, in Bradley & Gardiner (1984), note 26, pp. 189–218.
30. Woodhenge: M. Cunnington (1929). The deposits: Burl, *Prehistoric Henges* (Shire, Princes Risborough, 1991), pp. 50–51.
31. Woodlands and Ratfyn pits: J.F.S. Stone & W.E.V. Young, *WAM 52*, 1948, pp. 257–306.
32. F. Vatcher *Ant 43*, 1969, pp. 310–11.
33. Secondary cremations: Hawley (1924), p. 37.
34. Long bone pins: Atkinson, Piggott & Sandars, *Excavations at Dorchester, Oxon, I* (Oxford, Ashmolean Museum, 1951), pp. 142–44.
35. Flint blades: Chippindale (2004), p. 193.
36. Hawley (1924), p. 37; Hawley (1926), p. 45.
37. Cremations at the east: Hawley (1928), p. 170; Atkinson (1979), p. 62.
38. The macehead: Hawley (1925), p. 34.
39. Skilled craftsmen: T.G. Manby, *Grooved Ware in the North of England* (British Archaeological Reports [BAR], Oxford, 1974), p. 98.
40. Hoare (1812), p. 124.
41. Large posthole: Hawley (1926), p. 2; Cleal et al. (1995), table 69, p. 149. 1c large, 2 smaller just to its NW, 1a, 1b. Midsummer moonrise. Declination for parallax = 30.115°.

   Equation: $\cos az = \dfrac{\sin d - (\sin 51.18° \times 0.5°)}{(\cos 51.18° \times \cos 0.5°)} = az.\ 144.2°$

42. Breton axes as amulets: Burl (1985), pp. 19–20.

Chapter 7

1. Geoffrey of Monmouth (1969 ed.), pp. 172–73.
2. Aubrey (1980 ed.), p. 116.
3. Hawley (1921), pp. 39, 41; Thomas (1923).
4. Stone (1924), pp. 64–65, 137–39.
5. Aubrey (1980 ed.), p. 127.
6. Gerald of Wales (1982 ed.), pt. 2, p. 51.
7. Merlin: Geoffrey of Monmouth (1969 ed.), p. 198.
8. C-14 assays: Cleal et al. (1995), pp. 204–205, 331, 524. Q/R Holes cut by sarsens: Allen, in Cleal et al. (1995), p. 183.
9. Snowdonia: H. Howard, *PPS 48*, 1982, p. 117.
10. Glaciation: Kellaway, *Nature 233* (1971), pp. 30–35; Kellaway (2002), pp. 57–71; Geddes (2000), p. 65. Near the Cursus: Kellaway (2002), p. 65.
11. The source of the Altar Stone: Kellaway (1991), pp. 245, 267; Thorpe et al. (1991), pp. 119, 153.
12. OU9: Cleal et al. (1995), pp. 99, 377, 394. 'Not the Cosheston Beds': Thorpe et al. (1991), p. 141.

13. Excavation of Q and R Holes: Hawley (1928), pp. 172–73; Atkinson (1979), pp. 204–206.
14. The two adjacent stoneholes, WA3654, WA3648: Allen, in Cleal et al. (1995), pp. 187–88, fig. 80, plan 171.
15. Number of stones, the 'entrance' and the alignment: Allen, in Cleal et al. (1995), p. 181, fig. 79, plan 170; fig. 80, plan 171.
16. The great stonehole and the Altar Stone: Allen, in Cleal et al. (1995), p. 178, hole WA3639. fig. 180.
17. Pitts, *Nature 290*, 1981, pp. 40–41; *PPS 48*, 1982, pp. 75–132, fig. 3.
18. 'Grace-note': Burl, *WAM 87*, 1994, pp. 93–94.
19. Dyfed: Daniel, *Ant 56*, 1982, p. 64. Insanity: R. Muir, *Riddles in the British Landscape* (Thames & Hudson, London, 1981), p. 70.
20. Stone circles in Pembrokeshire: Thorpe et al. (1991), pp. 115–16, table 3.
21. Worn-down schist: *WAM 21*, 1884, p. 142.
22. Atkinson, in Heggie (1982), p. 109.
23. Glaciation unlikely: C.P. Green, *Nature 243*, 1973, pp. 214–16; Cunliffe & Renfrew (1997), pp. 257–70; J.D. Scourse, in Cunliffe & Renfrew (1997), pp. 271–314.
24. Boles Barrow: W. Cunnington, in R.H. Cunnington (1975), pp. 15–16, 38.
25. 'More than fantasy?': *Hamlet*, Act I, Scene 1, line 54.
26. Bluestone in Salisbury Museum: Accession no. 68/1934.
27. Provenance of the bluestone: Petrie (1880), p. 16; Wood (1747), pp. 41, 53, plan, p. 66.
28. Burl (1999), pp. 118–21.
29. W/MR beakers earlier than the sarsens of Stonehenge: Clarke (1970), vol. 1, p. 105.
30. Epic feat from the Preselis: Clarke (1970), vol. 1, p. 107.
31. Beaker chronology: Gibson (2002), pp. 92–93.
32. Fruitless search in the Preselis: Drewett (1987), pp. 15–16. Further fieldwork: Darvill & Wainwright, *Ant 76*, 2002, pp. 623–24; *Arch Wales 43*, 2003, pp. 3–12; *Brit Arch 83*, 2005, pp. 28–31.
33. Ixer & Turner (2006), p. 8. See also *OJA 25 (1)*, 2006, pp. 26–46.
34. Unusual setting of the bluestones: Burl, 'Myth-Conceptions', *3rd Stone 37*, 2000, pp. 6–9.
35. Clarke (1970), vol. 1, p. 107; Pitts (2000), pp. 211–12.
36. Giot (1960), p. 52; Patton (1993), pp. 87–89; Twohig (1981), p. 114.
37. Daniel (1950), pp. 155–56; Powell, in Powell et al. (1969), pp. 259–60.
38. Hoare (1812), p. 7.

Chapter 8

1. 'Rude': Fergusson (1872). 'Rough': T.E. Peet, *Rough Stone Monuments and Their Builders* (Harper, London, 1912).
2. Aubrey (1980 ed.), pp. 76, 91, 93, plate VIII.
3. Stukeley (1724), p. 78 (p. 61); Stukeley (1740), p. 14.
4. Wood (1747), pp. 43–44; Smith (1771), p. 52.
5. Upcast earth: E.H. Stone (1924), p. 116.
6. Hawley (1923), pp. 14–16.

7. Stone 94's pit: Cleal & Walker, in Cleal et al. (1995), p. 273, plan 277. A resistivity examination: Allen, in Cleal et al. (1995), p. 50.

8. Measurements for the Four Stations: Atkinson (1978), p. 51. 'Operation of field-geometry': Atkinson (1979), p. 33.

9. Newall (1953), p. 10.

10. The Stations as 'symbolic memorials': Atkinson (1979), p. 33.

11. Rev. Edward Duke: Marsden (1999), p. 25; E. Cunnington (1979), pp. 97–99.

12. The large skull: Stukeley (1724), p. 102 (p. 89).

13. The solar stations: Duke (1846), p. 144.

14. Hawkins (1966), pp. 132–35.

15. Lockyer (1906), p. 93.

16. Ruggles, in Cunliffe & Renfrew (1997), pp. 218–20. See also Castleden (1993), p. 134.

17. King Arthur's Hall: Lewis, *JRAI 25*, 1986, p. 5; Burl (1995), p. 34.

18. Fortingall: F. Coles, *PSAS 42*, 1907–8, pp. 121–25; Thom, Thom & Burl (1980), pp. 336–37. Preliminary excavation report: Burl (1988), pp. 9–11, 166–73.

19. Alignments in Finistère: Pontois (1929), pp. 96–125; 'Le loi': Pontois (1929), p. 106.

20. Crucuno: Giot, l'Helgouach & Monnier (1979), p. 409; Thom, Thom, Merritt & Merritt, *Curr Anthr 14* (1973), pp. 450–52.

21. Exmoor stones: L.V. Grinsell, *The Archaeology of Exmoor. Bideford Bay to Bridgewater* (David & Charles, Newton Abbot, 1970), p. 12.

22. Exmoor: Grinsell (1970), note 21, pp. 22–27. Exmoor surveys: Rev. J.F. Chanter & R.H. Worth, 'The rude stone monuments of Exmoor and its borders, I', Trans. *Dev. Assoc. 37*, 1905, pp. 375–97; *ibid*, II, 1906, pp. 538–52; N.V. Quinnell, 'Lithic monuments within the Exmoor National Park', ed. C.J. Dunn (Royal Commission on the Ancient and Historical Monuments of Wales [RCAHM], Aberystwyth, 1992).

23. Woodburrow Hangings: Chanter & Worth (1905), pp. 392–93; Quinnell (1992), 'Challcombe 15'.

24. F. Elgee, *Early Man in North-East Yorkshire* (Gloucester, John Bellows, 1930), pp. 105–106.

25. Anglesey: F. Lynch, *Prehistoric Anglesey* (Llangefni, Anglesey Ant. Soc., 1970), p. 116.

26. The Crucuno triangle: W. Sitwell, *Stones of Northumberland and Other Lands* (Andrew Reid & Co., Newcastle, 1930), pp. 95–97.

27. Camden (1637), p. 203.

28. *Caxton. The Description of Britain*, selected and modernized by M. Collins (Sidgwick & Jackson, London, 1988), pp. 41–46. Ranulf Higden: S.A.E. Mendyk, *'Speculum Britanniae': Regional Study, Antiquarianism, and Science in Britain to 1700* (Toronto University Press, 1989), pp. 41–42, 259, notes 20, 21; C. Given-Wilson, *Chronicles. The Writing of History in Medieval Britain* (Hambledon & London Ltd, London, 2004), pp. 55–56 et al..

29. Burl (1976a), p. 53 (written in 1973).

30. Thom, Thom, Merritt & Merritt, *Curr Anthr 14* (1973), p. 451.

Chapter 9

1. Durrington Walls, 1951–52: *Ant 34*, 1954, pp. 155–70
2. Circular buildings and the south circle: Wainwright & Longworth (1971), plan 1, p. 26, fig. 11; plan II, p. 30, fig. 12; pp. 204–8, fig. 84.
3. Feasting: 'Journey to Stonehenge', *Time Team Special*, Channel 5 television programme (November 2005).
4. Sexual symbolism: *Brit Arch 80*, 2005, p. 11.
5. Stanton Drew: A. David et al., *Ant 78*, 2004, pp. 341–56; Gibson (2005), pp. 31. 53, 155, 170, 171, 173.
6. Timber rings in the Netherlands and Britain: Gibson (1998), pp. 111–12.
7. Cross-Channel contacts: Pearson (1993), p. 95; Cunliffe (2001), p. 211.
8. Early Beaker burials near Stonehenge: Burl (1987), pp. 116, 129, fig. 9.
9. Rollright Stones: Stukeley (1743), p. 20.
10. Radiocarbon assays. Stone 1: 2073±21 bc (UB-3821); trilithon 53–54: 1945±45 bc (OxA-4840); trilithon 56: 1720±150 bc (BM-46); trilithon 57: 1910±40 bc (OxA-4839). Bayliss, Housley & McCormac, in Cleal et al. (1995), pp. 524–25, 532, 533.
11. Recumbent stones: Burl (2000), pp. 222–23.
12. Sarsens: H.C. Brentnall, 'Sarsens', *WAM 51*, 1946, p.426; India: P. Singh, *Burial Practice in Ancient India* (Prithvi Prakashan, Varanasi, 1970), pp. 104, 137, 154; Aubrey: *The Natural History of Wilts. By John Aubrey, FRS, written between 1656 and 1691*, ed. J. Britton (Wilts Top Soc, 1847), p. 44. 'The Wanderer', *Anglo-Saxon Poetry*, ed. S.A.J. Bradley (Dent, London, 1982), p. 232.
13. Polished sarsens: Aubrey (1980 ed.), p. 91.
14. Transport of the sarsens: Atkinson (1979), pp. 114–15, 116–22.
15. Shaping sarsens: Stone (1924), pp. 4–7, 87; Atkinson (1979), pp. 122–29.
16. Raising the uprights: Stone (1924), pp. 104–8.
17. Raising the lintels: Atkinson (1979), pp. 134–39.
18. The ramp for Stone 56: Hawley (1926), p. 12; Atkinson (1979), p. 207; Allen, in Cleal et al. (1995), pp. 188, 202.
19. Graded heights: Petrie (1880), pp. 6, 12.
20. The sarsen entrance: Stukeley (1740), p. 17.
21. Inner faces of stones: Stukeley (1740), p. 15.
22. Number of trilithons: Jones (1655), p. 63; Stukeley (1740), p. 22.
23. Stone 60: Atkinson, letter to *Stonehenge Viewpoint 71*, 1988, p. 2.
24. *Entasis*: Stone (1924), p. 11; Atkinson (1979), p. 37.
25. Stonehenge architects – Mycenaean architect: Atkinson (1979), pp. 92–93. Egyptians: J. Ivimy, *The Sphinx and the Megaliths* (London, Turnstone Books, 1974). Martians: T.C. Lethbridge, *The Legend of the Sons of God* (Sidgwick & Jackson, London, 1973), p. 110.
26. Paired bluestones: Atkinson (1979), p. 212.
27. Imposing interior of Stonehenge: Stukeley (1740), p. 25.
28. On top of trilithons: Stukeley (1724), p. 67 (p. 46), plenty of room; Stukeley (1740), p. 28, 'frightful'. Canadian cyclists: Long (1876), p. 62; Harrison (1900), p. 17. Quoting a report in *The King*, February, 1900, p. 148.

29. Breton *fers-à-cheval*: Burl (1985) for specific sites. Plans of sites near Carnac: A. & A.S. Thom, *La Géométrie des Alignements de Carnac (suivi de plans Comparatifs)*, (Université de Rennes, Rennes, 1977). For Er-Lannic: P. Gouezin & E. Le Gall, *Le Site Mégalithique d'Er-Lannic* (Archeo Douar Mor, 1998).
30. The trilithon horseshoe: Stukeley (1724), p. 59 (p. 41).
31. Brittany and Britain: Derek Simpson, in Megaw & Simpson (1979), pp. 223, 227.
32. Avebury, circle or horseshoe: Aubrey (1980), p. 44; Ucko et al. (1991), p. 227, Transparency 26.
33. L. Myatt, *The Standing Stones of Caithness. A Guide* (Privately printed, 2003), pp. 24–25; Sir Henry Dryden, in Fergusson (1872), pp. 530–31; Thom, Thom & Burl (1990), vol.II, pp. 288–89.
34. Hethpool: P. Topping, *Northern Archeology 2 (2)*, 1981, pp. 3–10; Burl (1995), p. 71.
35. Missionaries: V.G. Childe, *The Prehistory of European Society* (1958), p. 129.
36. Lucy: an early fourth-century Syracusan saint and martyr. Her Feast Day is 13 December which, before the change to the Gregorian calendar in 1752, was the shortest day of the year. Donne's poem was written around 1617 almost a century and a half earlier. See chapter one, note 48, for Stukeley's similar midsummer mistake.

Chapter 10

1. A.L. Owen, *The Famous Druids . . .* (Clarendon Press, Oxford, 1962), p. 118.
2. *Macbeth*, Act III, Scene 4, line 122.
3. King: Harrison (1901), p. 78. Horrid sacrifice: T. Maurice, *Indian Antiquities VI* (London, 1796), p. 128.
4. Cleal et al. (1995), fig. 8, p. 14; Cleal & Walker, in Cleal et al. (1995), pp. 285–87.
5. Aubrey (1980 ed.), p. 97; Stukeley (1740), p. 12.
6. Slaughter Stone as an obstacle: Hawley (1924), pp. 36–37. Inigo Jones: Webb (1725), p. 11; Aubrey (1980 ed.), p. 76.
7. De Heere: J.A. Bakker, *Ant 53*, 1979, pp. 107–11; Burl (1994), p. 88. It was not until 1662 that 'the earliest perspectively correct view known' of Stone-henge was drawn, by Willem Schellinke: J.A. Bakker, *In Discussion with the Past . . .* (Foundation for Promoting Archaeology, Zwolle, 1999), pp. 9–22.
8. Webb (1725), p. 16.
9. Dates for Stone E: Cleal & Walker, in Cleal et al. (1995), pp. 283–87; Bayliss, Housley & McCormac, in Cleal et al. (1995), pp. 524–25.
10. Atkinson (1979), p. 78; Stone (1924), p. 119.
11. Stone D: Hawley (1924), p. 36; Cleal & Allen, in Cleal et al. (1995), fig. 13, p. 37.
12. Partner to the Slaughter Stone: Stukeley (1724), p. 76 (p. 57).
13. Unexcavated area: Cleal et al. (1995), fig. 156, p. 269.
14. Uncertainty about the solar alignments: Ruggles (1997), pp. 220–21.

15. Stukeley, 'or nearly': Stukeley (1740), p. 56.
16. 'Ground Plan of Stonehenge': Hoare (1812), p. 143.
17. The avenue: Atkinson (1979), pp. 66; *RCAHM-England* (1979), p. 11. The excavation: G. Smith 'Excavation of the Stonehenge Avenue at West Amesbury, Wilts', *WAM 48*, 1973, pp. 42–56, fig. 3. Stonehenge Bottom: Richards (1991), pp. 15–16.
18. The walk: Exon et al. (2000), p. 75.
19. C-14 assays from the avenue NW ditch: 1985 ± 50 bc (OxA-4884); 1728 ± 68 bc (BM 1164); 1770 ± 70 bc (HAR-2013). SE ditch: 1915 ± 40 bc (OxA-4905). Bayliss, Housley & McCormac, in Cleal et al. (1995), pp. 526–27. For a provisional chronology of avenues in Britain and Ireland, 2600–2000 BC, see Burl (1993), p. 23.
20. Discovery of the Avenue: Stukeley (1724), p. 77 (p. 59); Stukeley (1740), p. 35.
21. Deletions: Stukeley (1724), p. 78 (p. 59).
22. Gale's letter: Lukis (1885), p. 268.
23. Avenue stones at Stonehenge: Stukeley, 'History of the temples . . . Part I': Bodleian Eng. Misc. c.323, p. 129.
24. Avenues near Stonehenge: Burl (2000), pp. 409–10.
25. The Beckhampton avenue – Lukis' scepticism: *PSAL 9*, 1881–83, pp. 344–46. The 1999 excavation: Gillings, Pollard & Wheatley, *Wiltshire Archaeological & Natural History Magazine, 93* (2000), pp. 1–8.
26. Tudor vandalism at Stonehenge: Jones (1655), p. 57.
27. Amesbury and the avenue: Stukeley (1724), p. 77–78 (p. 59).
28. Stukeley's drawings of the Stonehenge avenue – Bodleian Library, Gough Maps 229: August, 1721, f.16; 6 June 1724, f.24.
29. Atkinson (1979), p. 44.
30. Wheeler, *The Times*, 26 February 1958, p. 9.
31. The Stonehenge carvings: Lawson & Walker, in Cleal et al. (1995), pp. 31–33. The genuine dagger: *British Archaeology 73*, 2003, pp. 8–13; *British Archaeology 74*, 2004, p. 28.
32. British weapons: Burgess (2001), p. 334. Lintel 121: Atkinson (1979), p. 209.
33. Lighting: O.G.S. Crawford, *Ant 28* (1954), pp. 25–31.
34. Le Tiemblage: P-R Giot, *Gallia Préhistoire 16*, 1973, pp. 401–26; Burl, *Ant 60*, 1986, pp. 147–48.
35. Camden (1637), p. 253.
36. Corpora of art – Britain: R.W.B. Morris, 'The prehistoric rock art of Great Britain: a survey of all sites bearing motifs more complex than simple cupmarks', *PPS 55*, 1989, pp. 45–88. Ireland: C. O'Kelly, 'Passage-grave art in the Boyne Valley, Ireland', *PPS 39*, 1973, pp. 352–82. Also: M. O'Sullivan, *Megalithic Art in Ireland* (Dublin, Country House, 1993; no index). Brittany: Twohig (1981). Figures for sites: Twohig (1981), pp. 83–148. Breton motifs: Twohig (1981), table 4, pp. 55–57. Possible daggers: Twohig (1981), p. 90 (Penhape, Prajou-Menhir and others).
37. Rectangles and axes in Britain: R.W.B. Morris (1989), pp. 62, 66, 87.20
38. Ardross: J. Milne, *Trans. Banffshire Field Club* (1910–11), p. 35.
39. Ri Cruin: *PSAS 65*, 1931, pp. 269–75. Nether Largie: *PSAS 8*, 1870, p. 380.
40. Badbury: *Ant J 19*, 1939, pp. 291–99.
41. Drombeg: E.M. Fahy, *J. Cork HAS 64*, 1959, pp. 4–5.
42. Er-Lannic: M. St-J. Péquart & Z. le Rouzic, *Corpus des Signes Gravés des Monuments Mégalithiques du Morbihan* (Picard & Berger-Levrault, Paris,

1927), p. 20, plates 7–9; P. Gouezin, *Le Site Mégalithique d'Er Lannic* (Association Archeo Douar Mor, Morbihan, 1998), p. 13.

43. Breton axe-carvings: Twohig (1981), p. 89. 'Daggers': Twohig (1981), p. 90.
44. Anthropomorphic *stelae*: Twohig (1981), pp. 91–92. Figures of plain rectangles – Mané Bras: Twohig (1981), fig. 84; Penhape: Twohig (1981), p. 123; Goërem, Gâvres: Twohig (1981), p. 134; Les Pierres-Plates: Twohig (1981), p. 147; Prajou-Menhir: Twohig (1981), p. 153.
45. Les Pierres-Plates: Burl (1985), pp. 160–63, fig. on p. 160.
46. Menhirs in Brittany – Kerloas: Burl (1985), pp. 62–64; Kerzerho: Burl (1985), pp. 145–46; Le Grand Menhir Brisé: Burl (1985), pp. 135–36.
47. Prehistoric numeracy: Burl (1976b).
48. Recumbent stone circles: Burl, 'Science or symbolism: problems of archaeoastronomy', *Ant 54*, 1980, pp. 191–200.
49. F. Lynch, 'Colours in prehistoric architecture', in Gibson & Simpson, eds., *Ritual and Religion in Prehistoric Britain. Essays in Honour of Aubrey Burl* (Thrupp, Sutton, 1998), p. 62. Barrows: L.V. Grinsell, *Dorset Barrows* (Dorchester, Dorset Natural History and Archaeological Society, 1959), p. 99; L.V. Grinsell, 'Somerset barrows, part I, West & South', reprint from *Somerset Archaeology & Natural History Society*, vol. 113, 1969, p. 34. Yorkshire: J.C. Atkinson, *Forty Years in a Moorland Parish* (Macmillan, London, 1891), p. 148; F. Elgee, *Early Man in North-East Yorkshire* (John Bellows, Gloucester, 1930), p. 91. Brittany: Brocéliande: J. Briard, ed., *Mégalithes du Haute Bretagne* (Editions de la Maison des Sciences de l'Homme, Paris, 1989), pp. 41–56; Alignements du Moulin: Burl (1985), p. 91. Recumbent stone circles, Balquhain: Burl, *Prehistoric Astronomy and Ritual* (Shire, Princes Risborough, 2005), pp. 59–65. Stukeley's barrow: Stukeley (1724), pp. 97–97 (pp. 82–83, 85); Stukeley (1740), p. 44.
50. Burial inside Stonehenge: Hawley (1923), p. 18.
51. The gallows on the Wansdyke: Stukeley (1740), p. 4, table II.

Chapter 11

1. Stukeley (1740), p. 12.
2. Altar Stone: Petrie (1880), p. 18.
3. Second Altar: Aubrey (1980 ed.), pp. 94–95.
4. St James's Palace: *WAM 11*, 1869, pp. 112, 349.
5. Stones for bridges: Aubrey (1980 ed.), p. 93; Stukeley (1724), p. 26 (p. 5); Stukeley (1740), p. 37.
6. The Berwick St James' stones: G.M. Engleheart, *WAM 46*, 1933, pp. 395–97; Burl (1987), pp. 139–40; Thorpe et al. (1991), p. 119.
7. St James' churches in Wiltshire: Nikolaus Pevsner, *Wiltshire* (Penguin Books, Harmondsworth, 1975), p. 93 ff. Berwick St James: Pevsner, *Wiltshire* (1975), p. 108. The chalice: *WAM 26*, 1892, pp. 328, 332.
8. Inigo Jones (1655), p. 57. 'Wherein the *Victims* for oblations were slain': Inigo Jones (1655), p. 5.
9. Stukeley (1740), p. 30.
10. Dimensions of the Altar Stone: Atkinson (1979), p. 56.
11. Stukeley (1724), pp. 65–66, (p. 45); Stukeley (1740), pp. 30–31.

12. R.H. Cunnington (1975), p. 41.
13. Atkinson (1979), pp. 211–12.
14. Stukeley (1740), p. 28.
15. Stone 55: Petrie (1880), p. 11.
16. Roman coins around Stone 55a, 55b: Gowland (1903), pp. 27–28.
17. Barclay (1895), p. 57.
18. Centre stones: Burl (2000), p. 394.
19. Stone (1924), p. 19.
20. Niel (1975), p. 50; Freeman (1998), p. 10.
21. R.H. Cunnington (1935), pp. 96–97.
22. Stukeley (1724), p. 45, (p. 25).
23. The Sanctuary: M. Cunnington (1931), p. 308, Hole 3.
24. Woodhenge: M. Cunnington (1929), p. 14.
25. Carvings near the Altar Stone: Lawson and Walker, in Cleal et al. (1995), pp. 30–33.
26. Les Combarelles: A. & G. Sieveking, *The Caves of France and Northern Spain; a Guide* (Vista Books, London, 1962), pp. 56–65.
27. The 'window': Stone (1924), p. 20, plate 5. Latitude, 51.8°; horizon, +0.5°; declination – 23.979°. The midwinter sun would rise near 128° and set at about 232°. Over eight hours it would be moving at a speed of some 40ft (12m) a minute. The inverted triangle of the 'window' is no more than $3\frac{1}{2}$ft (1m+) wide at the utmost.
28. Stukeley (1740), p. 12, table VII.

Chapter 12

1. 'European', Wessex/Middle Rhine Beaker barrows near Stonehenge: Clarke (1970), vol. II, pp. 500–505.
2. The killing of the Beaker man: *Ant 52*, 1978, pp. 235–36; *WAM 78*, 1983, pp. 7–30, the burial: pp. 13–24.
3. Arrowheads: S. Green, 'Flint arrowheads: typology and interpretation', *Lithics 5*, 1984, pp. 19–29. The five assays: 2010+60 bc (OxA-4886); 1835+70 bc (OxA-5044); 1875+60 bc (OxA-5045); 1825+55 bc (OxA-5046); 1765+70 bc (BM-1582). Bayliss, Housley & McCormac, in Cleal et al. (1995), pp. 524–25.
4. Callis Wold 100: J. Mortimer, *Forty Years Digging . . .* (1905), p. 104. Germany: S. Piggott, 'Beaker bows: a suggestion', *PPS 37* (11), 1970, p. 91. Corpus of British arrowheads: Clarke (1970), vol. II, pp. 438–47.
5. The Stonehenge Archer: *CA 184*, 2003, pp. 146–52.
6. The mass Beaker grave: *CA 186*, 2003, p. 231.
7. Independent authorities: Professor M.P. Pearson, Department of Archaeology & Prehistory, University of Sheffield; Dr Alison Sheridan, Head of Early Prehistory, National Museums of Scotland.
8. Amesbury 11 bell barrow: Hoare (1812), p.128. Finds: Annable & Simpson (1964), pp. 53, 108, item 327, the tweezers. The urn is lost, possibly smashed in the Cunningtons' hasty and slipshod removal of Hoare's collections from Stourhead to Devizes in 1878: L. Phillips, 'An investigation into the life of A.D. Passmore, a most curious specimen', *WAM 97*, 2004, p. 281.

9. Y and Z Holes: Hawley (1925), pp. 27–31, pp. 37–50; Walker, in Cleal et al. (1995), pp. 256–65. Radiocarbon assays: Bayliss, Housley & McCormac, in Cleal et al. (1995), pp. 524–25.

10. Social stagnation: C. Burgess, 'Population, climate and upland settlement', *BAR 143*, Oxford, 1985, p. 213.

11. Sir Thomas Browne: *Hydriotaphia; or Urne-Buriall* (printed for Hen. Brome, London, 1658), chapter 5; S. Piggott, 'Sir Thomas Browne and antiquity', *Oxford J Arch 7 (3)*, 1988, p. 267.

12. Breton menhirs – Kerzerho: Burl (1985), pp. 145–46; Kerloas: Burl (1985), pp. 62–64; Grand Menhir Brisé: Burl (1985), pp. 135–36.

13. Antrobus (1900), p. 19.

14. Amesbury: Gover et al. (1970), pp. 358–59. Saxon burials: Grinsell (1957), Amesbury, p. 30, Durrington, p. 66. Also: D.J. Bonney, 'The pagan Saxon period, *c.*500–700 AD, in R.B. Pugh. ed., *A History of Wiltshire I, Pt 2* (Oxford Univerity Press, Oxford, 1973), pp. 468–84.

Appendix 1

1. There are dictionaries for the Atlantic Fringe languages. Brittany: L. Stéphan & V. Séité, *Léxique Breton-Français et Français-Breton* (Éditions Emgleo-Breiz, Bannalec, 1984). Cornwall: C. Weathergill, *Cornish Place-Names and Language* (Sigma Leisure, Wilmslow, 1995). Wales: H. Lewis, ed., *Collins-Spurrell Welsh Dictionary* (Collins, London, 1960).

Appendix 2

1. Grid references and sources for the great ovals and the horseshoes listed in this Appendix can be found in Burl (2000), pp. 395–435.

Appendix 3

1. R.W.B. Morris, 'The prehistoric rock art of Great Britain: a survey of all sites bearing motifs more complex than simple cupmarks', *PPS 55*, 1989, pp. 45–88. For the variety of carvings: figs 1, 2, pp. 46, 47.

2. The Ardross cist-slab: the reference cited by Morris, *Trans Banff Field Club* (1910), p. 36, is incorrect.

3. Kilmartin Valley: Morris (1989), p. 66.

4. Badbury bowl barrow: Morris (1989), p. 87. *Ant J 3*, 1923, pp. 348–52; *Arch J 19*, 1939, pp. 291–99.

5. Drombeg: E.M. Fahy, *J Cork Hist Arch Soc 64*, 1959, pp. 1–27.

6. Twohig (1981), p. 89, table 4, pp. 55–57. Also figures 83–148 following the text.

7. Axe-carvings: Twohig (1981), p. 89.

8. Carvings in Breton tombs, see Twohig (1981), figures following p. 259: Gavr'inis, fig. 113; Grah Niaul, fig. 128; Kercado, fig. 94; Mané Kerioned B, figs 87, 89; Mané Lud, fig. 99; Mané Ruthuel, fig. 106; Penhape, fig. 123; Petit-Mont, fig. 125 and Table des Marchands, figs 102, 104.

9. 'Bucklers': Twohig (1981), pp. 91–92.

10. Figurines, see Twohig (1981), note 8: Gavr'inis, fig. 117; Goërem, Gâvres, figs 134, 135, 136; Ile Longue, fig. 108; Kercado, fig. 93; Luffang, now open to the sky and the stone removed, fig. 139; Les Pierres Plates, figs 143, 144, 146, 147, 148; Mané Bras, fig. 84; Mané Ruthuel, fig. 105; Penhape, fig. 123; Table des Marchands, fig. 102.

11. Table des Marchands and other carved slabs, see: M. & St.-J. Péquart & Z. le Rouzic, *Corpus des Signes Gravès des Monuments Mégalithiques du Morbihan* (Éditions Auguste Picard, Paris, 1927)

12. The statue-menhirs of the Aveyron: *Statue-Menhirs. Des Enigmes de Pierre Venues de Fond des Ages*, ed. d'A. Philippon (Éditions de Rouergues, Rodez, 2002).

BIBLIOGRAPHY

Andrews, J. & Dury, A., 1952. *Map of Wiltshire, 1773* (Wiltshire Archaeological & Natural History Society, Devizes).

Annable, K. & Simpson, D.D.A., 1964. *Guide Catalogue to the Neolithic and Bronze Age Collections in Devizes Museum* (Wiltshire Archaeological & Natural History Society, Devizes).

Anon., 1776. *A Description of Stonehenge, Abiry, &c, in Wiltshire* . . . (Anon, Salisbury).

Anon., 1898. *The Illustrated Guide to Old Sarum and Stonehenge* (Browne & Co., Salisbury).

Antrobus, Lady Florence, 1900. *A Sentimental and Practical Guide to Amesbury and Stonehenge* (Estate Office, Amesbury).

Ashbee, P., 1966. 'The Fussell's Lodge long barrow excavations, 1957', *Arch 100*, pp. 1–80.

Ashbee, P., 1984. *The Earthen Long Barrow in Britain*, 2nd ed. (Geo Books, Norwich).

Ashmore, P.J., 1996. *Neolithic and Bronze Age Scotland* (Batsford, London).

Atkinson, R.J.C., 1956. *Stonehenge* (Hamish Hamilton, London).

Atkinson, R.J.C., 1978. 'Some new measurements at Stonehenge', *Nature 275*, pp. 50–52.

Atkinson, R.J.C., 1979. *Stonehenge. Archaeology and Interpretation* (Penguin, Harmondsworth).

Atkinson, R.J.C., 1982. 'Aspects of the astronomy of Stonehenge', in Heggie (1982), pp. 107–26.

Atkinson, R.J.C., 1985. 'William Stukeley and the Stonehenge sunrise', *Archaeoastronomy 8*, S61–2.

Atkinson, R.J.C., Piggott, S. & Stone, J.F.S., 1952. 'Excavation of two additional holes at Stonehenge, 1950, and new evidence for the date of the monument', *Ant J 32*, pp. 14–20.

Aubrey, J., 1980. *Monumenta Britannica, I, c.1665–93* (Dorset Publishing, Milborne Port).

Aubrey, J., 1982. *Monumenta Britannica, II, c.1665–93* (Dorset Publishing, Milborne Port).

Bakker, J.A., 1979. 'Lucas de Heere's Stonehenge', *Ant 53*, pp. 107–11.

Balfour, M., 1979. *Stonehenge and its Mysteries* (Macdonald & Jane's, London).

Barber, M., 2003. *Bronze and the Bronze Age. Metalwork and Society in Britain, c.2500 – 800 BC* (Tempus, Brimscombe Port).

Barclay, A. & Harding, J., eds, 1999. *Pathways and Ceremonies. The Cursus Monuments of Britain and Ireland* (Oxbow, Oxford).

Barclay, E., 1895. *Stonehenge and its Earthworks* (Nutt, London).

Barron, R.S., 1976. *The Geology of Wiltshire, a Field Guide* (Moonraker Press, Bradford-on-Avon).

Bender, B. et al.., 1998. *Stonehenge. Making Space* (Berg, Oxford).

Browne, H., 1867. *An Illustration of Stonehenge and Abury, in the County of Wilts . . .*, 8th ed. (J. Browne, Salisbury).

Burgess, C., 1980. *The Age of Stonehenge* (Dent, London).

Burgess, C., 2001. *The Age of Stonehenge* (Phoenix, London, with new Note).

Burl, A., 1976a. *The Stone Circles of the British Isles* (Yale University Press, London).

Burl, A., 1976b. 'Intimations of numeracy in the Neolithic and Bronze Age societies of the British Isles', *Arch J 133*, pp. 9–32.

Burl, A., 1979. *Rings of Stone* (Frances Lincoln, London).

Burl, A., 1981. 'Holes in the argument', *Archaeoastronomy 4 (4)*, pp. 19–21.

Burl, A., 1984. 'Geoffrey of Monmouth and the Stonehenge bluestones', *WAM 79*, pp. 178–83.

Burl, A., 1985. *Megalithic Brittany. A Guide to over 350 Ancient Sites and Monuments* (Thames & Hudson, London).

Burl, A., 1987. *The Stonehenge People* (Dent, London).

Burl, A., 1991. 'The Heel Stone, Stonehenge: a study in misfortunes', *WAM 84*, pp. 1–10.

Burl, A., 1993. *From Carnac to Callanish. The Prehistoric Rows and Avenues of Britain, Ireland and Brittany* (Yale University Press, London).

Burl, A., 1994. 'Stonehenge: slaughter, sacrifice and sunshine', *WAM 87*, pp. 85–95.

Burl, A., 1995. *A Guide to the Stone Circles of Britain, Ireland and Brittany* (Yale University Press, London).

Burl, A., 1997. 'The sarsen horseshoe inside Stonehenge: a rider', *WAM 99*, pp. 1–12.

Burl, A., 1999. *Great Stone Circles. Fables, Fictions, Facts* (Yale University Press, London).

Burl, A., 2000. *The Stone Circles of Britain, Ireland and Brittany* (Yale University Press, London).

Burl, A., 2001a. 'Stonehenge. How did the stones get there?', *History Today 51 (3)*, pp. 19–25.

Burl, A., 2001b. 'The Altar Stone: prone to doubt', *3rd Stone 40*, pp. 48–55. See also Thom, Thom & Burl.

Burl, A., & Mortimer, N. eds 2005. *Stonehenge. An Unpublished Manuscript by William Stukeley, 1721–4* (Yale University Press, London).

Burnett, J.J., 1985. *The Ancient Kingdom of Wessex* (Book Guild, Lewes).

Camden, W., 1637. *Britain, or a Chorographicall Description of the most flourishing Kingdomes, England, Scotland, and Ireland* . . . (G. Latham, London).

Camden, W., 1695. *Camden's Britannia, newly translated into English: with large Additions and Improvements*, ed. E. Gibson (A. Swalle, London).

Captain, E.R., 1979. *Stonehenge and Druidism* (Artisan Sales, Thousand Oaks).

Case, H.J., 'Circles, squares, triangles and hexagons', in Cleal & Pollard (2004), pp. 114–16, pp. 120–29.

Castleden, R., 1987. *The Stonehenge People* (Routledge, London).

Castleden, R., 1992. *Neolithic Britain. New Stone Age Sites in England, Scotland and Wales* (Routledge, London).

Castleden, R., 1994. *The Making of Stonehenge* (Routledge, London).

Castleden, R., 1999. 'New views across an old landscape: re-assessing Stonehenge (1)', 3rd *Stone 35*, pp. 12–18.

Castleden, R., 2003. *Britain 3000 BC* (Sutton, Thrupp).

Charleton, W., 1663. *Chorea Gigantum; or the Most Famous antiquity of Great-Britan, vulgarly called Stone-Heng, standing on Salisbury Plain, Restored to the Danes* (Herringman, London).

Chippindale, C., 1987. *Visions of Stonehenge, 1350–1987* (Southampton City Art Gallery, Southampton).

Chippindale, C., 2004. *Stonehenge Complete*, 3rd ed. (Thames & Hudson, London).

Chippindale, C., Devereux, P., Fowler, P., Jones, R. & Sebastian, T., 1990. *Who Owns Stonehenge?* (Batsford, London).

Clarke, D., 1970. *Beaker Pottery of Great Britain and Ireland, I, II* (Cambridge University Press, Cambridge).

Cleal, R.M. & Pollard, J., eds 2004. *Monuments and Culture. Papers in Honour of an Avebury Archaeologist: Isobel Smith* (Hobnob, East Knoyle).

Cleal, R.M., Walker, K.E. & Montague, R., 1995. *Stonehenge In Its Landscape, Twentieth-Century Excavations* (English Heritage, London).

Cochrane, C., 1969. *The Lost Roads of Wessex* (David & Charles, Newton Abbot).

Collis, J., 2003. *The Celts. Origins, Myths, Inventions* (Tempus, Brimscombe Port).

Cope, J., 1998. *The Modern Antiquarian. A Pre-Millennial Odyssey through Megalithic Britain* (Thorstons, London).

Corcoran, J.X.W.P., 1969. 'The Cotswold-Severn group', in Powell et al. (1969), pp. 13–104.

Crampton, P., 1967. *Stonehenge of the Kings* (Baker, London).

Cunliffe, B., 2001. *Facing the Ocean* (Oxford University Press, Oxford).

Cunliffe, B., & Renfrew, C., eds, 1997. *Science and Stonehenge* (The British Academy, London).

Cunnington, M.E., 1929. *Woodhenge* (Wiltshire Archaeological Society, Devizes).

Cunnington, M.E., 1931. 'The "Sanctuary" on Overton Hill, near Avebury', *WAM 45*, pp. 300–35.

Cunnington, R.H., 1935. *Stonehenge and its Date* (Methuen, London).

Cunnington, R.H., 1975. *From Antiquary to Archaeologist. A Biography of William Cunnington, 1754–1810*, ed. J. Dyer (Shire, Princes Risborough).

Daniel, G., 1950. *The Chamber Tombs of England and Wales* (Cambridge University Press, Cambridge).

Darvill, T., 1996. *Prehistoric Britain from the Air. A Study of Space, Time and Society* (Cambridge University Press, Cambridge).

Darvill, T., 'Ever decreasing circle: the sacred geographies of Stonehenge and its landscape', in Cunliffe & Renfrew (1997), pp. 167–202.

Darvill, T., Wainwright, G., 2003. 'Stone circles, oval settings and henges in south-west Wales and beyond', *Ant J, 83*, pp. 9–45.

David, A. & Payne, A., 1997. 'Geophysical surveys within the Stonehenge landscape; a review of past endeavour and future potential', in Cunliffe & Renfrew (1997), pp. 73–113.

Dibble, W.E., 1976. 'A possible Pythagorean triangle at Stonehenge', *JHA 7*, pp. 141–42.

Dick, O.L., ed., 1949. *John Aubrey's 'Brief Lives'* (Secker & Warburg, London).

Diodorus Siculus (of Sicily). See Oldfather (1929).

Drewett, P.L., 1987. 'An archaeological survey of Mynedd Preseli, Dyfed', *Arch W 27*, pp. 14–16.

Duke, Rev. E., 1846. *The Druidical Temples of the County of Wilts* (Russell Smith, London).

Easton, J., 1815. *Conjectures on that Monument of Ancient Art, Stonehenge on Salisbury Plain* (J. Easton & C. Law, Salisbury).

Emerson, R.W. 1914. *Stonehenge* (LCC Central School of Arts and Crafts, London).

Evans, J., 1978. 'Recent excavations at Stonehenge', *Ant 52*, pp. 235–36.

Exon, S., Gaffney, V., Woodward, A. & Yorston, R., 2000. *Stonehenge Landscapes. Journeys through Real-and-Imagined Worlds* (Archaeopress, Oxford).

Fergusson, J., 1872. *Rude Stone Monuments in all Countries. Their Age and Uses* (John Murray, London).

Fowles, J. & Brukoff, B., 1980. *The Enigma of Stonehenge* (Jonathan Cape, London).

Freeman, G.R. & P.J., 1998. 'Stonehenge: winter solstice sun rise and set lines accurate to 0.2' in 4000 B.P. Unpublished paper, Edmonton, Canada.

Geddes, I., 2000. *Hidden Depths. Wiltshire's Geology and Landscapes* (Ex Libris, Bradford on Avon).

Geoffrey of Monmouth, *c.*1136. *The History of the Kings of Britain*, ed. L. Thorpe (Folio Society, London, 1969).

Gerald of Wales, *c.*1185. *The History and Topography of Ireland*, trans. J.J. O'Meara (Penguin, Harmondsworth, 1982).

Gibson, A., 1998. *Stonehenge & Timber Circles* (Tempus, Brimscombe Port).

Gibson, A., & Sheridan, A. eds, 2004. *From Sickles to Circles. Britain and Ireland at the Time of Stonehenge* (Tempus, Brimscombe Port).

Giot, P-R., 1960. *Brittany* (Thames & Hudson, London).

Giot, P-R., l'Helgouac'h, J. & Monnier, J.L., 1979. *Préhistoire de la Bretagne* (Ouest France, Rennes).

Gover, J.E.B., Mawer, A., & Stenton, F.W., 1970. *The Place-Names of Wiltshire* (Cambridge University Press, Cambridge).

Gowland, W., 1902. 'Recent excavations at Stonehenge', *Arch 58*, pp. 37–118.

Gowland, W., 1903. 'Recent excavations at Stonehenge', *WAM 33*, pp. 1–62.

Green, C. P., 1995. 'Stonehenge: geology and prehistory', *Proc Geologists' Association 108*, pp. 1–10.

Green, C. P., 1997. 'The provenance of rocks used in the construction of Stonehenge, in Cunlifffe & Renfrew (1997), pp. 257–70.

Grinsell, L.V., 1957. 'Archaeological gazetteer', in Pugh, R.B. & Crittall, E., eds, *A History of Wiltshire I (1)* (Victoria County History, London).

Grinsell, L.V., 1958. *The Archaeology of Wessex* (Methuen, London).

Grinsell, L.V., 1975. *The Legendary History and Folklore of Stonehenge* (Toucan Press, St Peter Port).

Grinsell, L.V., 1976. *Folklore of Prehistoric Sites in Britain* (David & Charles, Newton Abbot).

Grinsell, L.V., 1978a. *The Druids and Stonehenge. The Story of a Myth* (Toucan Press, St Peter Port).

Grinsell, L.V., 1978b. *The Stonehenge Barrow Groups* (Salisbury Museum, Salisbury).

Hanning, R.W., 1966. *The Vision of History in Early Britain* (Columbia University Press, New York & London).

Harding, A. & Lee, G.E., 1987. *Henge Monuments and Related Sites of Great Britain* (BAR 175, Oxford).

Harding, J., 2003. *Henge Monuments of the British Isles* (Tempus, Brimscombe Port).

Harrison, R.J., 1980. *The Beaker Folk. Copper Age Archaeology in Western Europe* (Thames & Hudson, London).

Harrison, W.J., 1901. 'A bibliography of the great stone monuments of Wiltshire – Stonehenge and Avebury', *WAM 32*, pp. 1–169.

Hawkins, G.S., 1973. *Beyond Stonehenge* (Hutchinson, London).

Hawkins, G.S., with White, J.B., 1966. *Stonehenge Decoded* (Souvenir Press, London).

Hawley, W., 1921. 'Stonehenge: interim report on the exploration', *Ant J 1*, pp. 17–41.

Hawley, W., 1922. 'Second report on the excavations at Stonehenge, *Arch J 2*, pp. 36–52.

Hawley, W., 1923. 'Third report on the excavations at Stonehenge', *Arch J 3*, pp. 13–20.

Hawley, W., 1924. 'Fourth report on the excavations at Stonehenge', *Arch J 4*, pp. 30–9.

Hawley, W., 1925. 'Report on the excavations at Stonehenge during the season of 1923', *Arch J 5*, pp. 21–50.

Hawley, W., 1926. 'Report on the excavations at Stonehenge during the season of 1924', *Arch J 6*, pp. 1–25.

Hawley, W., 1928. 'Report on the excavations at Stonehenge during 1925 and 1926', *Arch J 8*, pp. 149–76.

Haycock, D.B., 2002. *William Stukeley. Science, Religion and Archaeology in Eighteenth-Century England* (Boydell, Woodbridge).

Heath, R., 1993. *A Key to Stonehenge* (Bluestone Press, St Dogmaels).

Heggie, D., 1980. *Megalithic Science. Ancient Mathematics and Astronomy in Northwest Europe* (Thames & Hudson, London).

Heggie, D., 1982. *Archaeoastronomy in the Old World* (Cambridge University Press, Cambridge).

Henry of Huntingdon, editions 1129–1154. *Historia Anglorum*, trans. & ed. T. Forrester, 1853, as *The Chronicle of Henry of Huntingdon* (Llanerch Press, Felinfach, 1991).

Hoare, Sir Richard Colt, 1812. *The Ancient History of Wiltshire. I: South Wiltshire* (William Miller, London).

Hoskin, M., 1985. 'Stukeley's cosmology and the Newtonian origins of the Olberg paradox', *JHA 16*, pp. 77–112.

Hoyle, F., 1977. *On Stonehenge* (Heinemann, London).

Hunter, M., 1975. *John Aubrey and the Realm of Learning* (Duckworth, London).

Hutton, R., 2005. 'The religion of William Stukeley', *Ant J 85*, pp. 381–384.

Ixer, R.A. & Turner, P., 2006. 'A detailed re-examination of the petrologu of the Altar Stone and other non-sarsen sandstones from Stonehenge as a guide to their provenance', *WAM 99*, pp. 1–9.

Jones, I., 1655. *The Most Notable Antiquity of Great Britain, vulgarly called Stone-Heng* (Daniel Pakeman, London).

Jones, L.E., 1998. *Druid Shaman Priest. Metaphors of Celtic Paganism* (Hissarlik, Enfield Lock).

Jordan, P., 2004. *North Sea Saga* (Pearson, Harlow).

Kellaway, G., 1971. 'Glaciation and the stones of Stonehenge', *Nature 232*, pp. 30–35.

Kellaway, G., ed., 1991. *Hot Springs of Bath* (Bath City Council, Bath).

Kellaway, G., 2002. 'Glacial and tectonic factors in the emplacement of the bluestones of Salisbury Plain', *The Survey of Bath & District No. 17*, Bath, pp. 57–71.

Lawson, A. J., 1992. 'Stonehenge: creating a definitive account', *Ant 66*, pp. 934–41.

Leapman, M., 2003. *Inigo. The Troubled Life of Inigo Jones, Architect of the English Renaissance* (Review, London).

Legg, R., 1986. *Stonehenge Antiquaries* (Dorset Publishing, Milborne Port).

Lockyer, Sir N., 1906, 2nd edition 1909. *Stonehenge and Other British Stone Monuments Astronomically Considered* (Macmillan, London).

Long, W., 1876. 'Stonehenge and its barrows', *WAM 16*, pp. 1–244.

Lukis, Rev. W.C., 1880. *The Family Memoirs of the Rev. William Stukeley, M. D. and the Antiquarian and Other Correspondence of William Stukeley, Roger and Samuel Gale etc., I* (Surtees Society, Durham).

Lukis, Rev. W.C., 1883a. *The Family Memoirs . . ., II* (Surtees Society, Durham).

Lukis, Rev. W.C., 1883b. 'Report on the prehistoric monuments of Stonehenge and Avebury', *PSAL 9*, pp 141–57.

Lukis, Rev. W.C., 1885. *The Family Memoirs . . ., III* (Surtees Society, Durham).

Marshall, P., 2004. *Europe's Lost Civilisation. Uncovering the Mystery of the Megaliths* (Headline, London).

Meaden, G.T., 1992. *The Stonehenge Solution. The Secret Revealed* (Souvenir, London).

Megaw, J.V.S. & Simpson, D.D.A., 1979. *An Introduction to British Prehistory* (Leicester University Press, Leicester).

Mendyk, S.A.E., 1989. *Speculum Britanniae. Regional Study, Antiquarianism and Science in Britain to 1700* (University of Toronto Press, Buffalo).

Michell, J., 1985. *Stonehenge. Its Druids, Custodians, Festival and Future* (RTP, London).

Midgey, M.S. 2005. *The Monumental Cemeteries of Prehistoric Europe* (Tempus, Brimscombe Port).

Mohen, J-P., 1999. *Megaliths. Stones of Memory*, trans. D.B. & D.J. Baker (Abrams, New York).

Morse, M.A., 2005. *How the Celts came to Britain. Druids, ancient Skulls and the Birth of Archaeology* (Tempus, Brimscombe Port).

Mortimer, N., 2003. *Stukeley Illustrated. William Stukeley's Rediscovery of Britain's Ancient Sites* (Green Magic, Shepton Mallet).

Mortimer, N. See also: Burl & Mortimer.

Newall, R.S., 1929. 'Stonehenge', *Ant* 3, pp. 78–88.

Newall, R.S., 1953. *Stonehenge, Wiltshire* (HMSO, London).

Newham, C.A., 1964. *The Enigma of Stonehenge, and its Astronomical and Geometrical Significance* (Newham, Leeds).

Newham, C.A., 1972. *The Astronomical Significance of Stonehenge* (Moon Publications, Shirenewton).

Niel, F., 1975. *The Mysteries of Stonehenge*, trans. L. Blair (Avon, New York).

North, J., 1996. *Stonehenge. Neolithic Man and the Cosmos* (HarperCollins, London).

Oldfather, C.H., 1929. *Diodorus of Sicily, II* (Heinemann, London).

Oswald, A., Dyer, C. & Barber, M., 2001. *The Creation of Monuments. Neolithic Causewayed Enclosures in the British Isles* (English Heritage, London).

Parker Pearson, M., 1993. *Bronze Age Britain* (English Heritage, London).

Parker Pearson, M., & Ramilisonina, 1998. 'Stonehenge for the ancestors: the stones pass on the message', *Ant* 72, pp. 308–26.

Patton, M., 1992. 'Megalithic transport and territorial markers: evidence from the Channel Islands', *Ant* 66, pp. 392–95.

Patton, M., 1993. *Statements in Stone. Monuments and Society in Neolithic Brittany* (Routledge, London).

Pavel, P., 1992. 'Raising the Stonehenge lintels in Czechoslovakia', *Ant* 66, pp. 389–91.

Petrie, W.M.F., 1880. *Stonehenge: Plans, Description, and Theories* (Stanford, London).

Piggott, S., 1971. 'Introduction': *Inigo Jones, STONE-HENG; Walter Charleton, CHOREA GIGANTUM; John Webb, A VINDICATION, London 1725* (Gregg International, Farnborough).

Piggott, S., 1985. *William Stukeley. An Eighteenth-Century Antiquary*, 2nd edition (Thames & Hudson, London).

Piggott, S., 1989. *Ancient Britons and the Antiquarian Imagination* (Thames & Hudson, London).

Pitts, M., 1981. 'Stones, pits and Stonehenge', *Nature 290*, pp. 46–47.

Pitts, M., 1982. 'On the road to Stonehenge: report on investigations beside the A344 in 1968, 1979 and 1980, *PPS 48*, pp. 75–132.

Pitts, M., 2000. *Hengeworld* (Century Press, London).

Pontois, B. le, 1929. *La Finistère Préhistorique* (Librairie Émile Nourry, Paris).

Postins, M. W., 1982. *Stonehenge. Sun, Moon and Wandering Stars* (Postins, Kenilworth).

Powell, A., 1988. *John Aubrey and His Friends*, 3rd edition (Hogarth Press, London).

Powell, T.G.E., Corcoran, J.X.W.P., Lynch, F. & Scott, J., 1969. *Megalithic Enquiries in the West of Britain* (Liverpool University Press, Liverpool).

RCAHM-England, 1979. *Stonehenge and Its Environs. Monuments and Land Use* (Edinburgh University Press, Edinburgh).

Richards, J., 1985. *Beyond Stonehenge. A Guide to Stonehenge and its Prehistoric Landscape* (Trust for Wessex Archaeology, Salisbury).

Richards, J., 1990. *The Stonehenge Environs Project* (English Heritage, London).

Richards, J., 1991. *Stonehenge* (English Heritage, London).

Richards, J., 2004. *Stonehenge. A History in Photographs* (English Heritage, London).

Ross, A., 2004. *Druids. Preachers of Immortality* (Tempus, Brimscombe Port).

Ruggles, C.L.N., 1997. 'Astronomy and Stonehenge', in eds. Cunliffe, B & Renfrew, C. (1997), pp. 203–30.

Ruggles, C.L.N., 1999. *Astronomy in Prehistoric Britain & Ireland* (Yale University Press, New Haven & London).

Russell, M., 2002. *Monuments of the British Neolithic. The Roots of Architecture* (Tempus, Brimscombe Port).

Scourse, J.D., 1997. 'Transport of the Stonehenge bluestones: testing the glacial hypothesis', in Cunliffe & Renfrew (1997), pp. 271–314.

Smith, G., 1973. 'Excavation of the Stonehenge avenue at West Amesbury, Wiltshire', *WAM 68*, pp. 42–56.

Smith, J., 1771. *Choir Gaur; the Grand Orrery of the Ancient Druids, commonly called Stonehenge* (J. Smith, Salisbury).

Souden, D., 1997. *Stonehenge. Mysteries of the Stones and Landscape* (English Heritage, London).

Stevens, E.T., 1882. *Jottings on some of the Objects of interest in the Stonehenge Excursion* (Brown & Co., Salisbury).

Stevens, F., 1938, *Stonehenge Today and Yesterday* (HMSO, London).

Stone, E.H., 1924. *The Stones of Stonehenge* (Robert Scott, London).

Stone, J.F.S., 1953. *Stonehenge in the Light of Modern Research* (The Three Winterbournes III, Salisbury).

Stone, J.F.S., 1958. *Wessex* (Thames & Hudson, London).

Stover, L.E. & Kraig, B., 1979. *Stonehenge and the Origins of Western Culture* (Heinemann, London).

Stukeley, W., 1724. 'The history of the temples and religion of the antient Celts, 1721–4', MS. 4, 253, Cardiff Public Library.

Stukeley, W., 1740 . *Stonehenge a Temple Restor'd to the British Druids* (Innys & Manby, London).

Stukeley, W., 1743. *Abury, a Temple of the British Druids, with Some Others Described* (Innys, Manby, Dod & Brindley, London).

Stukeley, W. See also: Burl & Mortimer; Haycock; Lukis; Mortimer; Piggott.

Sweet, R., 2004. *Antiquaries. The Discovery of the Past in Eighteenth-Century England* (Hambledon & London, London).

Taylor, C., 1979. *Roads & Tracks of Britain* (Dent, London).

Thom, A., 1967. *Megalithic Sites in Britain* (Clarendon Press, Oxford).

Thom, A. & Thom, A.S., 1978. *Megalithic Remains in Britain and Brittany* (Clarendon Press, Oxford).

Thom, A. & Thom, A.S., 1975. 'Stonehenge as a possible lunar observatory', *JHA 6 (1)*, pp. 19–30.

Thom, A., & Thom, A.S. & Burl, A., 1980. *Megalithic Rings. Plans and Data for 229 Monuments in Britain* (BAR, 81, Oxford).

Thom, A., & Thom, A.S. & Burl, A., 1990. *Stone Rows and Standing Stones, II* (BAR, S560, Oxford).

Thom, A.A.S. & A.S., 1974. 'Stonehenge', *JHA 5 (2)*, pp. 71–90.

Thomas, H.H., 1923. 'The source of the stones of Stonehenge', *Arch J 23*, pp. 236–60.

Thorpe, R.S., Williams-Thorpe, O., Jenkins, D.G. & Watson, J.S., 1991. 'The geological sources and transport of the bluestones of Stonehenge, Wiltshire, UK', *PPS 37 (2)*, pp. 103–57.

Timperley, H.W. & Brill, E., 1983. *Ancient Trackways of Wessex* (P. Drinkwater, Shipston-on-Stour).

Thurnam, J., 1869. 'On ancient British barrows, especially those of Wiltshire and the adjoining counties (Part 1. Long Barrows)', *Arch 42*, pp. 161–224.

Tuck C., 2003. *Landscape and Desire. Revealing Britain's Sexually Inspired Sites* (Sutton, Thrupp).

Twohig, E., 1981. *The Megalithic Art of Western Europe* (Oxford University Press, Oxford).

Ucko, P., Hunter, M., Clark, A.J. & David, A., 1991. *Avebury Reconsidered. From the 1660s to the 1990s* (Institute of Archaeology, London).

Vatcher, L. & F., 1973. 'Excavation of three post-holes in Stonehenge car park', *WAM 68*, pp. 57–63.

Wainwright, G.J. & Longworth, I.H., 1971. *Durrington Walls: Excavations 1966–1968* (Society of Antiquaries, Dorking).

Wayland, J., c.1845. *The Highwaymen of Wiltshire* (N.B. Randle, Devizes).

Weaver, Rev. R., 1840. *Monumenta Antiqua* (J.B. Nichols & Son, London).

Wheatley, D., year unknown. *A New View of Stonehenge* (Braden Press, Stratton St Margaret).

William of Newburgh, c.1180. *Historia de Gestis Anglorum*, trans. & ed., J. Stevenson, 1856, as *The History of William of Newburgh* (Llanerch Press, Felinfach, 1996).

Williams-Thorpe, O. & Thorpe, R.S., 1991. 'Geochemistry, sources and transport of the Stonehenge bluestones', *PBA 77*, pp. 133–61.

Wood, J., 1747. *Choir Gaure, vulgarly called Stonehenge, on Salisbury Plain . . .* (privately published, Oxford).

Wood, J.E., 1978. *Sun, Moon and Standing Stones* (Oxford University Press, Oxford).

Woodward, A., 2000. *British Barrows. A Matter of Life and Death* (Tempus, Brimscombe Port).

INDEX

Important page references are givein in **bold**.
Illustrations are *italicized*.